BARTH AND BONHOEFFER AS CONTRIBUTORS TO A POST-LIBERAL ECCLESIOLOGY

BARTH AND BONHOEFFER AS CONTRIBUTORS TO A POST-LIBERAL ECCLESIOLOGY

Essays of Hope for a Fallen and Complex World

Tom Greggs
edited with Robert W. Heimburger

LONDON • NEW YORK • OXFORD • NEW DELHI • SYDNEY

T&T CLARK

Bloomsbury Publishing Plc

50 Bedford Square, London, WC1B 3DP, UK
1385 Broadway, New York, NY 10018, USA
29 Earlsfort Terrace, Dublin 2, Ireland

BLOOMSBURY, T&T CLARK and the T&T Clark logo are trademarks of
Bloomsbury Publishing Plc

First published in Great Britain 2022
Paperback edition published 2023

Copyright © Tom Greggs (with Robert W. Heimburger), 2022

Tom Greggs has asserted his right under the Copyright, Designs and Patents Act, 1988, to be identified as Author of this work.

For legal purposes the Acknowledgements on pp. ix–x constitute an extension of this copyright page.

Cover design: Terry Woodley

All rights reserved. No part of this publication may be reproduced or transmitted in any form or by any means, electronic or mechanical, including photocopying, recording, or any information storage or retrieval system, without prior permission in writing from the publishers.

Bloomsbury Publishing Plc does not have any control over, or responsibility for, any third-party websites referred to or in this book. All internet addresses given in this book were correct at the time of going to press. The author and publisher regret any inconvenience caused if addresses have changed or sites have ceased to exist, but can accept no responsibility for any such changes.

A catalogue record for this book is available from the British Library.

Library of Congress Cataloging-in-Publication Data
Names: Greggs, Tom, author.
Title: Barth and Bonhoeffer as contributors to a post liberal ecclesiology : essays of hope for a fallen and complex world / Tom Greggs.
Description: London ; New York : T&T Clark, 2022. |
Includes bibliographical references and index. |
Identifiers: LCCN 2021019009 (print) | LCCN 2021019010 (ebook) |
ISBN 9780567701565 (hb) | ISBN 9780567701572 (paperback) |
ISBN 9780567701596 (epdf) | ISBN 9780567701602 (epub)
Subjects: LCSH: Postliberal theology. | Barth, Karl, 1886–1968. |
Bonhoeffer, Dietrich, 1906–1945. | LCGFT: Essays.
Classification: LCC BT83.595 G74 2022 (print) | LCC BT83.595 (ebook) |
DDC 230/.046–dc23
LC record available at https://lccn.loc.gov/2021019009
LC ebook record available at https://lccn.loc.gov/2021019010

ISBN: HB: 978-0-5677-0156-5
PB: 978-0-5677-0157-2
ePDF: 978-0-5677-0159-6
ePUB: 978-0-5677-0160-2

Typeset by Newgen KnowledgeWorks Pvt. Ltd., Chennai, India

To find out more about our authors and books visit www.bloomsbury.com and sign up for our newsletters.

This book is dedicated to the six theologians who in their markedly different ways inspired, shaped and influenced my readings of Karl Barth and Dietrich Bonhoeffer over the last quarter of a century:

*To the memory of Daniel W. Hardy and John B. Webster;
And to Mark J. Edwards, David F. Ford, Paul T. Nimmo and Stephen J. Plant.*

CONTENTS

Acknowledgements	ix
List of Abbreviations	xi
INTRODUCTION	1

Part I
READING BARTH AND BONHOEFFER TOGETHER

Chapter 1
THE INFLUENCE OF KARL BARTH ON DIETRICH BONHOEFFER   11

Chapter 2
THE INFLUENCE OF DIETRICH BONHOEFFER ON KARL BARTH   35

Part II
ENGAGEMENTS WITH BARTH

Chapter 3
BARTH ON SALVATION   51

Chapter 4
BARTH ON ETERNITY   65

Chapter 5
JESUS IS VICTOR!   83

Chapter 6
BRINGING BARTH ON RELIGION TO THE INTER-FAITH TABLE   99

Chapter 7
THE LORD OF ALL   117

Part III
ENGAGEMENTS WITH BONHOEFFER

Chapter 8
RELIGIONLESS CHRISTIANITY IN A COMPLEXLY RELIGIOUS AND
SECULAR WORLD   133

Chapter 9
RELIGIONLESS CHRISTIANITY AND THE POLITICAL IMPLICATIONS
OF THEOLOGICAL SPEECH   147

Chapter 10
BEARING SIN IN THE CHURCH   163

Chapter 11
PRIESTLY MEDIATION IN THE CHURCH   183

Part IV
READING BARTH AND BONHOEFFER TOGETHER IN A FALLEN PLURALIST WORLD

Chapter 12
PESSIMISTIC UNIVERSALISM   195

CONCLUSION   211

Bibliography   215
Index   225

ACKNOWLEDGEMENTS

The author would like to thank Dr Rob Heimburger for his detailed editorial assistance with the collation of this volume. The care and work he has undertaken is exemplary, and without his support the production of the volume would not have been possible, especially during an exceptionally busy time as head of divinity at Aberdeen. Thanks are also due to Dr Declan Kelly for work at the proofing and indexing stages, as well as to colleagues at Bloomsbury for their editorial assistance. Any errors which remain are, of course, the fault of the author.

The author also thanks the following for their permission to reproduce copyright material, thoroughly updating it to appear in this volume.

'Bonhoeffer's Influence on Barth' appeared as 'The Influence of Dietrich Bonhoeffer on Karl Barth'. In *Engaging Bonhoeffer: The Impact and Influence of Bonhoeffer's Life and Thought*, edited by Matthew D. Kirkpatrick, 45–64. Minneapolis, MN: Fortress Press, 2016.

'Barth on Salvation' appeared as 'Karl Barth on Salvation'. In *Christian Theologies of Salvation: A Comparative Introduction*, edited by Justin S. Holcomb, 300–17. New York: New York University Press, 2018. https://doi.org/10.18574/nyu/9780814724439.001.0001.

'Barth on Eternity' appeared as 'The Order and Movement of Eternity: Karl Barth on the Eternity of God and Creaturely Time'. In *Eternal God, Eternal Life: Theological Investigations into the Concept of Immortality*, edited by Philip G. Ziegler. London: Bloomsbury, 2016.

'Jesus Is Victor!' appeared as ' "Jesus Is Victor": Passing the Impasse of Barth on Universalism'. *Scottish Journal of Theology* 60, no. 2 (2007): 196–212. https://doi.org/10.1017/S0036930607003201.

'Bringing Barth on Religion to the Inter-faith Table' appeared as 'Bringing Barth's Critique of Religion to the Inter-faith Table'. *Journal of Religion* 88, no. 1 (2008): 75–94. https://doi.org/10.1086/522280.

'The Lord of All' appeared as 'The Lord of All: Rediscovering the Christian Doctrine of Providence for a Pluralist Society'. In *Transforming Exclusion: Engaging with Faith Perspectives*, edited by Wayne Morris and Hannah Bacon, 44–62. London: Continuum, 2011. http://public.eblib.com/choice/publicfullrecord.aspx?p=732115.

'Religionless Christianity in a Complexly Religious and Secular World' appeared as 'Religionless Christianity in a Complexly Religious and Secular World: Thinking through and beyond Bonhoeffer'. In *Religion, Religionlessness and Contemporary Western Culture: Explorations* in *Dietrich Bonhoeffer's Theology*, edited by Stephen Plant and Ralf K. Wüstenberg, 111–25. Frankfurt am Main: Peter Lang, 2008.

'Religionless Christianity and the Political Implications of Theological Speech' appeared as 'Religionless Christianity and the Political Implications of Theological Speech: What Bonhoeffer's Theology Yields to a World of Fundamentalisms'. *International Journal of Systematic Theology* 11, no. 3 (2009): 293–308. https://doi.org/10.1111/j.1468-2400.2009.00450.x.

'Bearing Sin in the Church' appeared as 'Bearing Sin in the Church: The Ecclesial Hamartiology of Bonhoeffer'. In *Christ, Church, and World: New Studies in Bonhoeffer's Theology and Ethics*, edited by Michael G. Mawson and Philip G. Ziegler, 77–99. London: Bloomsbury T&T Clark, 2016.

'Priestly Mediation in the Church' appeared as 'Ecclesial Priestly Mediation in the Theology of Dietrich Bonhoeffer'. *Theology Today* 71, no. 1 (2014): 81–91. https://doi.org/10.1177/0040573613518642.

'Pessimistic Universalism' appeared as 'Pessimistic Universalism: Rethinking the Wider Hope with Bonhoeffer and Barth'. *Modern Theology* 26, no. 4 (2010): 495–510. https://doi.org/10.1111/j.1468-0025.2010.01630.x.

Every effort has been made to obtain permission to reproduce copyright material. If any proper acknowledgement has not been made, we would invite copyright holders to inform us of the oversight.

Unless otherwise noted, Bible quotations are from the New Revised Standard Version (NRSV), copyright © 1989 the Division of Christian Education of the National Council of the Churches of Christ in the United States of America. Used by permission. All rights reserved.

ABBREVIATIONS

CD	Barth, Karl. *Church Dogmatics*. Edited by Geoffrey W. Bromiley and Thomas F. Torrance. 2nd edn. London: T&T Clark, 2004
ChrL	Barth, Karl. *The Christian Life: Church Dogmatics IV/4 Lecture Fragments*. Translated by Geoffrey W. Bromiley. Edinburgh: T&T Clark, 1981
DBW	*Dietrich Bonhoeffer Werke*. München/Gütersloh: Chr. Kaiser Verlag, 1986–98
DBW 1	*Sanctorum Communio*
DBW 3	*Schöpfung und Fall*
DBW 4	*Nachfolge*
DBW 6	*Ethik*
DBW 8	*Widerstand und Ergebung*
DBW 13	*London: 1933–1935*
DBWE	*Dietrich Bonhoeffer Works (English)*. Minneapolis, MN: Fortress Press, 1995–2014
DBWE 1	*Sanctorum Communio*
DBWE 2	*Act and Being*
DBWE 3	*Creation and Fall*
DBWE 4	*Discipleship*
DBWE 6	*Ethics*
DBWE 8	*Letters and Papers from Prison*
DBWE 10	*Barcelona, Berlin, New York: 1928–1931*
DBWE 12	*Berlin, 1932–1933*
DBWE 13	*London: 1933–1935*
LW	Luther, Martin. *Luther's Works*. American edn. St. Louis: Concordia, 1955–86
PG	Migne, J. P., ed. *Patrologia Graeca*. Paris: Imprimerie Catholique, 1857–66
PL	Migne, J. P., ed. *Patrologia Latina*. Paris: Imprimerie Catholique, 1841–55
ST	Aquinas, Thomas. *Summa Theologiae*

INTRODUCTION

The theologies of Karl Barth and Dietrich Bonhoeffer mark both my earliest and most enduring theological influences. At the age of sixteen, I read Bonhoeffer's *Discipleship* and *Letters and Papers from Prison* and found myself captivated by the description of the Christian faith he offered. Bonhoeffer's own discussion of religionless Christianity was the gateway through which at the same age I began to read Barth – initially the paragraph (§17) on religion in *Church Dogmatics* 1/2 and, from there, *The Humanity of God* and volume 1/1. Indeed, the late John Webster (both my former teacher and later colleague) used to enjoy teasing me when we taught together by reminding me and informing the students we taught that when he first met me I didn't even know how to say 'Barth' (pronouncing the 'th' at my Oxford interview aged seventeen) never mind know enough to teach him. Through my initial undergraduate training, while I was principally focused on patristics, it was Barth and Bonhoeffer's theologies I read in my free time and it was they who accompanied me on my journey of faith in intellectual discipleship. I found in reading them a joy that I have rarely found elsewhere; and the delight I had when first reading them continues to this day. While Barth would become a principal interlocutor in my doctorate (which sought to straddle patristics and systematics), Bonhoeffer has also remained a cantus firmus in my theological reflection, in no small part because of the encouragement of my friend, Stephen Plant, who challenged me to 'become a theologian' rather than an historian of Barth and to do so by spreading my theological horizons a little wider: who better, he thought, to begin with in this than with Bonhoeffer? While they were written for a very different context and about an utterly different subject, the words of Keats seem so apt to my experience of what is now a quarter of a century of engaging with these two thinkers:

> A thing of beauty is a joy for ever:
> Its loveliness increases; …
> All lovely tales that we have heard or read:
> An endless fountain of immortal drink,
> Pouring unto us from the heaven's brink.

While there are areas over which I disagree with each of their theologies (not least over the discussion of gender), I find joy every time I return to Barth and Bonhoeffer.

I realize, however, that this is not so for many students of theology. But I am struck how those who have been critical of them have often done so not out of an engagement with the details and insights of their work, but rather out of a rejection of the approach to theology which is deeply 'theological'. It is, in fact, this feature which is most attractive of all to me. All too often theology in the past fifty years, and especially that field of theology which has traditionally been called 'systematics', has valorized and determined itself by external academic discourses and by a desire to conform to a mode of modern intellectualism associated with the university which diminishes tradition-specific thinking and modes of thought that relate to practice. The historic sense of a theology department which stood alongside law and medicine within the university as a subject focused not only on intellectual research but also on the training of and engagement with practitioners has been forgotten and replaced with an approach to theological discourse which stands more alongside history, classics, social studies, philosophy or psychology, borrowing their forms and horizons to speak of the horizon of God – an object of study intractable because of the sheer self-sufficient plenitude of the creator who can never be treated by creatures as an object of study as if God stood as a 'thing' alongside other 'things' in creation. There are two reasons for this focus on external discourses – both related to the divorce between theology and the church. Firstly, churches have themselves retreated from the intellectual sphere, the public university and the critical contexts in which theology can be pursued, despite the fact that university education in society increases year on year. Confessionally driven, 'teaching' seminaries have replaced in many cases the requirement for trainee ministers to take degrees in divinity at public, research universities. Alongside this, secondly, university departments of theology have sought to find their worth and place in the university not by virtue of engagement in living traditions through research with impact in theses loci (as might very well be the case with disciplines such as politics and economics) but by virtue of aping the forms of discourse found in other disciplines and lacking confidence in the practice of doing (to borrow a phrase from Webster) 'theological theology'. There is in much theological writing a kind of what I have come to think of as an academic 'orientalism': it both glorifies in the otherness of these other fields to which it aspires and considers there to be something implicitly irrational and primitive in more traditionally theological theology in contrast to the exotic newness of social scientific, culture-based, analytic methods to which theological discourse must become subject, regardless of the uniqueness of theology's own object and the distinctive communities to which theology belongs. Such approaches to theology are often Nietzschean in outlook, operating with the idea that God is dead and, thereby, that living traditions are nothing but museum pieces to be analysed from afar with a chilly scientific objectivity.

It is on account of the desire to reclaim a sense of a living tradition in which we can be traditioned and from which we can think that I have collected these essays together. In one sense, they are working essays *in via* – along the path of my becoming (my ever becoming) a theologian with a commitment to the church in the complexly religious and secular contexts to which I belong.[1] Indeed, the essays in this volume span over fifteen years. While I hope there has been some development of voice and theological maturity during this period, there has nevertheless been a clear degree of continuity in the themes and issues which I have addressed. My earliest interest (ten years before I ever dared to write anything on them!) in Barth and Bonhoeffer was sparked by their desire and capacity to speak *as theologians* into the distinctive modern contexts in which they lived – not simply reflecting those cultures but thinking theologically about them. Their work on the theological critique of religion captivated me as a very young person living in an overtly secular intellectual and ethical context who wanted to work for the church. Some of the fruit of that reflection would later become my book *Theology against Religion*. However, I have also realized in writing my large constructive work, *Dogmatic Ecclesiology*, the extent to which these themes have followed me in all avenues of my theological work: understanding the purpose of the church in a post-Christendom world; recognizing the need for a critical voice in relation to the constant threat of 'religion' (as both an ecclesial and academical origin and end); seeking to speak the good news in a way that desires the *shalom* (the salvation, indeed) of the world; desiring to be orientated radically on the interruptive grace of the God of grace; understanding the dimensions of salvation which take place in the here and now of the given quotidian of creation; avoiding unbiblical and unwise binaries in theological thought; not reducing God to being a 'thing' among other things (including in our intellectual conceptualizations). While these are not terms, concepts or phrases that necessarily correlate at all points with the work of Barth and Bonhoeffer, they are inspired by reading them, and by the seriousness with which they thought and wrote theologically about the church in their age of ever-increasing secularism and with which they interacted with the community of prayer, faith and the gospel: they theologize the critique of secularism, rather than secularize in their academic speech the theological discipline. They engage with the occasions in the quotidian givenness of their lives which demanded theologians to speak, rather than reflecting through some soft correlationism these occasions as if they might be determinative of their theological method or *telos*.

While there is every desire in this book to engage seriously the process of exegeting these theologians, indeed even to the level of discussing their relationship and the possibility of collecting essays together from them both in one volume, it may well be that the gatekeepers of each school (Barth and Bonhoeffer) find themselves dissatisfied with the discussions; this matter is, in fact, dealt with and challenged in the first chapters (Chapters 1 and 2). The essays included in this volume seek, however, not only to think *towards* and *about* the theologies of Barth and Bonhoeffer but to think *with*, *from* and – even at times in relation to the different context in which we

---

1. I borrow this turn of phrase from my other great mentor, alongside John Webster, David Ford (my Doktorvater).

now find ourselves – *beyond* their theologies.² Since neither of them desired to found a 'school' of thought but wished others, like them, to be theologians in their own right, there is an approach of *ressourcement* in the way in which their theologies are utilized at various points in this book to address questions which they, themselves, did not address directly. As with their own approaches to the theologies from which they draw, these essays not only mark a careful listening to the voices of the past (Barth and Bonhoeffer in particular) and a desire to listen carefully to them, but they also mark an activity of – having listened – *speaking*, and doing so not simply as an historian of dogma but also as a theologian. While historical theology and systematics are deeply intertwined subjects, these essays seek collectively to engage overtly in their interrelation. They are not only exercises in historical theology and retrieval but also attempts to speak to the current (changed) ecclesial and academic context theologically. To quote the words of John Webster:

> Much of the best constructive theology tends to be undertaken by those who study and seek to retrieve something from earlier theological practices. Retrieval ought not to be nostalgia, but the expectant search for new possibilities.³

> All one can do is – following the example of the grand old man of Basel, or of those *ressourcement* theologians who pored over Migne for years looking for buried treasure – dig deeply and lovingly into the thoughts of the church thinkers of the past and above all into Holy Scripture, and say as clearly and vividly and generously as one can what one finds, in the hope that it may well prove to be just what church and culture really need.⁴

There is a desire in these essays to speak, through retrieval, into the church and culture in the age in which we currently live.

Theologically speaking, one might well think of these exercises in historical theology and systematics to be engagements in, within and with the communion of saints – listening to and conversing with the living voices of the best of the recent theological past. For some, these essays will lack at points the purism of history and listening, saying too much in a contemporary voice to a contemporary context; even the engagement of putting the two together will be too great a stretch for the guardians of the boundaries. For others, there will be concerns about the constructive moves. Indeed, there are some who, without engaging in or with the details of the arguments I have set out on other occasions have drawn strange

---

2. There is a certain indebtedness in this approach to John de Gruchy, and especially his essay 'With Bonhoeffer, Beyond Bonhoeffer: Transmitting Bonhoeffer's Legacy', in *Dietrich Bonhoeffer's Theology Today: A Way between Fundamentalism and Secularism?*, ed. John W. de Gruchy et al. (Güterslohr: Gütersloh Verlag, 2009).

3. John Webster, *Word and Church: Essays in Christian Dogmatics* (London: T&T Clark, 2015), xiii.

4. Webster, *Church and Word*, 6.

conclusions about the approach I take both historically and constructively.[5] Others still have understood the very process of theological writing to be distinct from my own understanding, wishing God to be an analytic object of study comparable to (and among) all other objects in terms of conceptual reflection in a way which is antithetical to Barth or Bonhoeffer's own approaches.[6] And there will be many who simply think that theology should not be formed by the living inheritance of the past, but must do away with this to start afresh 'constructively'.

These essays, however, seek to be true to both Barth and Bonhoeffer, *and* to their senses of what the task of theology is. But they do so in a way which builds from them. There is a desire in them not to engage in the kinds of 'hands off' secular approaches to theology that exist, nor the exercise of spuriously academicizing theology which has taken hold in certain quarters (in which theology becomes a handservant to philosophy or another external discipline), nor the kinds of internal and sectarian approaches to theology which do not engage in the place of the church in the world in its current and complex forms. There is in the essays, instead, a desire to speak theologically from within a traditioned form of theological speech in a way which can address theologically and speak theologically about the church within the world today – especially in its post-Christendom form.[7] The essays note the modern nature of Barth and Bonhoeffer alongside their orthodoxy,[8] and the reflection of both Barth and Bonhoeffer on the conditions and context of modernity and its features. In this sense, while they address a range of different

---

5. Principal among these would be Barry Harvey, who presents me as suggesting a Kantian exclusion of religion from the public sphere (the opposite of what I argue), and whose earlier review of my previous work sadly makes no detailed engagement with the material content of the evidence of my argument beyond the first few pages: see Barry Harvey, *Taking Hold of the Real: Dietrich Bonhoeffer and the Profound Worldliness of Christianity* (Eugene, OR: Wipf and Stock, 2015), 131, 142.

6. I see this at play in Oliver Crisp, 'I Do Teach It, but I also Do Not Teach It: The Universalism of Karl Barth', in *All Shall Be Well: Explorations in Universal Salvation and Christian Theology, from Origen to Moltmann* (Eugene, OR: Wipf and Stock, 2011), 305–24. See also the reply to Crisp's general position (and more positive reading of my account) by David W. Congdon, 'Apokatastasis and Apostolicity: A Response to Oliver Crisp on the Question of Barth's Universalism', *Scottish Journal of Theology* 67, no. 4 (2014): 464–80. The approach pertaining to logical, analytic presupposition does not work well with Barth's Christocentric personalism.

7. The concern to address theologically the context in which we live is something which was deeply instilled in me by my Doktorvater, David Ford. The public role of the systematician and the need for the theologian to think concretely and urgently about the situation of pluralism are themes I learned deeply from him.

8. In this sense, the readings offered are very influenced by Bruce McCormack. See his *Orthodox and Modern: Studies in the Theology of Karl Barth* (Grand Rapids, MI: Baker Academic, 2008).

topics, each of the essays in some ways is an attempt at discussing the church and the gospel it preaches in a post-liberal age: these essays take seriously the very particularity of the claims of the gospel in its rational explication but do so in a way that does not retreat into a sectarian context but addresses the church's speech in a context especially of secularism and pluralism. Speaking with and from Barth and Bonhoeffer, and seeking to use their theological wisdom, the essays desire to offer a generously particularist set of theological reflections on the realities of the church and its speech in a complexly secular and pluralist context. Chuck Mathewes identifies this issue well when he states: 'If the fundamental problem of modern politics is pluralism, this is a fundamentally religious problem and must be confronted as such.'[9] He also notes: 'The challenge of otherness is very profound, for it reveals that in religious pluralism theology confronts a primordial theological problem: the problem of otherness. What the contemporary world calls pluralism we should see, in theological terms, as the fundamental challenge of otherness.'[10] Both liberal and sectarian approaches to theology are ill-equipped to deal with these issues. The theological modes of theology in which Barth and Bonhoeffer write, however, offer a tradition of theological discourse within modernity which seek, in Barth's words, to avoid 'pietistic sterility on one hand, and the sterility of the Enlightenment on the other'.[11] Or else in the words of Bonhoeffer, there is a need to avoid 'a spiritual existence that takes no part in worldly existence, and a worldly existence that can make good its claim over and against the sacred sector. The monk and the cultural protestant of the nineteenth century represent these two possibilities.'[12] Moreover, overly secularized or spuriously academicized forms of theology are not well placed to speak to faith communities or to politics in general, choosing instead either to represent and reflect the secular discourses which are already in operation or to speak in the manner of the philosopher or quasi-scientific historian who is only interested in discussing the rational explication of the gospel to the narrow field of self-identified specialists.

While Part I of the book considers the relationship between Bonhoeffer and Barth, advocating a hermeneutical approach to understanding their work in relation to each other and accounting for why they might be discussed together in one book, the remainder of the essays consider the themes of salvation (and interrelated themes), God's relation to the whole of creation (both Christian and non-Christian), the critique of religion and religious pluralism, and the relation of the church to the world. Two essays on the mutual influence of Barth and Bonhoeffer on each other, and the manner in which their thought should be considered in relation to each other, are followed by a series of essays on Barth's

---

9. Charles Mathewes, *A Theology of Public Life* (Cambridge: Cambridge University Press, 2007), 111.

10. Ibid., 108.

11. Karl Barth, *Community, State and Church* (Garden City, NY: Doubleday, 1960), 105.

12. DBWE 6, 57; cf. DBWE 8, 428: 'The weakness of liberal theology was that it allowed the world the right to assign to Christ his place within it.'

theology on themes pertaining to the church and its speech in a post-Christendom world. The first of these essays (Chapter 3) offers a reading of Barth's account of salvation. This essay considers the content of the church's speech about the God of the gospel and God's relation to humanity. For Barth, the word of God is the word of the creator directed at us, which has become necessary and remains so for the renewal of the original relation between God and humanity. Revelation's purpose, therefore, is that it makes known to us the word of reconciliation, the word of the reconciler. In this event of revealing Godself to humanity, God promises Godself as the content of our future.[13] In light of this reality, the next chapter (Chapter 4) on Barth considers Barth's account of how the eternal God relates to the complexities of creaturely humanity in all its spatio-temporal quotidian givenness while at the same time offering an account of the eternal constancy of the God of the Gospel in God's relation to humanity. This chapter offers to some degree the revolutionary Barthian Christocentric (what we might call) 'metaphysics' in operation in relation to potentially Barth's most radical theological contribution – the doctrine of election. And from there, the book considers in Chapter 5 the implications of this account of eternity to the way in which the extent of salvation might be understood in a simultaneously hopeful and particularist way in a world of ongoing time and complexity. The final two chapters in the section on Barth (Chapters 6 and 7) deal with this multiplicity and complexity in a little more detail – firstly, in Chapter 6 from the perspective of Barth's critique of religion and what this might mean for the church's speech and activity in a complexly secular and pluralist world; secondly, in Chapter 7 from the perspective of what Barth's account of providence might mean for discussions of other religions.

The following set of chapters focuses on Bonhoeffer's contributions to the themes of this book. It begins with an initial pair of essays which were written together on the way in which Bonhoeffer's religionless Christianity might be understood and might speak to the contemporary context. The first of these essays (Chapter 8) considers the way in which Bonhoeffer's discussions in *Letters and Papers from Prison* might be translated for the different sociological context in which the church now exists compared to Bonhoeffer's own context, considering the importance of treating Bonhoeffer's work on these matters as a *theological* and not a sociological trope. The second of the essays (Chapter 9) builds from this discussion, looking at what Bonhoeffer's theology might be able to say to the theo-political context of the world today and what Bonhoeffer might be able to teach the church about its place within and speech to the world in its current forms. The book then turns to more directly ecclesiological implications of these themes. Chapter 10 discusses how to think about sin in relation to the church – both in terms of the fallenness of humanity in relation to God and creation, and the ways in which the church as a community offers an anticipatory, redemptive and political community of salvation. The chapter considers the act of God, for Bonhoeffer, in putting right the 'horizontal' disorder caused by sin both internal

---

13. CD I/1, 142.

to the church and in relation to the church's role in the world. This leads into the discussion of priestly mediation in Bonhoeffer's theology (Chapter 11), focused on his theological approach to the church. The chapter discusses how the priestliness of the church is felt internally: Christ establishes a mode of sociality in the church which arises from mediation not only between God and humanity but also between human beings and other human beings; and the external relationality which is established between the church and the world, whereby in Christ, the church shares in the task of vicarious representative responsibility for the world. A final chapter of the book (Chapter 12) brings Barth and Bonhoeffer together on the theme of sin and the scope of salvation in relation to the world, offering the church a hopeful and positive account of the salvation of God in relation to the world while at the same time emphasizing the priority of divine, interruptive grace and – through that – the church's relationship to the world in the continuation in sin in the believer.

Although these essays were written in their original forms as occasional pieces, attempts have been made throughout to show the interconnectedness of the chapters to each other in espousing a theology for a church after liberalism. Indeed, at times, there are components of overlap – even in the revision of the essays – between chapters. Although what is offered in the essays is something which might be considered 'generously particularist' in approach to the claims of theology, there is nevertheless a desire to approach the themes with a realness and, even, pessimism in relation to what humans and the world can achieve without the interruptive gracious activity of God, and in terms of the church's own existence within the world. In this way, the essays seek to understand systematically not only the way in which we can speak of the church's life and speech in a complexly religious and secular world in a manner that gives priority to the Spirit's bringing forth the fruit of humility but also the way in which the impact of theological taxonomy of loci and the significance of the dogmatic proximity of loci to the themes discussed are key to the need to treat the themes herein with an appropriate degree of coherence and theological proportionality. The essays are evidently occasional and do not engage with the sense of the priority of analytic (or any other) philosophy over theological speech which engages with an object of study which is other than creation and all other things in creation, but they are systematic in the attempt to think about these occasional themes with reference to the horizon of other proximate loci to the themes discussed in a manner which attempts a coherence which is not overdetermined.[14]

---

14. Cf. the extremely helpful account of systematicity in A. N. Williams, *The Architecture of Theology: Structure, System, and Ratio* (Oxford: Oxford University Press, 2011).

Part I

READING BARTH AND BONHOEFFER TOGETHER

Chapter 1

THE INFLUENCE OF KARL BARTH ON DIETRICH BONHOEFFER

One of the significant issues at stake in being able to engage in the same book, never mind at times the same essays, with both Karl Barth and Dietrich Bonhoeffer is the relationship of their theologies to each other. So much recent scholarship has been aimed at guarding the bounds and gates of the respective Barth and Bonhoeffer theological camps. In such approaches, the distinctive features of each theologian are stressed often in a manner which suggests a greater degree of dissimilarity than similarity: how could these approaches do otherwise when they are specifically looking for difference, careful nuance and scholastic detail? But this very method of study itself likely skews the proportions of the discussion such that in protecting the bounds and intricate contours of the individual thinker, the focus of the conversation comes to concern precisely those bounds and intricate contours, and not the vast areas of overlap and commonality. Thinkers come to be defined by the bounds of their thoughts and the detailed distinctions such that one might be forgiven thinking that conversation partners, who speak to each other from a shared sense of the main aspects of the theological agenda, are pitched anachronistically in opposition to each other. While there is truth in Hans Robert Jauss's hermeneutical insight that we understand the internal commitments of a given thinker in seeing her in contrast to another,[1] to focus only on the differences in a scholastic approach of gatekeeping is to form an account of a thinker which does not proportionately account for the broad approaches that a given thinker follows.

Certainly, there will be many who will suggest that an approach that seeks to give proportionate account to commonality in discussing two figures together is not historically detailed or theologically nuanced enough. However, in bringing Barth and Bonhoeffer together in discussion, there is no suggestion that differences do not exist; simply, that commonalities exist as well. Rather than conceiving of them as members of rival or competing theological camps (as those of all kinds of theological stripes following the lives of these theologians have done),

---

1. See, for example, *Question and Answer: Forms of Dialogic Understanding*, ed. and trans. Michael Hays (Minneapolis: University of Minnesota, 1989). I owe my engagement with Jauss to discussions with Anthony Thiselton.

it is surely more historically apt to view them as dialogue partners – who have enough agreement to enable them to converse together amidst commonality and difference – rather than considering them as an elephant and a whale who could never speak to each other.[2] Such an approach based on conversation and dialogue is, indeed, historically accurate, given the variety of interactions that Bonhoeffer and Barth had throughout Bonhoeffer's academic and ecclesial life.

Furthermore, to remember that they are conversation partners is to remember that both theologians (while confessionally Reformed and Lutheran) were *Protestant* and *moderns*. In studying historical theologians of our tradition, there is a danger in the modern period of presupposing that we can explain whatever a given person states by attending to the influence of some version of philosophy or another, or some influence of a preceding theological idea or thinker or another. The worst forms of this are such that one is left thinking why it was necessary for the thinker we are studying to write (and therefore why we should study them) if all they personify is an uncritical appropriation and repristination of an earlier thinker. One sees this in scholarship about Barth and Bonhoeffer which views them as (variously) uncritically indebted to Luther, Dilthey, Hegel, Kant, Calvin, Kierkegaard and others. Often these discussions have little sense of the appropriation of former figures through the refraction of those through whom their ideas have been received in future generations; this is particularly so (and importantly for Bonhoeffer) in relation to the appropriation of Luther following the Luther renaissance at the turn of the past century. Obviously, accounts of thinkers in terms of influence are important, but saying an idea stems from a particular preceding thinker is: firstly, controversial, as there is never a consensus about this among historians of these figures (as is evident in the wide variety of perspectives offered); secondly, conjectural, as there may well be parallel or transformative developments that we fail to observe or recognize; thirdly, tendentious, as for Christian historical theology, it is always the case that doctrines assumed to be biblical or theological in one theologian are rendered philosophical in other ones;[3] and, fourthly, inadequate as this tells us little about the doctrine or idea or figure we are studying.[4] Therefore, rather than directly discuss Barth and Bonhoeffer principally in terms of the influences upon them and the details of distinction in relation to distinctive thinkers, it is best to consider the paths along which these thinkers walk and the conversations (with their shared interests and conversations) that took place on these paths, including with those from previous generations.

---

2. As was Barth's description of his relationship with Bultmann in *Karl Barth – Rudolf Bultmann Letters, 1922–1966*, ed. Bernd Jaspert and G. W. Bromiley, trans. G. W. Bromiley (Grand Rapids, MI: Eerdmans, 1981), 105.

3. Compare Luther, Kierkegaard and Calvin.

4. I owe these insights to my former teacher, Professor Mark Edwards, in relation to patristic study. However, the same principles apply for these figures, and indeed all modern theologians.

There will always be influences on thinkers, but there will be *transformations* of these influences in their distinctive appropriations by given thinkers.

In this chapter, therefore, in addressing the influence of Barth on Bonhoeffer, what is advocated is a more fluid account of influence and of boundaries to reflect the fluidity of ongoing conversation. This is particularly important given that there is asymmetry in these figures which must be accounted for: Barth is evidently the senior person and yet writes for a period of twenty-two years after Bonhoeffer's untimely death. And there are also changes in both their thought over time.[5] But the key point to consider will be the manner in which these two thinkers interact, and particularly the influence of Barth on Bonhoeffer's thought. These are two thinkers walking along the same modern, theological path, and they are conversing on it – initially with Barth as the teacher to whom Bonhoeffer asks questions as the thoughtful and engaged student. Even in these critical questions, what one sees are movements along shared trajectories as Barth and Bonhoeffer engage in similar theological projects and similar problems in similar ways.[6] Indeed, in many of the critical moments, Bonhoeffer calls Barth to follow through on the theological foundations he has laid.

The influence of Barth on Bonhoeffer's earlier theology

Certainly, in reading the early Bonhoeffer and reading about the early Bonhoeffer, there can be little sense that Bonhoeffer was anything other than positively influenced and impressed by Barth. Following their first meetings in 1931, Bonhoeffer famously wrote: 'Barth was even better than his books.'[7] And even later, when at Finkenwalde, Bonhoeffer and his students treated Barth as a hero of contemporary theology. Of course, there was a respectful difference and disagreement between the two which followed throughout Bonhoeffer's life, but this came in the context of repeated conversation and correspondence and significant shared theological commitment. In this way, Bonhoeffer's appreciation of Barth is akin to the kind of approach to senior theological figures which Barth himself advocates. Take, for example, Barth's own approach to the work of Calvin. For all his movement and deviation from Calvin, and for all of his appreciation, Barth is careful to maintain that the activity of engaging appreciatively with Calvin does not involve repetition of his thought, or uncritical appropriation:

---

5. There is, of course, Barth's famous shift in 1936 in relation to election, and Bonhoeffer's own maturation and the changes that one sees in *Letters and Papers from Prison*, DBWE 8.

6. We might consider the responses to the Church Struggle and the dissatisfaction with liberal theology.

7. Eberhard Bethge, *Dietrich Bonhoeffer: A Biography*, rev. edn (Minneapolis, MN: Augsburg Fortress, 1999), 132.

> Those who simply echo Calvin are not good Calvinists, that is, they are not really taught by Calvin. Being taught by Calvin means entering into dialogue with him, with Calvin as the teacher and ourselves as the students, he speaking, we doing our best to follow him and then – this is crux of the matter – making our own response to what he says. If that does not happen we might as well be listening to Chinese; the historical Calvin is not present. For that Calvin wants to teach and not just to say something that we will repeat.[8]

The same must surely be true of the relationship between Bonhoeffer and Barth. To have been taught by Barth was to enter into *dialogue* with him. Eberhard Bethge captures this well when he writes,

> There is no disputing the fact that there was no contemporary to whom Bonhoeffer opened his heart so completely as he did to Karl Barth. 'I have, I think, seldom regretted anything in my theological past so much as the fact I did not go to him sooner', he wrote from Bonn in July 1931 to Sutz.[9]

The same affection was felt even in the latest stages of Bonhoeffer's life, during his time in Tegel: 'Karl's cigar is on the table in front of me, and that is something really indescribable.'[10] In the words of Godsey (for all he ends up playing the two off each other): 'Barth and Bonhoeffer, Bonhoeffer and Barth! They make quite a team!'[11]

The presence of Barth's theology in Bonhoeffer's doctoral dissertation is all too plain to see. In terms of the theological context of the 1920s, despite his training in Berlin and the influence of both Seeberg and von Harnack, Bonhoeffer clearly sided with Barth in his belief that the subject of theology could not be humanity but God in God's works. For all that *Sanctorum Communio*'s subtitle suggests the role of sociology in the study of the church, the study is (as the start of the subtitle suggests) a *theological* one and moves in the direction from Seeberg towards Barth. Yes, there were disagreements – disagreements around the concreteness of the neighbour who is to be loved[12] – but this was hardly a fierce rejection of Barth and was rather a conversation and disagreement with him around a point of discussion. Bonhoeffer was already moving towards the position which he would later confirm upon meeting with Barth and *conversing with* him in dialogue – that in Barth was his greatest dialogue partner and influence.

---

8. Karl Barth, *The Theology of John Calvin*, trans. Geoffrey W. Bromiley (Grand Rapids, MI: Eerdmans, 1995), 4.

9. Bethge, *Dietrich Bonhoeffer: A Biography*, 142.

10. Ibid., 142.

11. John D. Godsey, *The Theology of Dietrich Bonhoeffer* (Philadelphia, PA: Westminster Press, 1960), 27.

12. DBWE 1, 167. The editor's introduction makes much more of this than the evidence in the chapter affords; see DBWE 1, 3.

While ostensibly *Act and Being* seems critical of Barth's approach to revelation which it sees as too free – a freedom from humanity rather than for humanity – and of Barth's uneasy relation to Immanuel Kant compared to Bonhoeffer's desire that revelation should bring about an (ecclesial) epistemology of its own, it is in and of itself instructive that Bonhoeffer uses Barth as the conversation partner (in contrast to Heidegger) with whom he shapes his own position and converses. For sure, Bonhoeffer is concerned with the danger of the potential for a lack of continuity in Barth's understanding of revelation in his dialectical approach: God is so free from creation in Barth's actualism that there is instability, claims Bonhoeffer. However, there is tremendous worth in the words of Pangritz:

> The acuity of the critique of Barth present in the habilitation dissertation should not deceive one into ranking Bonhoeffer with the colleagues at the Berlin faculty in their opposition to Barth. The converse is more likely: precisely because he feels close to him – the many approvingly cited quotations affirm this perception – Bonhoeffer endeavours to work out as clearly as possible the differences which nevertheless exist between them.[13]

Furthermore, it may well be that Bonhoeffer is behind the point at which Barth had already arrived – a place, indeed, much closer than the argument of *Act and Being* might suggest. The presumption of freedom as the base account of Barth's actualism is true of *Romans*, but by the time of Göttingen and Münster, there had already begun a decidedly Christocentric turn. Hence, in the *Münster Dogmatics*, Barth asserts: 'Offenbarung Gottes an den Menschen wird von Gott aus so und nicht anders möglich, daß Gottes Sohn oder Wort Mensch wird, und zwar Mensch in demselben Sinn wie wir alle es sind, also Fleisch, d.h. Träger unseres Widerspruchs zu Gott und zu uns selbst.'[14]

There is a clear grounding of revelation's objectivity in the incarnation: it is the singularity of this act which is the ground of the continuity of revelation in the context of divine freedom, just as Barth will later in the lectures give the security for the possibility of human knowledge in the work of the Holy Spirit. He asserts: 'Offenbarung Gottes an den Menschen wird vom Menschen aus so und nicht anders möglich, daß er durch den heiligen Geist in der Taufe wird und ist, was er aus sich selber nicht werden und in sich selber nicht sein kann: ein Hörer und Täter des Wortes Gottes.'[15]

This is certainly Barth's own offering of an epistemology yielded by revelation. Whether it is one with which Bonhoeffer agrees can be debated, though the Christological and personal dimension is certainly key. Indeed, it may be that

---

13. Andreas Pangritz, *Karl Barth in the Theology of Dietrich Bonhoeffer* (Grand Rapids, MI: Eerdmans, 2000), 29.
14. Karl Barth, *Die christliche Dogmatik im Entwurf* (Zürich: Chr. Kaiser Verlag, 1927), §14, 289.
15. Ibid., §17, 380.

the Trinitarian and Christological pattern of thinking in Barth's theology is far more akin to the kind of person-centred account Bonhoeffer desires. Moreover, there is a clear ecclesial dimension to this receiving of revelation in freedom.[16] Barth, in this sense, was clearly a moving target regarding the critiques offered by Bonhoeffer, and quite possibly already ahead of where Bonhoeffer had pinned him: Barth was soon to move to a *church* dogmatics himself, from his previously conceived *Christian* dogmatics – a point which minimizes the distance between the thinkers. These points would, indeed, explain why Bonhoeffer engaged in such detail with Barth over the coming years. It is noteworthy that immediately following the acceptance of his second dissertation, Bonhoeffer would hardly ever offer the kind of critical engagement in lectures in Berlin or other contexts with epistemology which he does in *Act and Being*. His trip to New York saw him marked as a 'Barthian' in the context of Union Theological Seminary.

Of course, there are significant differences between the two. But these differences cannot be reduced to some suggestion of straightforward disagreement, or indeed the idea that they are part of two overarching rival theological camps. Their closeness grew from these earlier engagements following the Bonn meeting and culminated in their joint engagement in the Church Struggle.[17]

Lutheran Christocentric personhood versus Reformed divine otherness?

Yet, all too often, too simplistic an account of the differences which exist between these two thinkers is offered – with too great a focus on the difference at the expense of commonality.[18] Where differences are usually located by scholars, they tend to come in terms of one of two foci (or, indeed, in terms of the coalescence of the two): Lutheran versus Reformed confessional assumptions, and a Christocentric approach versus an approach based on divine otherness. However, it is a misrepresentation of Barth to presume his theology can simplistically be considered a classical Reformed confessional theology with its theocentric emphasis on divine otherness. And if this is the case, these kinds of one-dimensional critiques cannot be used as the basis for strongly demarcating Barth and Bonhoeffer.

---

16. Ibid., §12, 257.

17. And, in fact, while there is often the assumption that Bonhoeffer was more helpful than Barth in relation to the church's teaching about Judaism and Jews, Andreas Pangritz has complexified this image in his '"To Fall within the Spokes of the Wheel": New-Old Observations Concerning "The Church and the Jewish Question"', in *A Spoke in the Wheel: The Political in the Theology of Dietrich Bonhoeffer*, ed. Kirsten Busch Nielsen, Ralf K. Wüstenberg and Jens Zimmerman (Gütersloh: Gütersloh Ver.-Haus, 2013), 94–108.

18. I consider the approach of Michael DeJonge, *Bonhoeffer's Theological Formation: Berlin, Barth, and Protestant Theology* (Oxford: Oxford University Press, 2012), to be such an engagement.

Barth's own theological convictions are certainly Reformed, but there are two ways in which such a description falls short of an accurate presentation – even of the early Barth. The first consideration is the significance of Luther for Barth's theology. Certainly, during the Göttingen era, Barth explores (in his often polemical modality) the differences he holds in relation to Lutheran theology, especially in its confessional mode in his *The Theology of the Reformed Confessions*.[19] However, even in this Göttingen period (before the Münster period so significant for Bonhoeffer), Luther is among the three most significant theologians used in his *Dogmatics*. These uses are far from negative or pejorative but often affirmatory and positive. Of course, there are many points at which Reformed and Lutheran theologies agree, and it may simply be that Barth is offering positive comment on those moments, and this is certainly the case. But it is also the case that in some of the most contested areas at stake between Lutherans and Calvinists, there is a positive assessment of Luther and a movement which is at least closer to Luther's position than is often recognized.[20] Let us consider the related issues of the *extra Calvinisticum* and the *capax* debates: Barth presents the issues with a conciliatory tone, seeking to identify the dangers of both Lutheran and Reformed presentations:

> The older Lutherans said that the flesh of Christ was so united to the Logos that wherever the Logos is, there it has the flesh most present with it. With this statement they wanted to do justice to the concern that we stressed in §5.1.1, that God totally reveals himself in his revelation and that a hidden portion of his essence does not remain unrevealed. The older Reformed recognized this concern. For this reason they did not contest the fact that the whole Logos dwells in the human nature of Christ. What they did contest was that he is enclosed in the human nature: 'we do not imagine that he was confined therein.' …
>
> The Lutherans, however, hear in all this only the word 'outside' (*extra*), and they thus termed this doctrine the Calvinistic *extra*. I have three reasons for fully accepting this Calvinistic extra. (a) It does not really damage the justifiable Lutheran concern that God is wholly in his revelation.[21]

---

19. Karl Barth, *The Theology of the Reformed Confessions*, trans. Darrell L. Guder and Judith J. Guder, Columbia Series in Reformed Theology (Louisville, KY: Westminster John Knox, 2002).

20. Randall C. Zachmann notes particularly the significance of Luther to Barth's conceptualization of the task of theology, as well as other key themes. He concludes: 'Barth first engages the Reformers in general, and Luther in particular, to argue against Aquinas and Schleiermacher that the subject matter of theology is the proclamation of the Word of God', 'Barth and Reformation Theology', in *The Oxford Handbook of Karl Barth*, ed. Paul Dafydd Jones and Paul T. Nimmo (Oxford: Oxford University Press, 2019), 114.

21. Karl Barth, *The Göttingen Dogmatics: Instruction in the Christian Religion*, ed. Hannelotte Reiffen, trans. Geoffrey W. Bromiley (Grand Rapids, MI: Eerdmans, 1991), §6 IV 158–9.

What we see here is that Barth finds significance in the reasoning behind the Lutheran conceptualization, rather than pejoratively or polemically reacting against it. Certainly, the tenor of his engagement is more strongly Reformed in his Münster *Dogmatics in Outline*,[22] but the engagement around this theme is hardly straightforwardly oppositional in terms of an antagonistic engagement with the ideas which have led to this Lutheran conceptualization. While Bonhoeffer did clearly differ with Barth on this front,[23] Barth's own approach is more nuanced, and becomes ever more so. Indeed, in *Church Dogmatics*, the theme is not terribly present, and in terms of its early volumes, Barth can say:

> In what acknowledgment of God's Word in our experience, then, can there be anything like a sure and necessary correspondence to the Word of God? If there really is, then it is in virtue of the acknowledgment which man cannot achieve and therefore cannot assert, but which comes by grace upon his work that is corrupt and dead through sin, for Christ's sake and not for the sake of his inner disposition. How else can it be even in the religious man, the believing Christian? He it is specifically who knows, who alone knows, that this is how it is and not otherwise. The saying *finitum non capax infiniti* cannot really prove what has to be proved at this point. If the real experience of the man addressed by God's Word is against this saying, then the saying must go, as every philosophical statement in theology that is in contradiction with this experience must go. As a philosophical saying it does not interest us in the slightest. We do not say *finitum* but *homo peccator non capax* and we do not continue *infiniti* but *verbi Domini*. The real experience of the man addressed by God's Word is the very thing that decides and proves that what makes it possible lies beyond itself.[24]

The difference between the two on this point, certainly as Barth matures, is more limited than is often suggested: simply pointing to the fact Barth is Reformed and Bonhoeffer is Lutheran is not sufficient to suggest they do not belong within the same broad modern, theological movement and should not be considered together and brought into conversation.

The second consideration in relation to a simple demarcation of Barth and Bonhoeffer in terms of their confessional identities comes in terms of the fact that they are not simply orthodox representatives of their personal confessions but are also *moderns* in terms of their theological identity. Their engagements with post-Kantian philosophical contexts, as well as their predisposition to be able to sit critically (albeit respectfully) to their respective traditions, are indicative of this and important to remember when reading them. We see this, significantly, not only in Bonhoeffer's later (and more radical – albeit in a manner contiguous with his

---

22. Barth, *Die christliche Dogmatik im Entwurf*, 251, 269, 360.

23. *Act and Being*, DBWE 2, 84, 126. This doctrine is not, in fact, as key *to Act and Being* as one might think in terms of its dominance in terms of Bonhoeffer's critique.

24. CD I/1, 220–1.

earlier) writings from prison but also in Bonhoeffer's *Discipleship* in its capacity to offer critical engagement with the appropriation of Lutheranism. Similarly, Barth's preparedness to rethink radically his own confessional tradition (and the broader Augustinian tradition behind that) in relation to double predestination, as well as the significance of his actualistic approach to theology, are indications of the extent to which Barth is a modern even as he is orthodox.[25] If on the basis principally of their different confessional commitments we fail to see Barth and Bonhoeffer as theologians who have shared theological propensities and commitments, and as theologians engaged in constructive dialogue and with whom we might jointly dialogue, we fail not only to see the commonalities between these traditions and their own nuanced engagement with their confessions but also their own shared identities as moderns.[26]

Alongside these issues of confessional identity, there has been a propensity to contrast Barth and Bonhoeffer in terms of Bonhoeffer's so-called Christological personalism and Barth's emphasis on divine otherness.[27] However, while this might be fair to the pre-1924 Barth, as Bruce McCormack has demonstrated powerfully, through Barth's discovery of the significance of the anhypostatic-enhypostatic Christological dogma of the early church, Barth's shift to a Christocentric approach had begun in 1924, and these theological assumptions and basic approach continued through Barth's works to the first volume of *Church Dogmatics*.[28] McCormack states in relation to Barth's development in this period:

> Christology was as much a *critically* realistic theology as the previous theology in the shadow of a consistent eschatology had been. There was no relaxation here of Barth's fundamental radicalism. What is in view here is an advance along the same line which Barth had first entered in 1915; not a break with it. But second, and equally important, the incarnation could now be given its due. No longer did Barth need to reduce the 'site' of revelation to a single 'mathematical

---

25. On this, see Bruce McCormack's excellent and stimulating collection of essays, *Orthodox and Modern: Studies in the Theology of Karl Barth* (Grand Rapids, MI: Baker Academic, 2008).

26. There is great insight in Zachmann's comments, 'Barth and Reformation Theology', 114–15:

> Barth's conviction that Jesus Christ is the one Word of God leads him to become increasingly critical of the Reformers for the way they distinguish God in Godself from Jesus Christ, first with regard to the eternal election. Of God, and then with regard to the knowledge of God the Creator and the knowledge of ourselves as sinners, and finally with regard to the relationship between Jesus Christ as the one sacrament of God and the other alleged sacraments of the Church.

27. See DeJonge, *Bonhoeffer's Theological Formation*.

28. Bruce McCormack, *Karl Barth's Critically Realistic Dialectical Theology: Its Genesis and Development, 1909–1936* (Oxford: Oxford University Press, 1997), chaps. 8–9.

point' – the event of the cross. Now, the dialectic of veiling and unveiling on its objective side could comprehend the whole of the incarnate existence of the Mediator.[29]

Pre-1936, Barth mediates this Christologically grounded theology pneumatologically (in a way which echoes in fact, some of the pneumatological material in Bonhoeffer's early writings especially in *Act and Being*),[30] but it is clear that the Christological personalism of Barth's theology is set. Judging Barth by his theology before 1924 without recognizing the development in his thought, and presuming the Barth of the two editions of *Romans* is saying the same as he is even within five years of the first edition's publication (and utilizing this theology as a means of differentiating Barth and Bonhoeffer) is simply unhelpful. Where protests and questions come from Bonhoeffer, we might say, they come from Bonhoeffer wanting to make Barth *even more committed* to the Christological personalism to which Barth is already committed, and into which he journeys ever more. As Pangritz makes clear, what Bonhoeffer does in light of Barth's Christological theology is thus: 'Bonhoeffer protested wherever he thought Barth too [like Bonhoeffer's own teachers] was neglecting Christology.'[31] In other words, we might say Bonhoeffer is pushing Barth to be more committed to that which he is already committed, to follow through with his Christological turn to the thorough-going Christocentrism at which Barth arrives within less than a decade of the publication of Bonhoeffer's *Habilitationschrift*. The propensity to arbitrarily cut off Barth's theology at an early point in Bonhoeffer's life as if this were the point at which Barth arrived ultimately is one which unhelpfully suggests a greater chasm between Barth and Bonhoeffer than there in fact was: Barth is a moving target, and while he is moving, Bonhoeffer asks questions to propel Barth along the path on which they were already walking together. There is great worth in Bethge's comments: 'Whatever the implications of Bonhoeffer's earlier or later criticisms of Barth may be, in all four phases [of Bonhoeffer's engagement with Barth] he wanted them to be regarded as coming from inside and not outside the Barthian movement.'[32]

This is not to say that there were no points of difference. In one sense, the two had different projects, and Bonhoeffer found Barth's rejection of concreteness in discussion as confusing as Barth found the ideas frustrating. Bonhoeffer desired a discussion of the concrete situation and concrete ethics, as his lectures in 1932–3 made plain.[33] Indeed, we can find in some sense this commitment to concretion present even in the first doctoral dissertation, *Sanctorum Communio*. However,

---

29. Ibid., 328.

30. See David Emerton, *God's Church-Community: The Ecclesiology of Dietrich Bonhoeffer* (London: T&T Clark, 2020).

31. Pangritz, *Karl Barth in the Theology of Dietrich Bonhoeffer*, 22.

32. Bethge, *Dietrich Bonhoeffer: A Biography*, 134.

33. Ibid., 140.

following intense conversation and discussion with Barth around these issues, it is also worth noting that – while there were some moments of concretion in his ethical writings – both *Discipleship* and *Ethics* are not 'concrete' in the way one might imagine with clear ethical commands in given particular situations. And, even though the emphasis in all three of the aforementioned books is no doubt different to Barth's in significant ways (though even Bonhoeffer's commitment to 'mandates' is something Barth does not *polemically* reject), the form of concretion Bonhoeffer ultimately arrives at is one of which generally Barth approves, and Barth's immense affirmation of each of these volumes.[34] Clearly, there are differences between the two (in terms of emphasis around the question of the *capax* and in terms of emphasis over concretion), but both – as dialogue partners – walk along the same path.

Theologizing the critique of religion

Part of the problem in terms of the way in which these two figures are understood together (and in terms of the extent to which there is influence of Barth on Bonhoeffer) is that where there is perhaps some of the greatest commonality between the two is precisely where those who look only to the motif of 'positivism of revelation' as a critique of Barth in Bonhoeffer's discussion of religionlessness ironically find the greatest dissimilarity. This tagline, as if it existed *in abstracto* and without both the surrounding materials in the letters and the relationship between the two thinkers, has been a rallying call for those who wish to guard the boundaries of Bonhoeffer's theological distinctiveness. However, the immense similarity the two thinkers have in relation to this incredibly radical and distinctive theological discussion of religion far outweighs the distinctions, and the very phrase itself needs to be unpacked with tremendous care.

As with Barth's engagement with religion in paragraph 17 of *Church Dogmatics* I/2, Bonhoeffer's 'religionless Christianity' and 'non-religious interpretation' belong to a line of thought begun in the nineteenth century with certain critics of religion, including Feuerbach, Freud, Nietzsche and Marx. Rather than defending Christianity against such critiques, Bonhoeffer seeks to think with them in order to engage in a truer articulation of theology proper. As with Barth, for Bonhoeffer the critiques levelled at Christianity actually help the self-articulation of Christian theology to correspond more genuinely to the subject it seeks to describe; while the critics are ostensible enemies of religion, they are unexpected friends of theology. Bonhoeffer's most significant interlocutors are Nietzsche and Freud, in comparison to Barth for whom the dominant interlocutors were Feuerbach, Marx and (to a lesser degree) Freud.[35] However, Bonhoeffer's purpose and method is

---

34. Barth, CD III/4, 4; CD IV/2, 533; and Godsey, *The Theology of Dietrich Bonhoeffer*, 21n6.

35. On this, see Dumas (although he overstates the distinction between Barth and Bonhoeffer): André Dumas, *Dietrich Bonhoeffer: Theologian of Reality*, trans. Robert

entirely congruous with Barth on this point: he seeks to think theologically around such themes. Again, they are walking on the same path – a path which is radical and distinct from the surrounding theological thinkers of the age, and on which Bonhoeffer could not have journeyed without Barth's insights.

As with Barth, there is a primarily *theological* purpose to religionless Christianity for Bonhoeffer rather than a sociological description of some form of unidirectional aggressive form of secularization.[36] Importantly, human autonomy and secularization are not for Bonhoeffer primarily sociological categories but theological ones for a world which has not simply come of age by itself but which has come of age *by Jesus Christ*.[37] Nor can one think simply of religionless Christianity as in some ways being a translation of terms from religious to equivalent secular ones:[38] despite some suggestions that tend in this direction, there is no evidence of this remotely in Bonhoeffer, who continues to use terminology (in both German and Greek) such as church, baptism, sacrament and repentance; Bonhoeffer's work is far more profound than simple translation into the language of 'modern

---

McAffee Brown (London: SCM, 1971), 183, cf. 294. On Nietzsche and Bonhoeffer, see Peter Frick, 'Friedrich Nietzsche's Aphorisms and Dietrich Bonhoeffer's Theology', in *Bonhoeffer's Intellectual Formation*, ed. Peter Frick (Tübingen: Mohr Siebeck, 2008), 175–200; Stephen Plant, *Bonhoeffer* (London: Continuum, 2004), 49–52; and Bethge, *Dietrich Bonhoeffer: A Biography*, 84–5. On Bonhoeffer and Freud, see Clifford J. Green, *Bonhoeffer: A Theology of Sociality* (Grand Rapids, MI: Eerdmans, 1999), 17–18. On Bonhoeffer and Feuerbach, see Ralf K. Wüstenberg, *Bonhoeffer and Beyond: Promoting a Dialogue between Religion and Politics*, International Bonhoeffer Interpretations 2 (Frankfurt am Main: Peter Lang, 2008), 29–30; and Sabine Dramm, *Dietrich Bonhoeffer: An Introduction to His Thought*, trans. Thomas Rice (Peabody, MA: Hendrickson, 2007), 217.

36. For Bonhoeffer's sociological reading of a unified secularization thesis, see DBWE 8, 362–4, 425–8, 450, 475–81 and 499–504. On the problematic nature of a unified secularization thesis, see, for example, David Martin, *The Religious and the Secular: Studies in Secularization* (London: Routledge & Kegan Paul, 1969); David Martin, *Reflections on Sociology and Theology* (Oxford: Clarendon Press, 1997); Peter Berger, ed., *The Desecularization of the World: The Resurgence of Religion in World Politics* (Grand Rapids, MI: Eerdmans, 1999); and Talal Asad, *Formations of the Secular: Christianity, Islam, Modernity* (Palo Alto: Stanford University Press, 2003). On Bonhoeffer's limited engagement with sociology, see Peter Selby, 'Christianity in a World Come of Age', in *The Cambridge Companion to Dietrich Bonhoeffer*, ed. John W. de Gruchy (Cambridge: Cambridge University Press, 1999), 237–8.

37. DBWE 8, 342. I have tackled this theme in more detail in Chapter 8, and the reader is directed there for a more nuanced justification of this point. There is a point to be made about translation here: the new translation in DBWE interprets 'durch Jesus Christ' as attached to 'Inanspruchnahme', while LPP translation sticks more closely to the German word order.

38. Heinrich Ott, *Reality and Faith: The Theological Legacy of Dietrich Bonhoeffer*, trans. Alex A. Morrison (London: Lutterworth Press, 1971), 60–1; Dumas, *Dietrich Bonhoeffer: Theologian of Reality*, 183.

man and woman'. Rather, Bonhoeffer transforms the critique of religion (as Barth does) into the tantalizing suggestion that there is now a need to think in a religionless way[39] – not simply because this critique determines the need to do so but, according to him, also because it accords with the very message of God in scripture. The critique of religion moves from being an indicative description of human sinfulness (as one sees in Barth) to becoming a subjunctive or an optative theological possibility of or desire for religionlessness,[40] following Barth's theology through further, and pushing Barth through interrogative engagement to be more fully committed to his own theological journey (as Bonhoeffer had done at earlier points in their relationship as well).

Many helpful historical summaries of Bonhoeffer's work on religionless Christianity exist. But it is not the purpose of this chapter simply to rehearse summaries already made with scholarly precision elsewhere, and their sensitive identification of the careful turns of phrase in the letters relating to religionlessness and the secular interpretation of scripture.[41] Instead, it is advocated that Bonhoeffer's discussion of religionless Christianity should be understood in relation to Barth's thought as only a partially formed (but programmatic nonetheless) pointer of his theology, and where he is taking it. In this call, Bonhoeffer is building upon Barth's thought – Barth's extraordinarily original §17 of *Church Dogmatics*. It important to remember that Bonhoeffer's theology in prison is not considered for him an end point of his theology but a *midpoint* – a suggestion of the *trajectory* he is on. That religionlessness has been seen by scholars as an end point has arisen by virtue of the tragic circumstances of Bonhoeffer's untimely death. But the very genre of this theology (the letter and outline of the book), and the interrogative mood of much of his writing, determines that these are ideas *in via* rather than mature and final assertions. Bonhoeffer has clearly journeyed to a point and is thinking at this stage about where to take his theology further; however, he is not on a different path or journey to the one he has thus far taken, and remains on a path on which he is walking with and talking to Barth. Bonhoeffer does not repeat Barth simply: what point would there be to that? But Bonhoeffer is inspired by Barth in his theological

---

39. On the critique of religion and nonreligious Christianity, see Pangritz, *Karl Barth in the Theology of Dietrich Bonhoeffer*, 87–94.

40. On indicative, subjunctive and optative moods in theology, see David F. Ford, *Self and Salvation: Being Transformed* (Cambridge: Cambridge University Press, 1999), 257–62; and David F. Ford, *Christian Wisdom: Desiring God and Learning in Love* (Cambridge: Cambridge University Press, 2007), 45–51. The desire for a religionless Christianity is something Barth believed one could not hope for this side of the fall; see Matthew Myer Boulton, *God against Religion: Rethinking Christian Theology through Worship* (Grand Rapids, MI: Eerdmans, 2008), xvii.

41. For an introduction to the issues surrounding Bonhoeffer's religionless Christianity, see Selby, 'Christianity in a World Come of Age'. A more fulsome and detailed account is provided in Ralf K. Wüstenberg, *A Theology of Life: Dietrich Bonhoeffer's Religionless Christianity*, trans. Doug Stott (Grand Rapids, MI: Eerdmans, 1998).

imagination and thought, posing questions and offering critiques in private letters. Trajectories are important in assessing the relationship of Bonhoeffer's thought to that of Barth, and Bonhoeffer clearly sees himself as on the same trajectory as Barth.[42]

However, rather than realizing this commonality, all too often (as with the disproportionate focus on particular distinctions without understanding them in terms of broader agreement) the two-word charge (in German) of 'positivism of revelation' is not only rallied around but also becomes a hermeneutical lens through which to read the whole of the relationship between Barth and Bonhoeffer.[43] Bethge is surely right: 'Whoever had grown tired of Karl Barth found ample ammunition in the slogan "positivism of revelation".'[44] Following Bonhoeffer's seeming condemnation of Barth's theology under the epithet of 'positivism of revelation' and the occasional none too kind words of Barth about Bonhoeffer in light of this criticism,[45] there has been a wealth of mistrust and broken dialogue between the Barth and the Bonhoeffer 'camps'. However, there is far more continuity than has often been suggested between Barth and Bonhoeffer on the issue of theologizing the critique of religion. Crucially, it is necessary to attend to what Bonhoeffer actually says, and to the way in which he unpacks this charge, which is often thrown at Barth's theology with little sense of its true meaning. As Clifford Green helpfully reminds us: 'Bonhoeffer's unguarded remark about Barth in a private letter should not be used to drive a wedge between these two theologians.'[46]

'Positivism of revelation' appears in three letters of Bonhoeffer. The first time it is used (30 April 1944),[47] the charge is directed at Barth with regard to the way in which he has failed to unpack 'religionless Christianity'. Bonhoeffer

---

42. Bonhoeffer himself understood the issue of trajectories, seeing there as being a line for 'all genuine Christian thinking from Paul, Augustine, Luther, to Kierkegaard and Barth', DBWE 10, 461.

43. See, for example, Wolfhart Pannenberg, *Theology and the Philosophy of Science*, trans. Francis McDonagh (London: Darton, Longman and Todd, 1976), 275–6. For an introduction to what is meant more generally by 'positivist' approaches to revelation (in contrast to 'reductionist' approaches), see Ben Quash, 'Revelation', in *The Oxford Handbook of Systematic Theology* (Oxford: Oxford University Press, 2009), 332–40 (cf. 328–32).

44. Eberhard Bethge, *Dietrich Bonhoeffer: Theologe – Christ – Zietgenosse* (Munich: Chr. Kaiser Verlag, 1967), 999; translation from Pangritz, *Karl Barth in the Theology of Bonhoeffer*, 2.

45. For example, in Barth's letter to Superintendent Herrenbrück of 21 December 1952, in *World Come of Age: A Symposium on Dietrich Bonhoeffer*, ed. R. Gregor Smith (London: Collins, 1967), 70; Barth's letter to Bethge in Karl Barth, *Fragments Grave and Gay*, ed. Martin Rumscheidt (London: Collins, 1971), 121; and in Barth's comments (which notably do not name Bonhoeffer) in CD IV/3, 735.

46. Clifford Green, 'Trinity and Christology in Bonhoeffer and Barth', *Union Seminary Quarterly Review* 60, no. 1 (2006): 22.

47. DBWE 8, 280.

in this letter clearly affirms that Barth 'is the only one to have started along this line of thought' – a point which reflects more continuity than discontinuity with Bonhoeffer's own enterprise. Indeed, in this letter Bonhoeffer considers the need to unpack religionless Christianity by asking questions of Barth in terms of what his critique of religion means in reality for churches, sermons, liturgy, working people, doctrines, etc. Bonhoeffer points to his own distinction between the ultimate and the penultimate as having 'new importance here'.[48] The second occurrence of the term (5 May 1944)[49] is focused more on substantive doctrinal questions, criticizing Barth's doctrine of revelation for its 'like it or lump it' nature on such themes as the virgin birth and the Trinity: for Bonhoeffer the concern is that there is no engagement by Barth in degrees of doctrinal significance, with all loci deserving equal affirmation. Here, Bonhoeffer contends that the church stands for Barth in place where religion once dwelt, and the world is left to its own devices.[50] The third occurrence of this term (8 June 1944) is again directed at the lack of 'concrete guidance' for the 'non-religious interpretation of theological concepts'. This discussion is not in substantive disagreement with Barth but concerns the process of unpacking the meaning of his critique of religion, or allowing that critique to be the dominant guiding point that Bonhoeffer believes it should be, since it marks Barth's 'greatest service' to theology.[51]

Clearly, the content of the critique is not as harsh as it is sometimes presented as being when seen in context. Given the indebtedness and respect for Barth that Bonhoeffer shows throughout his theological career (see above), to see Barth's work on religion as his most significant insight is remarkable. Furthermore, it may well be that 'positivism of revelation', far from distancing Bonhoeffer from the trajectory on which Barth was headed, places Bonhoeffer firmly on that trajectory also.[52] Yet again, this can be seen as a critique aimed at making Barth follow through on the path to which he is already committed and to walk along it more speedily. There is scope for a monograph which alone attended to the vast array of interpretations scholars have offered with regard to the way in which one should understand Bonhoeffer's two-word charge. Indeed, there is almost as much (if not more) reflection on this than the meaning of religionlessness and non-religious interpretation.[53] For some theologians, the charge is aimed more at Barthians and

48. Ibid., 281.

49. Ibid., 286.

50. Clearly, one must remember that the latter point must be understood in light of Barth's early theology only; Bonhoeffer did not have access to the four-volume doctrine of creation found in CD III.

51. DBWE 8, 328.

52. In Chapter 3, there will be a discussion of the way in which this is further demonstrated in Barth's more mature work, including the two volumes of the Doctrine of God, which – while Bonhoeffer had read them – do not mark major interlocutors for Bonhoeffer.

53. Space cannot allow a thorough engagement into the details of these definitions, therefore, but certain aspects of them will be attended to in the footnotes. By far, the two most scholarly and useful engagements in English on the historical relationship between

the Confessing Church than Barth himself.⁵⁴ Others see it as arising from a degree of misunderstanding on the part of Bonhoeffer of Barth's purpose.⁵⁵ For others, it revolves around a shift towards existential thinking on Bonhoeffer's part, compared to Barth's overarching systematic principle of Christology which swallows up all else.⁵⁶ Still others consider the meaning to relate to the distinctive Christological method of Bonhoeffer compared to the Trinitarian method of Barth.⁵⁷ Some have suggested the ultimately positive role of religion in Barth in terms of leading humans to grace,⁵⁸ or the philosophical distinction between a theologian who is influenced primarily by Feuerbach, Freud and Marx (Barth), compared to one influenced

---

Barth and Bonhoeffer are Pangritz, *Karl Barth in the Theology of Dietrich Bonhoeffer*; and Wüstenberg, *A Theology of Life*. The reader should look to these for guidance on detailed issues.

54. See Pangritz, *Karl Barth in the Theology of Dietrich Bonhoeffer*, 77; cf. Green, 'Trinity and Christology in Bonhoeffer and Barth', 22. This seems to accord with Bonhoeffer's reaction to the Confessing Church's view of the theology of Rudolf Bultmann: see David Fergusson, *Rudolf Bultmann*, Outstanding Christian Thinkers (London: Continuum, 2000), 113. However, the charge of 'positivism' is still focused on Barth as well in this letter; for the Confessing Church is the charge of positivism as well as the related but distinct charge of 'conservative restoration' (DBWE 8, 328–9).

55. Hence Friedrich-Wilhelm Marquardt, *Theologie Und Sozialismus. Das Beispiel Karl Barths*, 3rd enlarged edn (Munich: Chr. Kaiser Verlag, 1985); Gerhard Krause, 'Dietrich Bonhoeffer and Rudolf Bultmann', in *The Future of Our Religious Past: Essays in Honour of Rudolf Bultmann*, ed. James M. Robinson (London: SCM, 1971), 279–305; and Stanley Hauerwas, *With the Grain of the Universe: The Church's Witness and Natural Theology* (London: Baker, 2001), 190, according to which Bonhoeffer 'mistakenly assumes that Barth is trying to answer a question that he thought should not be asked'. While Pangritz gives an excellent defence of Bonhoeffer's understanding of Barth on this point (Pangritz, *Karl Barth in the Theology of Dietrich Bonhoeffer*, 117–19), there may be a slight element of overstatement in his argument: certainly Bonhoeffer did have CD II/2 in sheet form, but not access to all of Barth's preceding works in his prison cell, and even the greatest of memories cannot hold all of the detail of a thinker such as Barth. Certainly, there is an element of 'impressionism' about Bonhoeffer's charge, innate indeed to the manner in which it is made – in a letter.

56. Ott, *Reality and Faith*, 123–30.

57. Green, 'Trinity and Christology in Bonhoeffer and Barth', 3–5. This makes a number of significant assumptions about Barth's theology, and is deeply complex to judge in light of recent debates regarding the immanent trinity in Barth's theology. On Barth on the immanent trinity, see the ongoing debates between (principally) Bruce McCormack, and George Hunsinger and Paul Molnar.

58. Dumas, *Dietrich Bonhoeffer: Theologian of Reality*, 178–84; cf. Green, *Bonhoeffer*, 258, who makes a similar point. This rests on a misreading of Barth's §17. Cf. chap. 2 of this book: religion fulfils no more positive a role than sin does; and Barth does not replace religion with grace; rather, *Jesus Christ* (the person) is the *Aufhebung* of religion.

by Nietzsche (Bonhoeffer).[59] Others point to the influence of the philosopher, Wilhelm Dilthey, on Bonhoeffer during the period of his prison writings.[60] For some, the issue is the dominant influence of Luther on Bonhoeffer compared to Calvin on Barth, particularly over the issue of the *extra Calvinisticum*.[61] Still others see the issue as resting in the positive meaning of 'religion' for the two theologians, with Bonhoeffer adopting an 'operational or behavioural' concept of religion in comparison to a 'morphological or institutional' one.[62] For others, it is Barth's 'all or nothing' approach that should be emphasized, especially around the issue of the virgin birth, at the heart of 'positivism of revelation'.[63] For others, the matter is Barth's inability to relate revelation to the world,[64] or his strong distinction of the church from the world.[65] At stake in some interpretations is Bonhoeffer's unpreparedness to create a theory of religion (and his critique of Barth's doing so) and the related

---

59. Dumas, *Dietrich Bonhoeffer: Theologian of Reality*, 183. There is worth in this point, but it should not be entirely over-emphasized. Bonhoeffer, too, is influenced by Freud, as much of the literature on this topic demonstrates, just as Barth is also aware of the work of Nietzsche. On the philosophical influences on Bonhoeffer, see further Peter Frick, ed. *Bonhoeffer's Intellectual Formation* (Tübingen: Mohr Siebeck, 2008).

60. Wüstenberg, *A Theology of Life*; Wüstenberg, *Bonhoeffer and Beyond*, 41–55; cf. Green, *Bonhoeffer*, 16. Dilthey does exercise an influence on Bonhoeffer at this point, but Bonhoeffer has already engaged with him in *Act and Being*, and therefore any suggestion of a radical, new and dramatic discontinuity with Barth cannot be accounted for on this basis.

61. Discussed and rebutted by Pangritz, *Karl Barth in the Theology of Dietrich Bonhoeffer*, 60. This is, indeed, hardly a fair reading of Barth who is in some ways almost as strongly influenced by Luther as he is by Calvin.

62. Green, *Bonhoeffer*, 262; cf. 258–68. However, this can hardly be used – as undoubtedly Green would not want it to be – as a wedge between Barth and Bonhoeffer. Indeed, Green's five-point summary of the critique of religion on 266–8 could equally well be applied to Barth as to Bonhoeffer, if one follows the interpretation of Barth offered in chap. 2 of this book.

63. Pangritz, *Karl Barth in the Theology of Dietrich Bonhoeffer*, 82–7, 99–14. Cf. Geffrey B. Kelly, 'Bonhoeffer and Barth: A Study of the Interaction with Karl Barht in Bonhoeffer's Theology of Revelation' (Université de Louvain, 1970). A focus on this issue seems to overestimate its importance somewhat, as it is only mentioned once in DBWE 8.

64. Regin Prenter, 'Dietrich Bonhoeffer und Karl Barths Offenbarungpositivismus', in *Mündige Welt*, ed. Eberhard Bethge (Munich: Chr. Kaiser Verlag, 1960), III, 13. To say this is to misunderstand Barth fundamentally. The issues Prenter addresses are ones I have addressed before in terms of human, historical, worldly particularity. See Tom Greggs, *Barth, Origen, and Universal Salvation: Restoring Particularity* (Oxford: Oxford University Press, 2009), especially the discussion of the Holy Spirit in Barth in Chapter 4. Also of note is the response to Prenter of Robert T. Osborn, 'Positivism and Promise in the Theology of Karl Barth', *Interpretation: A Journal of Bible and Theology* 25, no. 3 (1971): 289–90.

65. Brendan Leahy, '"Christ Existing as Community": Dietrich Bonhoeffer's Notion of Church', *Irish Theological Quarterly* 73, no. 1 (2008): 53.

issue of religion being a hamartiological concept for Barth compared to an historical concept for Bonhoeffer.⁶⁶ Still others analyse the distinction (helpfully) between Bonhoeffer and Barth in terms of different emphases in their theological approach – on the secondary objectivity of God in the former and the primary objectivity of God in the latter.⁶⁷

The problem with all these approaches is that there is a need to define which Barth that one is relating to which Bonhoeffer (as above!). However, it is certainly the case that the relationship between Bonhoeffer and Barth is far more *dynamic* than much of the secondary literature on the topic would suggest. Bonhoeffer may yet not have felt the revolutionary nature of Barth's doctrine of election, and we do well to remember that Barth had yet to embark fully on his four-volume doctrines of creation and of reconciliation. Certainly, the Barth that Bonhoeffer is aiming at is a moving target, and the concerns that underlie the charge of 'positivism of revelation' may not only be impressionistic at points. Aspects of the charge may, indeed, already have been answered not only by Barth's economic pneumatology which gives appropriate attention to the subjective appropriation of revelation but also in Barth's doctrine of God in *Church Dogmatics* volume II.⁶⁸ Crucially, one should recognize, however, that Bonhoeffer's work on religionlessness and the positivism of revelation marks a thinking *with* rather than a reacting against Barth, who himself is continuing to think through these matters. As Robert Osborn reminds us, the key thing is that 'Bonhoeffer himself said that Barth had "*not yet*" thought through to a solution'.⁶⁹ Barth's own reaction (and clear hurt) at Bonhoeffer's comment certainly did not do much to alleviate the sense that there was some genuine level of difference between them. Undoubtedly, Barth does not think that it is possible to ever escape from religion (as Bonhoeffer at least seems to), and in this much he never truly moves beyond his claim in *The Epistle to the Romans*: 'As men living in the world, and being what we are, we cannot hope to escape the possibility of religion.'⁷⁰ But this issue cannot simply be used to place

---

66. Wüstenberg, *A Theology of Life*, 64–5; cf. Wüstenberg, *Bonhoeffer and Beyond*, 49–50.

67. See Charles Marsh, *Reclaiming Dietrich Bonhoeffer: The Promise of His Theology* (Oxford: Oxford University Press, 1997), albeit with the proviso noted by George Hunsinger, 'Review of Charles Marsh, *Reclaiming Dietrich Bonhoeffer: The Promise of His Theology*', *Modern Theology* 12, no. 1 (1996), and supported by Green, 'Trinity and Christology in Bonhoeffer and Barth', 13-14. It should be noted, however, that the idea that Christ's humanity 'adds' anything to God (Marsh, 14) is never directly found in Bonhoeffer, and that the emphasis Marsh places on CD II/1 would find greater support for continuity between Bonhoeffer and Barth were Marsh to discuss II/2 in as much detail: in II/2, the *promeity* of God is seen at its theological heights (see Chapter 3 of this book).

68. Marsh, *Reclaiming Dietrich Bonhoeffer*, chap. 1 is helpful on these matters, if limited by not addressing CD II/2 in detail.

69. Osborn, 'Positivism and Promise in the Theology of Karl Barth', 286.

70. Karl Barth, *The Epistle to the Romans*, trans. Edwyn Hoskyns (Oxford: Oxford University Press, 1968), 230.

these theologians into distinctive (even opposed) theological camps. Charles Marsh is correct in stating that Barth is 'the very condition of the possibility of Bonhoeffer's theological pilgrimage';[71] and that we are wise to minimize rather than to maximize the differences between the two theological giants. Bonhoeffer expresses his desire for a religionless version of Christianity as a hope (in the optative mood); Barth's discussion of religion is a description of the current life of the Christian and the church (in the indicative).

Indeed, to some degree, it may be worth seeing Bonhoeffer's articulated struggles with Barth as struggles with himself. The charge that Bonhoeffer offers Barth of the church now standing in the place where religion once stood is a charge that could equally well be cited of his own theology up to that point.[72] Within the reflections on the *homo religiosus*, Bonhoeffer turns the critique into a self-examination with regard to *Discipleship*.[73] To some degree, his own self-struggle with his earlier church-orientated theology is expressed as a struggle with Barth,[74] as his major theological interlocutor. There is, indeed, a greater shift in many ways from Bonhoeffer's own *Discipleship* to his religionless Christianity than there is from Barth's critique of religion to Bonhoeffer's religionlessness. That Bonhoeffer articulates this self-struggle through discussion of Barth's work does not place distance between them, but already demonstrates that Bonhoeffer is seeking the assistance of his theological mentor in helping him to express his own constructive ideas: critically thinking from someone else's thoughts is, after all, the general practice of academic discourse in theology and the humanities. This does not serve to place Bonhoeffer outside the sphere of Barth's influence, but all the more firmly inside it.

Despite these points, problematically, in the literature, there has been a tendency to see Bonhoeffer's articulation of non-religious approaches to the Bible and of religionless Christianity as a shift from a more firmly Barthian perspective to a perspective that is more sympathetic to Bultmann.[75] However, this direction of movement is not the correct one to identify. Bonhoeffer's theological home was Berlin, and his thinking therefore was a thinking *from* liberalism *to* Barth: Barth was the means for Bonhoeffer's own sense of what was wrong with the liberal enterprise. One might do well, therefore, to think of Bonhoeffer's engagement with Bultmann and Barth on these themes not as a utilizing of Bultmann to identify what is wrong with Barth but as a recourse back to Barth to note what is wrong with Bultmann. The issue of Bonhoeffer's starting point may be of interest here, as starting with Bultmann and ending with Barth (as is the form in the letters)

---

71. Marsh, *Reclaiming Dietrich Bonhoeffer*, ix.
72. DBWE 8, 286.
73. Ibid., 369.
74. This is a point made by Gollwitzer in *Begegnung mit Dietrich Bonhoeffer: Ein Almanach*, ed. W.-D. Zimmermann (Munich: Kaiser, 1965), 112. An English translation can be found in Ott, *Reality and Faith*, 127.
75. See, for example, Krause, 'Dietrich Bonhoeffer and Rudolf Bultmann'.

certainly leads to Bonhoeffer ending in the Barth camp more fully than were the opposite the case. This point has greater implications, furthermore, than simply his relation to Bultmann, as Bultmann also engages directly with Dilthey in his 'New Testament and Mythology'.[76]

Even in Bonhoeffer's early letter of 5 December 1943, which begins his reflections on some of these themes, there are interesting points to note here. The concerns that underlie his reflections on the Old Testament in many ways parallel the concerns that are expressed by Bultmann with regard to the New Testament.[77] By the time that one gets to 30 April 1944, and the first charge against Barth, the language is even more akin to that of Bultmann. Bonhoeffer's concerns about religionless people today in light of nineteen hundred years of history feel redolent of Bultmann's statement that 'it is impossible to reinstate a past world picture'.[78] Similarly, Bonhoeffer's assertions that people cannot be religious any longer and that there is a dishonesty about being religious find close parallel to Bultmann's statement: 'We would affirm for our faith or religion a world picture that our life otherwise denied'.[79] Crucially, however, it is *from* these *questions* that Bonhoeffer arrives at *Barth's answers*:[80] while not arriving entirely satisfied with where Barth got to by that point, it is clear that there is a continued and sustained trajectory *not away from Barth but towards Barth*. One sees exactly the same point in the letter of 5 May 1944, with Bonhoeffer moving from the questions that Bultmann asks to the answers that Barth gives: it is on Barth's trajectory Bonhoeffer wishes to travel, and it is from Barth's answers that Bonhoeffer wishes to think in response to the liberal theological context in which the questions are posed.[81] When Bonhoeffer offers a similar analysis of intellectual history to Bultmann,[82] one again sees the same trajectory in the letter of 8 June 1944. Here, on first reading it might seem that Bultmann is given the crowning glory at the end of the successive responses to the issues Bonhoeffer has raised: Bultmann is used, indeed, by Bonhoeffer in response to Barth's failings. But what is the point on which Bonhoeffer ends? Bonhoeffer sets up a situation in which to respond to liberal theology (with Bultmann as a prime example of this), and his final interlocutor, who is seen as correct in seeking to overcome theological liberalism with his critique of religion, is Barth (even if Bonhoeffer does not think that he goes far enough).[83] The path

---

76. Rudolf Bultmann, *New Testament and Mythology and Other Basic Writings*, ed. and trans. Schubert M. Ogden (London: SCM, 1985), 23.

77. Cf. ibid., 3.

78. Ibid.

79. DBWE 8, 279–80, cf. Bultmann, *New Testament and Mythology and Other Basic Writings*, 4.

80. DBWE 8, 280.

81. Ibid., 285–6.

82. Ibid., 325–7, cf. Bultmann, *New Testament and Mythology and Other Basic Writings*, 2–7.

83. DBWE 8, 328–9.

on which Bonhoeffer was treading was certainly not the path of Bultmann, but the path away from Bultmann and from liberal theology. Bonhoeffer understood himself to be walking with Barth. This, indeed, is the path on which Bonhoeffer had walked from his earliest theological days in response to the liberal dominance of the Berlin faculty.[84]

A better way to understand Bonhoeffer's charge against Barth is to see it in relation to the theological father of liberalism, Friedrich Schleiermacher.[85] It may well be that Bonhoeffer believed that Barth was ultimately influenced (if negatively) by liberal theology, and that Barth was still allowing his work to be defined by the confines of liberal thought. Considering this point might help to unpack what Bonhoeffer meant by positivism of revelation, and to demonstrate that Bonhoeffer is seeking to be even more Barthian than Barth, rather than engaging in a different agenda.

Bonhoeffer had clearly engaged with Schleiermacher's work from the early stages of his theological formation. While still at school, Bonhoeffer read *Speeches*,[86] and worked through them a second time in the summer of 1923.[87] Discussion of Schleiermacher is found in both *Sanctorum Communio* and *Act and Being*.[88] Indeed, in the second thesis, Bonhoeffer affirms the 'theological right with which Barth reproached Schleiermacher for his "grand confusion" of religion and grace'.[89] Bonhoeffer, as Bethge recalls, had soon thought of Schleiermacher's work as an 'obscuration of the Reformation'.[90] However, it may well be in Schleiermacher's work that the clue to Bonhoeffer's concerns with Barth lie.

For Schleiermacher, 'religion in general' or religiosity is not the primary interest.[91] His concern is not 'natural religion' but individual instantiations of religion, and he spends a good deal of time discussing the various confusions of words related to religion.[92] He is concerned, indeed, that the terms are employed

---

84. Cf. Dumas, *Dietrich Bonhoeffer: Theologian of Reality*, 103–4. On Bonhoeffer's critique of Bultmann's demythologizing, see ibid., 188; and Pangritz, *Karl Barth in the Theology of Dietrich Bonhoeffer*, 78–82.

85. On the relationship between Schleiermacher and Bonhoeffer, see Christiane Tietz, 'Friedrich Schleiermacher and Dietrich Bonhoeffer', in *Bonhoeffer's Intellectual Formation: Theology and Philosophy in His Thought*, ed. Peter Frick (Tübingen: Mohr Siebeck, 2008), 121–43.

86. Bethge, *Dietrich Bonhoeffer: A Biography*, 27.

87. Ibid., 35.

88. For example, DBWE 1, 64, 133, 159; DBWE 2, 154.

89. DBWE 2, 154.

90. Bethge, *Dietrich Bonhoeffer: A Biography*, 49.

91. Friedrich Schleiermacher, *The Christian Faith*, ed. H. R. Mackintosh and J. S. Stewart, trans. D. M. Baillie, W. R. Matthews, Edith Sandbach-Marshall, A. B. Macaulay, Alexander Grieve, J. Y. Campbell, R. W. Stewart and H. R. Mackintosh, English translation of the 2nd German edn (Edinburgh: T&T Clark, 1968), 30.

92. In the postscript to §6, and the postscript to §10.

in a confused manner,[93] and is himself quite specific about their meaning. By 'positive' is signified 'the individual content of all the moments of the religious life within one religious communion, in so far as this content depends on the original fact from which the communion itself, as a coherent historical phenomenon, originated.'[94]

Revelation, on the other hand, is defined by Schleiermacher as that which 'signifies the *originality* of the fact which lies at the foundation of the religious communion.'[95] This original element, for Schleiermacher, has a divine causality. Thus, the relationship of religion as a general category to positive individual instantiations of religion is brought about by the divine causality of revelation: revelation brings about the individual and distinctive historical category of *positive* religion. Barth, in his lectures on Schleiermacher, discusses the relation of these concepts to each other helpfully and clearly:

> Natural religion ... is that which can be abstracted equally from the teachings of all pious societies of the top stage as the common element in all of them, even if in different determinations. What is differently determined, the individual element, is the positive element in a religion. ... A revelation denotes the fact that underlies a religion and conditions the individual content of its pious emotions but cannot itself be explained in terms of an earlier historical relationship.[96]

Given Bonhoeffer's time in Berlin, it is hardly thinkable that his reflections on religion and on Barth on religion would not have Schleiermacher in the background. Furthermore, Bonhoeffer became interested in Barth's thought in 1924 through his cousin, Hans-Christoph von Hase,[97] just months after Barth's lectures on Schleiermacher, which must no doubt have been freshly of interest in the minds of the students present in Göttingen. If this might have been a dim and distant point twenty years in the past for the middle-aged Bonhoeffer in the cell, Bonhoeffer's engagement with Dilthey surely places Schleiermacher back at the centre of Bonhoeffer's concerns. As Wüstenberg puts it: 'Given their substantive, proximity, one can mention Schleiermacher's and Dilthey's concepts of religion under a common denominator.'[98]

What, then, does this mean for Bonhoeffer's charge against Barth of 'positivism of revelation'? Firstly, it relates to the accusation of the 'take it or leave it' nature of revelation which, according to Bonhoeffer, exists in Barth's work. Positivism points to the givenness of the individual instantiation of Christianity, its unique

---

93. Schleiermacher, *The Christian Faith*, 47.
94. Ibid., 49.
95. Ibid., 50; italics original.
96. Karl Barth, *The Theology of Schleiermacher*, trans. Geoffrey W. Bromiley (Grand Rapids, MI: Eerdmans, 1982), 233.
97. Bethge, *Dietrich Bonhoeffer: A Biography*, 51.
98. Wüstenberg, *A Theology of Life*, 186, Cf. 73–6.

stand-aloneness which separates it not only from other religions but also from the world.[99] Secondly, and more fiercely, it seems that Bonhoeffer's term suggests a logical flaw in Barth's doctrine of revelation which separates it from all other potential engagements external to itself, creating a self-enclosed circle, self-sufficient in its entirety.[100] The argument of this would go thus: the positive aspect of a religion is its individuality and distinctiveness from all else. The cause of this (according to Schleiermacher) is revelation. Barth seems to agree with Schleiermacher in his presentation to some degree, since revelation contradicts religion. But, for Barth, the very thing which is distinctive is not only *caused by* revelation but *is* revelation. In other words, according to Bonhoeffer's critique of 'positivism of revelation', Barth says something akin to 'revelation makes Christianity a positive (unique) religion, and what is revealed is that Christianity is a religion based on revelation: the positivism of Christianity, which is caused by revelation, is, thereby, revelation.' Thus, revelation, rather than being the means of establishing the distinctiveness of Christianity, becomes the beginning and the end. However, it may well be that (written in a short letter, in a cell, without access to his library) this critique of Bonhoeffer's fails to do full justice to §17 of *Church Dogmatics*. Crucially, for Barth, it is not revelation or even grace which is the *Aufhebung* of religion,[101] but *Jesus Christ himself*. The trueness of Christian religion does not rest in revelation or grace, but its religion is contradicted in the same way in which sin is contradicted, not simply by the revelation of revelation but by the revelation of God in the person of Jesus Christ. To a degree, therefore, the charge rests on an insensitive reading of Barth, but nevertheless that reading does not stop Bonhoeffer sensing that Barth is on the path that he, too, should walk along: it means only that Bonhoeffer does not realize how closely and how much in step he and Barth are walking, and given the ongoing and dynamic nature of both of their works (see above), this can hardly be a charge of overt misrepresentation. Bonhoeffer builds upon Barth's indicative description of human religion and optatively hopes for a Christianity which can become religionless: for Bonhoeffer, there is the hope that religion need not be the 'given' (positive) for theology.[102] He charges Barth with

---

99. Cf. DBWE 8, 286.

100. Cf. Richard H. Roberts, 'Spirit, Structure and Truth', *Modern Theology* 3, no. 1 (1986), 77–106. Roberts claims that Barth vastly subordinates the Spirit to the central encounter with the Word of God, simply completing the circle of revelation.

101. The meaning of this term is much disputed. It stems from Hegelian philosophy, and means 'destruction' or 'sublation' or 'sublimation'.

102. It is because of this that it is so difficult to locate Bonhoeffer's model of understanding religion: '[Bonhoeffer] never really develops a theory of religion, nor is there a fixed place in him that one can point to and think they possess the interpretative key to Bonhoeffer's concept of religion. Some people find themselves agitated by Bonhoeffer's perspective' (Jeffrey Pugh, *Religionless Christianity: Dietrich Bonhoeffer in Troubled Times* (London: T&T Clark, 2008), 73). Pugh goes on to question himself whether Christianity could be separated from religion.

the task of moving *further away* from Schleiermacher's categories – otherwise put, with the task of becoming more intensely Barth. The critique is not against Barth's constructive work but of the continued Schleiermacherian categories which Barth still works with as a background: Bonhoeffer does not want less Barth; he wants more. Rather than 'mediating' Barth and liberal theology, throughout his career, Bonhoeffer called into question what he perceived as any liberal vestige remaining in Barth's theology (even if it is being shaped by opposition), calling Barth back to the Christological basis from which Barth claimed to work.

Conclusion

Rather than seeing these theological dialogue partners and compatriots as opponents or members of different (even opposed) theological camps, it is better to consider them as walking together along the same theological trajectories – holding each other to account, and conversing. There is no doubt that Barth was Bonhoeffer's most significant contemporary theological influence, nor can there be doubt of the immense shared theological vision. To work to build parapets in order to guard demarcations of the one from the other fails to understand the extent to which these figures can *together* be used in forming theology today. Where differences exist, it is often in terms of emphasis, and where Bonhoeffer is critical of Barth, it is often that he does not go far enough in the direction Barth himself is setting. Indeed, it is this latter point which is key to understanding the two-way dialogue and conversation between these major theologians: there is not only influence of Barth on Bonhoeffer but also of Bonhoeffer on Barth, and it is to this theme which this book now turns. These are two thinkers which have so much in common and so much to say to contemporary theology that it is a gross disservice to the theology of the twentieth century to read only one at the expense of the other.

Chapter 2

THE INFLUENCE OF DIETRICH BONHOEFFER ON KARL BARTH

Having considered the possibility and, indeed, advocated the wisdom of reading Karl Barth and Dietrich Bonhoeffer together from the perspective of Barth's influence on Bonhoeffer, this chapter turns to address the flip side of the discussion: whether there can be said to be any influence of Bonhoeffer on Barth. This may be seen as a strange issue to address. Born in 1886, Barth was a half-generation older than Bonhoeffer (born 1906). Bonhoeffer was only 12 years old when Barth published his theological epoch-making *Römerbrief*. Bonhoeffer studied Barth's work and was influenced by him as a student, such that his *Habilitationsschrift*, *Act and Being* was written in large part in dialogue with Karl Barth's work. Even though this work contains critical elements,[1] this criticism should, as has been advocated in the preceding chapter, be seen within a shared discourse – a discourse established by Barth into which Bonhoeffer enters. As has already been noted, in the words of Andreas Pangritz:

> The acuity of the critique of Barth present in the *Habilitation* dissertation should not deceive one into ranking Bonhoeffer with the colleagues at the Berlin faculty in their opposition to Barth. The converse is more likely: precisely because he feels so close to him – the many approving cited quotations affirm this perception – Bonhoeffer endeavours to work out as clearly as possible the differences which nevertheless exist between them.[2]

---

1. These are drawn out clearly (and polemically) by Michael P. DeJonge in *Bonhoeffer's Theological Formation: Berlin, Barth, and Protestant Theology* (Oxford: Oxford University Press, 2012). DeJonge argues that Bonhoeffer distances himself from Barth, offering an alternative to both Barth and Holl. Although the exegesis of *Act and Being* is thorough and compelling, the presentation of Barth in DeJonge's work seems to be a foil against which to describe Bonhoeffer and downplays the deep influence Barth has on Bonhoeffer and the shared dialogues in which they engage. Space does not allow a thorough development of this point, but suffice it to say that it is better to see the issue of influence more in the terms presented by Andreas Pangritz, *Karl Barth in the Theology of Dietrich Bonhoeffer* (Grand Rapids, MI: Eerdmans, 1999). For a detailed engagement with these points, see the previous chapter.

2. Pangritz, *Barth in the Theology of Bonhoeffer*, 29.

Bonhoeffer remained (even in his more critical comments) a theologian who was deeply influenced by Karl Barth both personally and theologically.

Furthermore, the different nature of their approaches to systematic theology itself suggests an intellectual legacy or foundation that moves in a particular direction: from regular to irregular dogmatics in Barth's terms;[3] or, as A. N. Williams describes it,[4] from a mode of systematic theology which marks an attempt at a *comprehensive* account of theology, arranged by loci, to a mode of systematic theology which is descriptive of a *single* locus, with an awareness of how it is shaped by or shapes other loci. The seeming comprehensiveness of Barth's various attempts at a regular dogmatics (culminating in his *Church Dogmatics*) offers a somewhat natural foundation for those engaged in the task of irregular dogmatics or in discussing singular issues in systematic theology, as Bonhoeffer was. It is less easy to imagine how the stream of influence might flow in the other direction, though on particular issues, one might imagine that it is possible.

The limitations of influence on Barth

Even in thinking of influence in the direction of Barth to Bonhoeffer, one might be, as many are and continue to be, minded to think that in the end their theologies existed in opposition. Bonhoeffer's infamous criticism of Barth's theology – that it was marked by a 'positivism of revelation' – has not helped the case that these two theologians should be thought of as conversing in a shared dialogue.[5] While Bonhoeffer offered this short telegrammatic phrase in critique of Barth, one which every student of modern theology knows, in response to this, Barth himself poured out some none-too-kind words about Bonhoeffer.[6] The most notable difficulty of all in tracing Bonhoeffer's influence on Barth is that Barth seems at points to be, at best, befuddled by Bonhoeffer's theology (and certainly hurt by the critique offered of revelatory positivism) and, at worst, straightforwardly critical of not only Bonhoeffer's theology but also some of his life decisions.

Barth was certainly confounded by the influence Bonhoeffer's theology had in the 1960s. He writes, for example: 'I knew Dietrich Bonhoeffer well. What he would have thought and planned and achieved had he lived, no one can say. The fragments of his theology (especially from his final years) have unfortunately become the fashion.'[7] The so-called unfortunate influence Bonhoeffer's theology

3. On the distinction between regular and irregular dogmatics, see CD I/1, 38, 275–87.

4. A. N. Williams, *The Architecture of Theology: Structure, System, and Ratio* (Oxford: Oxford University Press, 2011), 1–22.

5. The previous chapter has discussed this issue in detail and pointed towards the failure that many scholars have in reading Bonhoeffer on this topic.

6. Cf. Karl Barth, 'From a Letter to Superintendent Herrenbrück', in *World Come of Age: A Symposium on Dietrich Bonhoeffer*, ed. R. Gregor Smith (London: Collins, 1967), 70.

7. 'Barth: May 7, 1968', in Karl Barth, *A Late Friendship: The Letters of Karl Barth and Zuckermayer*, trans. Geoffrey W. Bromiley (Grand Rapids, MI: Eerdmans, 1982), 42.

exerted is also discussed in a letter concerning J. A. T. Robinson's work, in which Barth identifies the influence of Bonhoeffer on the Bishop of Woolwich, and states: 'darf natürlich auch nicht fehlen! Wer beruft sich heute nicht auf Bonhoeffer?'[8] Still seeing himself as an outlying voice in theological circles, Barth sees Bonhoeffer's theology much more as in vogue, and lists him alongside Tillich and Bultmann. As such, Bonhoeffer seems to fall prey to Barth's cutting wit. In part, this may have been in retaliation to Bonhoeffer's criticisms of Barth in his *Letters and Papers from Prison*. Barth expresses this critique directly in a letter of praise and thanks to Eberhard Bethge following the publication of what Barth describes as his 'masterpiece on Bonhoeffer'.[9] Amidst three lines of questioning, Barth states the following:

> Wholly obscure to me, even after reading your book, is the matter on which discussion has raged from several angles since it was provoked by *Letters and Papers from Prison*: the renewal of theology in both the narrower and the broader sense as he envisioned it. What is the 'world come of age'? What is meant by 'non-religious interpretation'? What is the 'positivism of revelation' ascribed to me? I know all the things, or most of the things, that the experts have made of this right up to Heinrich Ott. But to this day I do not know what Bonhoeffer himself meant and planned with it all, and very softly I venture to doubt whether theological systematics (I include his *Ethics*) was his real strength.[10]

This final sentence is a very cutting one, which seems to indicate something of Barth's hurt at the critique Bonhoeffer offered against his theology. Indeed, so strong was that sense that Barth wrote to Bethge of his surprise at discovering how influential he [Barth] had been on Bonhoeffer, stating that it was a shock to discover that he 'was always so important a figure to him [Bonhoeffer] – until at the end he charged me with a "positivism of revelation", an objection I could never clearly understand'.[11] Barth even states that he had, until reading the biography, 'always thought of [himself] as one of the pawns, not the knights or castles, on [Bonhoeffer's] chessboard'.[12]

Barth clearly questioned, furthermore, the very idea of religionless Christianity, and considered that all religious language was also secular. He thought that the

---

8. Karl Barth, 'Gespräch mit rheinischen Jugendpfarrern (4.11.1963)', in *Gespräche 1963*, ed. Eberhard Busch, Karl Barth Gesamtausgabe IV.41 (Zürich: Theologischer Verlag, 2005), 252. Translation: '[Bonhoeffer] of course must not be missed. Who today does not appeal to Bonhoeffer?'

9. 'To Rector Eberhard Bethge, Rengsdorf near Neuwied', in Karl Barth, *Letters 1961–1968*, ed. Jürgen Fangmeier and Hinrich Stoevesandt, trans. Geoffrey W. Bromiley (Grand Rapids, MI: Eerdmans, 1981), 250.

10. Ibid., 252.

11. Ibid., 250–1.

12. Ibid., 251.

idea of becoming more secular was misguided if not impossible, since all religious language by his account was both secular and sacred: there was no possibility of being more secular or entering into a more secular realm, since there is no such thing.[13] He saw *Letters and Papers from Prison* and the 'rather cryptic statements' it included as being part of a liberal agenda.[14] It is clear that Barth was not an unquestioning supporter of Bonhoeffer's theological insights.

It is also clear that Barth had questions to ask of some of Bonhoeffer's life decisions. Given Bonhoeffer's famous biography and status as a modern martyr, this is perhaps somewhat surprising, especially for someone who both called Bonhoeffer back to Germany ('your church's house is on fire ... you ought to return to your post by the next ship! ... If you did not matter so much to me, I would not have taken you by the collar in this fashion')[15] and was himself excluded from speaking in public and removed from his position in Bonn as a result of his unwillingness to swear the oath of allegiance to Hitler. However, speaking of the conspiracy of 1944, Barth wrote: 'I still remember as if it were yesterday how what Dietrich Bonhoeffer told me personally about the venture, or the conversations preceding it, gave me the impression of something hopelessly passé.'[16] This is a rather odd recollection for Barth, who seemed somewhat haunted at the end of his life by the urgency of his call to Bonhoeffer to return to Germany. Barth writes to reject Hendrikus Berkhof's request that Barth write to Boulon to ask Boulon to stay in Beirut. He writes: 'I am not able to accept responsibility: I have already in mind advice that I had once given Bonhoeffer to return from London to Germany, and by its observance he ended up in Flossenbürg.'[17] This is a letter which comes in the final months of Barth's life and shows how large an impact Bonhoeffer's untimely death had on Barth as a man.

While it is clear that we should not overstate the case of Bonhoeffer's influence on Barth, nevertheless, as I have argued elsewhere,[18] we should think of the two as walking along the same path together, conversing with one another. Influence does not always work in a static manner of building upon some intellectual insight, or offering citations from the other. Influence also works in shared conversation and interests, in indirect reflections that arise from dialogical engagement. Not always with absolute agreement, Bonhoeffer and Barth were nevertheless able to share a

---

13. CD IV/3, 735. Note that Bonhoeffer is not mentioned directly in the small print section here, but his ideas are clearly in the background.

14. ChrL, 200.

15. DBWE 13, 40-1; DBW 13, 32-3.

16. 'Barth: May 7, 1968', in Karl Barth and Carl Zuckmayer, *A Late Friendship: The Letters of Karl Barth and Carl Zuckmayer* (Grand Rapids, MI: Eerdmans, 1982), 53.

17. Karl Barth, 'An Prof. Dr. Hendrik Berkhof, Leiden, 1968', in *Briefe 1961-1968*, ed. Jurgen Fangmeier and Hinrich Stoevesandt, Karl Barth Gesamtausgabe V.6 (Zurich: Theologischer Verlag, 1979), 505; translation mine.

18. Tom Greggs, *Theology against Religion: Constructive Dialogues with Bonhoeffer and Barth* (London: T&T Clark, 2011), chap. 3.

discourse around a series of shared emphases, themes, theological commitments and ecclesial concerns. In certain of these, one can directly see the influence of Bonhoeffer on the theology of his theological mentor, Karl Barth.[19] Furthermore, Barth certainly indicates at various points in writings that he considered Bonhoeffer one of the major theological voices of the twentieth century. He lists, indeed, the heritage of Bonhoeffer's thought as one of various possibilities in theology in his 1962 lectures in America (*Evangelical Theology*), placing his thinking alongside the possible choices of his own thought, demythologization, the historical Jesus and so forth.[20] So significant a figure, in Barth's view, is bound to have had an influence on him; and it is to these influences it is now possible to turn.

The influence of a life

In the famous and telling letter to Eberhard Bethge, Barth recounts what he thinks some of Bonhoeffer's most significant contributions had been. Principal among these seems to have been an awareness of the prophetic foresight Bonhoeffer offered in terms of his response to the need for the church to stand up against the persecution of the Jews in Germany. Having noted that Bonhoeffer moved from the liberalism of his teachers to 'a living view of what the church … should be' during an early trip to Rome (which was a new discovery for Barth), he writes:

> Bonhoeffer was the first and almost the only one to face and tackle the Jewish question so centrally and energetically. I have long since regarded it as a fault on my part that I did not make this question a decisive issue, at least publicly in the church conflict (e.g., in the two Barmen Declarations I drafted in 1934). A text in which I might have done so would not, of course, have been acceptable to the mindset of even the 'confessors' of that time, whether in the reformed or the general synod. But this does not excuse the fact that since my interests were elsewhere I did not at least formally put up a fight on the matter. Only from your book [the Bethge biography] have I become aware that Bonhoeffer did so from the very first. Perhaps this is why he was not at Barmen nor later at Dahlem.[21]

Barmen's failure to address Jewish persecution is an embarrassing silence. While it is true that Barth was actively engaged in speaking out for Jewish people as early as 1934[22] – and some of his hesitancy was to do with (what would seem to us now as

---

19. The one attempt at an initial exploration of this direction of influence can be found in Matthew Puffer, 'Dietrich Bonhoeffer in the Theology of Karl Barth', in *Karl Barth in Conversation*, ed. W. Travis McMaken and David W. Congdon (Eugene, OR: Pickwick, 2014), 46–61.

20. Karl Barth, *Evangelical Theology* (Grand Rapids, MI: Eerdmans, 1963), 141.

21. Barth, *Letters 1961–1968*, 250.

22. Katherine Sonderegger, *That Jesus Was Born a Jew: Karl Barth's 'Doctrine of Israel'* (Pennsylvania: Pennsylvania State University Press, 1992), 22–3.

an inexcusable) attempt at avoiding unnecessary political involvement for which he felt ill-equipped – he said less than he ought.[23] Barth also famously stated that he found his personal relationships with genuine, living Jews (rather than the Jews of the Bible) difficult. He writes: 'in personal encounters with living Jews ... I have always, so long as I can remember, had to suppress a totally irrational aversion.'[24] Barth was clearly concerned to support baptized Jews, as we can see in the sixth point of his 'Theologische Existenz heute!'[25] and also offered complete support for Vischer's initial draft of ten theses on 'The Church and the Jews' for the Bethel Confession (the first five of which were more broadly focused on the question of biblical interpretation relating to the Jewish people as God's chosen).[26] However, in his comments on his decision to continue doing theology 'as if nothing had happened',[27] it is possible to witness a particular set of emphases in Barth's work that he was to question later in life in light of Bonhoeffer's recognition of the Jewish question, and the energy he gave to considering it and acting upon it.[28]

Indeed, Barth was generally impressed with the relationship Bonhoeffer recognized between Christian faith and political action. Recalling the influence of his own intellectual mentors (Blumhardt, Kutter and Ragaz), Barth questioned

---

23. Eberhard Busch, ed., *Karl Barth: His Life from Letters and Autobiographical Texts* (London: SCM Press, 2011), 226.

24. Barth, *Letters 1961–1968*, 262.

25. Karl Barth, 'Theologische Existenz heute!' (1933), Beiheft Nr. 2 von 'Zwischen den Zeiten', vol. 11 (1933) = *Theologische Existenz heute*, ed. K. Barth and E. Thurneysen, H. 1 (München: Kaiser, 1933), 45–6.

26. Karl Barth, 'Letter to Wilhelm Vischer, August 24, 1933', in *Briefe des Jahres 1933*, ed. Eberhard Busch, Bartolt Haase and Barbara Schenck (Zürich: Theologischer Verlag Zürich, 2004), 347. For more on the Bethel Confession and the role of Vischer and Bonhoeffer, see Andreas Pangritz, 'Wilhelm Vischer's Contribution to the "Bethel Confession"', paper presented to the American Academy of Religion, 2010, Montreal, Quebec.

27. Barth, 'Theologische Existenz heute!', 3.

28. For more on Barth and the Jews, see Sonderegger, *That Jesus Was Born a Jew*; Eberhard Busch, 'Indissoluble Unity: Barth's Position on the Jews During the Hitler Era', in *For the Sake of the World: Karl Barth and the Future of Ecclesial Theology*, ed. George Hunsinger (Grand Rapids, MI: Eerdmans, 2004), 53–79; Katherine Sonderegger, 'Response to Eberhard Busch', in *For the Sake of the World: Karl Barth and the Future of Ecclesial Theology*, ed. George Hunsinger (Grand Rapids, MI: Eerdmans, 2004), 80–7; Mark Lindsay, 'Dialectics of Communion: Dialectical Method and Barth's Defence of Israel', in *Karl Barth: A Future for Post Modern Theology?*, ed. Geoff Thompson and Christiaan Mostert (Hindmarsh, South Australia: Australian Theological Forum, 2000), 122–46; G. C. Berkouwer, *The Triumph of Grace in the Theology of Karl Barth* (London: Paternoster, 1956), 108–9; Clement Chia, 'Is Barth a Supercessionist? Reconsidering the Case in the Historical Context of The Nazi Jewish Question', presented at the Society for the Study of Theology, Leeds, 2006; and Eugene F. Rogers Jr, 'Supplementing Barth on Jews and Gender: Identifying God by Analogy and Spirit', *Modern Theology* 14, no. 1 (1998), esp. 55–6, 60–7.

his own movement away from more political issues following *Romans*, and during his time working in Germany from 1921 onwards: his focus had shifted to calling German theologians to reinterpret the reformation and make the reformation relevant. Barth now recognized that the Lutheran heritage of Germany required discussion of things he had taken for granted, and yet which Bonhoeffer rightly addressed:

> There was a genuine need in the direction which I now silently took for granted or emphasized only in passing: ethics, fellow-humanity, a serving church, discipleship, socialism, the peace movement, and in and with all these things, politics. This gap, and the need to fill it, Bonhoeffer obviously saw keenly from the very first, and he felt it with increasing intensity and expressed it on a broad front. This supplementation which had been missing so long and which he represented so vigorously, was and still remains to a great extent at least (and we hope decisively) the secret of the impression that he has rightly made especially when he became a martyr, too, for this specific cause.[29]

This interrelation of faith, life and action is something that seems to have impressed Barth and influenced him in a number of ways. Not only is it the case that Bonhoeffer's life and decisions about the way he would approach treatment of Jewish people influenced Barth, it was also the case that Bonhoeffer's concern for the Christian life, and what Barth identifies as 'discipline', further influenced Barth.[30] This might be thought about in two particular ways: the influence particularly of *Discipleship* and *Ethics*. We address each of these in turn.

Discipleship

Barth stated that, on the topic of discipleship and *imitatio Christi*, he was tempted in *Church Dogmatics* to reproduce the opening sections of *Discipleship* 'in an extended quotation'. His reasoning was simple: 'Easily the best thing written on this subject is to be found in *The Cost of Discipleship* [sic].' Not only that, but he also stated: 'I cannot hope to say anything better on the subject than what is said here by a man who, having written on discipleship, was ready to achieve it in his own life, and did in his own way achieve it even to the point of death.'[31] Whatever Barth might have thought of other decisions Bonhoeffer had made, Barth clearly saw the significance of a theologian who enacted his theological commitments in the life he led. For the polemically minded Barth, this is high praise.

The ideas of cheap and costly grace appear at various points in Barth's doctrine of reconciliation. In discussion of the judgement that human beings should receive and the grace with which God engages with humans, Barth writes that

---

29. Barth, *Letters 1961–1968*, 251.
30. Ibid.
31. CD IV/2, 353–4.

the grace with which God deals human beings is 'dear' and not 'cheap', citing Bonhoeffer in brackets after the phrase. The point Barth wishes to make in light of his description of God's reconciling grace is that grace does not remove or reduce the 'accusation and sentence' that human beings receive. Barth uses the idea of cheap and costly grace in order to make the point that the necessity of our confession of sin and guilt is not weakened by the grace of God, but that the necessity of that confession is grounded in the costly act of God in forgiving our sins, an act which God accomplishes in the event of the atonement. This means that the response to grace cannot be one of carelessness but only one of disciplined responsibility.[32]

The significance of discipleship and of costly grace is something Barth addresses particularly in his discussion of sanctification in *Church Dogmatics* IV/2. He points to the inseparability of justification and sanctification as two moments and aspects of one and the same event of God. Separating these two moments has the capacity to lead to two mistakes that have corresponding consequences for the life of faith. On the one hand, the mistake that the separation of justification and sanctification can lead to is some kind of semi-Pelagianism, or, as Barth describes it, an understanding which focuses on 'a favoured man who works in isolation'. This begets 'an illusory activism, where the relationship of sanctification to justification is forgotten'.[33] On the other hand, Barth draws upon Bonhoeffer's discussion of cheap grace to identify the other mistake – of forming the 'idea of a God who works in isolation, and His "cheap grace" (D. Bonhoeffer)'. This creates 'an indolent quietism, where the relationship of justification to sanctification is neglected'.[34] Barth makes the point in very much the same way that Bonhoeffer does in the opening pages of his *Discipleship*.[35]

Barth also draws significantly on Bonhoeffer's idea of 'simple obedience'.[36] In contrast with the old Adam who weighs and considers what is to be done, and ultimately denies the call of discipleship in Christ, the disciple to Christ is, according to Barth, to follow in simple obedience. This is a form of discipleship that does exactly as it is supposed to: 'nothing more, nothing less, and nothing different'.[37] It is a form of obedience in which the new Adam does exactly as he or she is commanded to by Christ. Barth writes:

> Bonhoeffer is ten times right when at this point he inveighs sharply against a theological interpretation of the given command and the required obedience, which is to the effect that the call of Jesus is to be heard but His command may be taken to mean that the obedience required will not necessarily take the form

---

32. CD IV/1, 70.
33. CD IV/2, 505.
34. Ibid.
35. DBWE 4, 43–56; DBW 4, 29–44.
36. DBWE 4, 77–83; DBW 4, 69–76.
37. CD IV/2, 540.

of the act which is obviously demanded but may in certain cases consist in the neglect of this act and the performance of others which are quite different.[38]

Barth is concerned in this that the outward activity of justified human beings is changed by the concrete command of Jesus, by the commanding grace of God. He insists that, for whatever seemingly justifiable reason a Christian might have not to follow in outward obedience, the command of God lays claim to the Christian's life and therefore must not be resisted: indeed, this seemingly justifiable reason often takes the form of the theological reasoning precisely to avoid the concrete and simple command of God. To demonstrate the point that is being made, Barth quotes Bonhoeffer:

> Where orders are given in other spheres, there can be no doubt how matters stand. A father says to his child: Go to bed, and the child knows what has to be done. But a child versed in this pseudo-theology might argue as follows. My father says: Go to bed. He means that I am tired. He does not want me to be tired. But I can dissipate my tiredness by going out to play. Therefore, when my father says: Go to bed, he really means: Go out to play. If this were the way in which children reasoned in relation to their fathers, or citizens in relation to the state, they would soon meet with a language that cannot be misunderstood-that of punishment. It is only in relation to the command of Jesus that things are supposed to be different.[39]

Barth draws on Bonhoeffer to rebuke this especially sanctimonious form of Christian rebellion, especially the use of theological means to question and subvert the commandment of Jesus.

Ethics

Related to this theme of discipleship and following the command of God, in which Barth draws on Bonhoeffer's thought, is Barth's engagement with Bonhoeffer's *Ethics*. Even though Barth is at moments less than positive about Bonhoeffer's ethical discussions,[40] on other occasions Barth recognizes the significance of Bonhoeffer's *Ethics* for contemporary theology. Barth is particularly impressed with Bonhoeffer's insight in terms of the importance of dogmatics for ethics. He writes: 'And the same attitude to the link with dogmatics is a commendable feature of the brilliant *Ethik* of Dietrich Bonhoeffer (German ed. 1949, E.T., 1955), which unfortunately exists only in a fragmentary and provisional form.'[41] Barth relates his discussion of ethics to that of human sanctification, and thereby to human action

---

38. Ibid., 540–1.
39. Ibid., 541–2, citing DBW 4, 71–2; cf. DBWE 4, 79.
40. E.g. Barth, *Letters 1961–1968*, 252.
41. CD III/4, 4.

that is effected by divine action. General ethics must therefore demonstrate both how the command is always an act and decision of God, and how the command of God invites the creature's response to freely accept and approve of God's merciful action and command.

However, this means that the final judgement on ethics always rests with God, since it is finally the act and decision *of God*. Ethics cannot be a casuistical ethics, therefore, even if there is a casuistry in the prophetic ethos of ethics.[42] As a result, in moving from general to special ethics, it is not the place of ethics to judge directly whether a particular instance of human activity and ethical decision is good or evil on the basis of a general rule that is equated with God's command.[43] Barth looks for support in this point from Bonhoeffer and quotes Bonhoeffer as follows:

> An ethics cannot be a book in which there is set out how everything in the world actually ought to be but unfortunately is not, and an ethicist cannot be a man who always knows better than others what is to be done and how it is to be done. An ethic cannot be a work of reference for moral action which is guaranteed to be unexceptionable, and the ethicist cannot be the competent critic and judge of every human activity. An ethic cannot be a retort in which ethical or Christian human beings are produced, and the ethicist cannot be the embodiment or ideal type of a life which is, on principle, moral.[44]

Here, Barth is in profound agreement with his younger colleague and goes on to offer a catena of Bonhoeffer quotations, each of which concerns the way that casuists often become so preoccupied with human understanding, negotiation and decision that they defer simple obedience to the divine command.[45] In some ways this is not surprising. In his review of Bonhoeffer's *Ethics*, Reinhold Niebuhr, in the context of many positive comments, was critical of it for what he perceived as the presence of Barth between the lines of Bonhoeffer's intended *magnum opus*.[46] Thus, it may well be that to see the influence of Bonhoeffer on Barth's ethics is simply to identify a reflection of Barth's own thought, which Barth commends: Barth may be influenced by Bonhoeffer's *Ethics*, where Bonhoeffer's *Ethics* has already been directly influenced by Barth's. Rather than influence, it may be the case that both theologians simply share a set of presumptions about how to approach ethics, and it is possible, thereby, to identify a shared conversation in which they engage.

---

42. CD IV/2, 9.
43. Ibid., 10.
44. Ibid., 10, citing DBW 6, 372; cf. DBWE 6, 369–70.
45. CD III/4, 14.
46. Reinhold Niebuhr, review of *Ethics* by Dietrich Bonhoeffer, *Union Seminary Quarterly Review* 11, no. 4 (1956): 57–8; cf. Robin W. Lovin, 'Reinhold Niebuhr and Dietrich Bonhoeffer on Responsibility', in *Engaging Bonhoeffer: The Impact and Influence of Bonhoeffer's Life and Thought*, ed. Matthew D. Kirkpatrick (Minneapolis, MN: Fortress Press, 2016), 65–86.

Nonetheless, Bonhoeffer's work on the mandates is also commended and in part appropriated by Barth. Barth sees the worth in Bonhoeffer's discussion of the mandates in relation to the constancy of divine command and human action, pointing to Bonhoeffer's central point that there is always an historical form (in Jesus Christ) in which the divine command is given.[47] Barth recognizes the benefits of using the term 'mandates' over and against more classical language of 'orders' or 'estates', and he lists the four mandates Bonhoeffer identifies – work, marriage (the family), the authorities and the church – as those things which involve both the whole of the human and all humans, and which are concrete forms of the command of God which are meaningful in all times and places.[48] Barth sees this presentation as being more helpful than those of Althaus and Brunner because Bonhoeffer recognizes that the constancy of ethical events can only be learned from the Word of God in order to be meaningful and legitimate. Barth writes:

> Bonhoeffer's 'mandates' are not laws somehow immanent in created reality and to be established at random by the moralist and proclaimed in a form which he himself discovers. On the contrary, they are 'from above', like the divine command itself, and indeed with it, as the 'form' which is quite inseparable from it. They do not emerge from reality; they descend into it. It is along these lines that we certainly have to think, and we may gratefully acknowledge that Bonhoeffer does this.[49]

This is not to say that Barth is uncritical of Bonhoeffer's discussion of the mandates. He sees the identification of four (or five) of them as somewhat arbitrary. Of particular concern is what Barth perceives to be Bonhoeffer's concern with the 'relationships of rank and degree'. Barth asks:

> Does the relationship always have to be one of superiority and inferiority? In Bonhoeffer's doctrine of the mandates, is there not just a suggestion of North German patriarchalism? Is the notion of the authority of some over others really more characteristic of the ethical event than that of the freedom of even the very lowest before the very highest?[50]

Ultimately, Barth also questions the term 'mandate', wondering if it is really distinguishable from 'command'. Barth wishes instead to speak of the constancy of the one command – the command in which God commands and humans must act. He poses the question: 'Would it not be advisable, then, to begin with the more cautious question what we have to learn from God's Word concerning this constancy rather than rushing on to the rigid assertion of human relationships arranged in a definite order, and the hasty assertion of their imperative

---

47. DBWE 6, 388–408; DBW 6, 392–408.
48. CD III/4, 21.
49. Ibid., 22.
50. CD III/4.

character?'[51] Nevertheless, Barth is in agreement with Bonhoeffer (over Brunner's consideration of orders of creation) that it is necessary to learn from the Word of God what the divine command is.[52] Bonhoeffer's *Ethik* is considered to have the right approach: it is not wrong, but unfulfilled or inadequate, perhaps, in Barth's view. Certainly, however, it is an ethics that he commends and which aids the development of his own thought.

Imago Relationis and Sanctorum Communio

Bonhoeffer is also influential on Barth in terms of Barth's understandings of human relationality. This is the case in two particular ways – one relating to human beings as relational creatures, and the other relating to the church as the communion of saints.

Firstly, in terms of Barth's account of the *imago dei*, various options are explored and rejected by him before Barth identifies, affirms and extends Bonhoeffer's account of the image of God in humanity. Barth draws attention to Bonhoeffer's *Creation and Fall*, in which Bonhoeffer asks how God can see, recognize and discover Himself in His work. Here, Barth draws on Bonhoeffer's account of the *analogia relationis* as a more faithful rendering of Gen. 1.26-27 than an *analogia entis*.[53] The image of God is seen in the freedom of humans for God who wills to be free for His creature. Humans are free in this particular way, because God created them as an earthly image of Himself. Barth quotes Bonhoeffer: 'Man is distinguished from other creatures by the fact that God Himself is in him, that he is the image of God in which the free Creator sees Himself reflected. … It is in the free creature that the Holy Spirit calls upon the Creator; uncreated freedom is worshipped by created freedom.'[54] This created freedom means that which is created is also related to something else created – other human beings. It means, in the words of Bonhoeffer, which Barth quotes, 'that man is free for man'.[55] Barth takes Bonhoeffer's account of the *anaologia relationis* in relation to the *imago dei* a step further, however. He uses it to explain the distinction between man and woman: 'The relationship between the summoning I in God's being and the summoned divine Thou is reflected both in the relationship of God to the man whom He has created, and also in the relationship between the I and the Thou, between male and female, in human existence itself.'[56] Barth offers a critical comment that this is an area that Bonhoeffer (and Vischer) could have explored further, albeit Barth does recognize that relating this to the male and female distinction can be nothing more than an analogy.

51. Ibid.
52. Ibid., 23.
53. See DBWE 3, 60–7; DBW 3, 56–63.
54. CD III/1, 195.
55. Ibid.
56. CD III/1, 196.

Secondly, in a similar way to that in which Barth commends *Discipleship*, he also offers uncritical praise for Bonhoeffer's *Sanctorum Communio*. Barth writes in his discussion of the growth of the community and the creedal concept of *communio sanctorum* that he will draw heavily on the work of Bonhoeffer.[57] Barth speaks with a degree of admiration and surprise that this is a dissertation written by a 21-year-old theologian. Indeed, he suggests that the only worth to be found in the Berlin school might be that it gave rise to Bonhoeffer:

> If there can be any possible vindication of Reinhold Seeberg, it is to be sought in the fact that his school could give rise to this man and this dissertation, which not only awakens respect for the breadth and depth of its insight as we look back to the existing situation, but makes far more instructive and stimulating and illuminating and genuinely edifying reading to-day than many of the more famous works which have since been written on the problem of the Church.[58]

Furthermore, Barth affirms the comments of Ernst Wolf that Bonhoeffer's work laid the foundations for and allowed the possibility of many other ecclesiological writings. Barth even comments: 'I openly confess that I have misgivings whether I can even maintain the high level reached by Bonhoeffer, saying no less in my own words and context, and saying it no less forcefully, than did this young man so many years ago.'[59] As with *Discipleship*, Barth openly acknowledges the quality of the work of Bonhoeffer and his indebtedness to it.

Barth identifies the operation of the Spirit in bringing humans together into communion. This communion takes place as the divine and human work together as the Spirit brings to fulfilment a corresponding human activity in creating union between those who are assembled by Him. As such a corresponding human activity, the incompleteness of human ecclesial communion exists between two moments of completion – between its origin and goal in God. Although they are participating incompletely in the completed act of union that lies behind and ahead of them in God's act, the Spirit nevertheless enables them to be genuine representatives of new humanity in the time between the times. Barth writes:

> As they now live and act on earth, in time, at the heart of world history (or as they have lived and acted, for those whose life is over have not dropped out of this fellowship), they are still the *communio peccatorum*, members of the race of Adam, participant in the transgression and fall and misery of all men. But in spite of this, and in triumph over it, they are already distinguished from all other men, constituting in fact and on behalf of the world the *communio sanctorum* – a provisional representation of the new humanity in the midst of the old. These

---

57. CD IV/2, 641.
58. Ibid.
59. Ibid.

men – the saints – who live and act in the communion of the one Holy Spirit, and therefore in communion one with another, are Christians.[60]

This description is highly redolent of Bonhoeffer's argument that the church is 'already completed and still in the process of growing' through an act of the Spirit.[61] Indeed, that Barth begins his section on 'The Growth of the Community'[62] with a small text acknowledgement of the significance of Bonhoeffer's *Sanctorum Communio* is indicative of the influence the work displays throughout Barth's discussion in this section of the paragraph.

Conclusion

In conclusion, although the relationship between Barth and Bonhoeffer is not entirely straightforward, even in those areas where Barth is not uncritical, there is nevertheless a sense of a shared discourse around certain themes, particularly relating to the Christian life. Therefore, rather than speaking in terms of direct influence, it might – as with the relationship and influence in the other direction – be better to think of an approach of critical and appreciative conversation between two theologians with shared approaches and concerns. That Bonhoeffer's theology does not directly and uncritically influence Barth at all points does not reduce the significance of Bonhoeffer for Barth. In comparison to the other major theologians of the twentieth century (Bultmann, Brunner, Tillich and even Moltmann), Barth's discourses with Bonhoeffer are exceptionally positive. Furthermore, Barth's method of appropriating the work of other theologians is always one that is engaged, critical and conversational.[63] Barth is clear that learning from other theologians does not simply mean repeating what they say but listening and then responding.[64] That Barth listens to Bonhoeffer and then responds is an indication of the seriousness with which he approaches this younger theologian. For Barth, to be a theologian who merits response and engagement within a shared discourse is, in one sense, the most significant influence a theologian can have.

60. CD IV/2, 642.
61. DBWE 1, 139; DBW 1, 86.
62. CD IV/2, §67.2.
63. See my chapter, 'Being a Wise Apprentice to the Communion of Modern Saints: On the Need for Conversation with a Plurality of Interlocutors', in *The Vocation of Theology Today: A Festschrift for David Ford*, ed. Tom Greggs, Rachel Muers, and Simeon Zahl (Eugene, OR: Cascade, 2013), 21–3.
64. Thus, at the opening of his lectures on Calvin, Barth writes: 'Calvin wants to teach and not just to say something that we will repeat. The aim, then, is a dialogue that may end with the taught saying something very different from what Calvin said but that they learned from or, better, thought through him', *The Theology of John Calvin*, trans. Geoffrey W. Bromiley (Grand Rapids, MI: Eerdmans, 1995), 4.

Part II

ENGAGEMENTS WITH BARTH

Chapter 3

BARTH ON SALVATION

Although Karl Barth is often caricatured as a theologian who was concerned singularly with the otherness of God and with the doctrine of revelation (someone preoccupied with saying *Nein!*), it is probably truer to say that Barth is above all else a theologian of the God *of salvation*. For Barth, theological abstraction consists of any point which is made separate to Jesus Christ – not to Christology or to conceptions of Jesus Christ, but to the God-man Himself in His life, death and resurrection. In one sense, it is only out of his prioritization of the reality that there is no god to be known except the God who is the God of our salvation that Barth's concern for revelation exists. For Barth, there is no distant God hidden behind God's economy, no God behind God as He is in His revelation to us in Jesus Christ: God is as God is in His act of revelation. In one sense, therefore, Barth's understanding of salvation is both foundational to and the purpose of his famous concern that theology be orientated only on the revelation of the Word of God. For Barth, the Word of God is the Word of the Creator directed to us, which has become necessary and remains so for the renewal of the original relation between God and humanity. Revelation's purpose, therefore, is that it makes known to us the Word of Reconciliation, the Word of the Reconciler. In this event of revealing Himself to humanity, God promises Himself as the content of our future.[1] Revelation is reconciliation, therefore, in certain ways for Barth.[2] As Barth summarizes in the thesis statement of §15 of *Church Dogmatics* (I/2) on 'The Mystery of Revelation': 'The mystery of the revelation of God in Jesus Christ consists in the fact that the eternal Word of God chose, sanctified and assumed human nature and existence into oneness with Himself, in order thus, as very God and very man, to become the Word of reconciliation spoken by God to man.' Barth is a theologian of salvation in a way comparable to Athanasius and Anselm. His concern is that there is no other God than the God who reveals Himself as for humanity.

Barth's radical manoeuvre of placing the doctrine of election within the doctrine of God demonstrates precisely this point. We can no longer think of God's act of election as being simply something that God does or wills. Instead,

---

1. CD I/1, 142.
2. Cf. ibid., 409–10.

for Barth, election is the decision in which God wills to be and actually is God.[3] God is, therefore, gracious in His own self-determination because in this self-determination, God wills to be God solely in Jesus Christ:[4] 'For this self-determination is identical with the decree of His movement towards man.'[5] God is, for Barth, the God of salvation, the God who determines Himself in Jesus Christ.

Even Barth's four part-volume account of creation is premised on salvation. For Barth creation and redemption are two points of one ellipse: they are conjoined as part of God's act of grace. Reconciliation and redemption are presupposed in creation:[6] 'It would be truer to say that creation follows the covenant of grace since it is its indispensable basis and presupposition.'[7] Creation tells humanity that the creature is predestined to participate in history whose ground and direction is in the will of God.[8] For Barth, creation is the beginning of the *Heilsgeschichte* which culminates in Jesus Christ.[9] Creation should not make us think of salvation as an afterthought, or a second plan after the failure of the principal plan of creation.[10] Quite the opposite: 'If by the Son or the Word of God we understand concretely Jesus, the Christ, and therefore very God and very man, as He existed in the counsel of God from all eternity and before creation, we can see how far it was not only appropriate and worthy but necessary that God should be the Creator.' Creation is an act of God which is preceded in the divine decrees by God's act of self-determination in His election to be Jesus Christ. Creation follows from God being the God for us, from the actuality that God is the God of salvation.

For Barth, the economy of God is the centrepiece of his thought. There is nothing in theology that cannot and should not be thought of in relation to the gracious turning of God to humanity in Jesus Christ. Where Barth differs in his Kantian propensities from his predecessors in the nineteenth century on this front is that he not only speaks of functional Christology but also sees this as grounded in both ontological Christology and in the doctrine of God proper. For Barth, it is not simply the case that we can only speak of God as He is for us, but it is also the case that God is God as He is for us. In this chapter, this theme will be explored in relation to Barth's account of the objectivity of salvation in the self-election of Jesus Christ. Following this, Barth's specific account of the doctrine of reconciliation, based on the *munus triplex* of Christ as Priest, King and Prophet, will be outlined in the second major section of this chapter. A final section of the chapter will provide some comment on the human response to salvation and the extent of salvation in Barth's account.

3. CD II/2, 76.
4. Ibid., 91.
5. Ibid., 91–2.
6. CD III/1, 42.
7. Ibid., 44.
8. Ibid., 46.
9. Ibid., viii.
10. Ibid., 46.

3. Barth on Salvation

Election and the God of salvation: In Christ

George Hunsinger has argued compellingly that to understand salvation for Barth it is necessary to note the centrality of the term 'in Christ' to his soteriology. Hunsinger writes:

> Perhaps no single observation can be of more assistance to the careful reader of the *Church Dogmatics* than to note that Barth always uses the ubiquitous but inconspicuous term 'in Christ' (and its cognates) in what is virtually a technical sense. Phrases, sentences, paragraphs, sometimes even entire sections … cannot be fully understood, unless it is seen that the argument turns on the objectivist soteriology conveyed by this little phrase.[11]

By soteriological objectivism, Hunsinger means that the life, death and resurrection of Jesus is the governing way in which salvation is to be understood: whatever humans do or whatever they experience in relation to salvation (what Hunsinger describes as 'soteriological existentialism') can only be understood as being radically subordinated to the person and work of Christ.[12] Salvation should be understood as 'entirely constituted, complete, and effective apart from and prior to any reception of it that may or may not occur here and now in our existence'.[13] Every account of salvation for Barth is an account of the life of Jesus Christ. This is, in some senses, a classical Reformed way of approaching soteriology: for example, Book II of Calvin's *Institutes* precedes Book III – the description of the person and the narrative of the life of Christ comes before the explanation of its benefits to humanity. All that soteriology should do is to indicate the narrative of the life of Christ and offer some reflection on it in relation to humanity: to Jesus Christ belongs salvation, and soteriology's role is to point to Him. As Barth puts it:

> 'In Christ' means that in Him we are reconciled to God, in Him we are elect from eternity, in Him we are called, in Him we are justified and sanctified, in Him our sin is carried to the grave, in His resurrection our death is overcome, with Him our life is hid in God, in Him everything that has to be done for us, to us, and by us, has already been done, has previously been removed and put in its place, in Him we are children in the Father's house, just as He is by nature. All that has to be said about us can be said only by describing and explaining our existence in Him; not by describing and explaining it as an existence which we might have in and for itself.[14]

---

11. George Hunsinger, *How to Read Karl Barth: The Shape of His Theology* (New York: Oxford University Press, 1991), 114.
12. Ibid., 105.
13. Ibid., 114.
14. CD I/2, 240.

But Barth sustains the objectivist account of salvation far beyond the imagination of Calvin.

For Barth, the ground of this objectivist salvation rests in his radical account of God's election. As Hans Urs von Balthasar reminds us, election is 'the heartbeat of Barth's theology'.[15] Indeed, Barth makes it clear that his governing soteriological principle 'in Christ' rests on his account of divine election:

> 'In Him' does not simply mean with Him, together with Him, in His company. Nor does it mean only through Him, by means of that which He as elected man can be and do for them. 'In Him' means in His person, in His will, in His own divine choice, in the basic decision of God which He fulfils over against every man.[16]

The ontological ground for salvation is to be found, therefore, in Barth's account of election.[17] By moving the doctrine of election into the doctrine of God, Barth gives content to his account of the divine life: God is the God of election, the God of salvation. Recognizing that it is not necessarily clear that election should be given place of precedence which Barth affords it, he asserts that election should be considered within the doctrine of God since in election we find the

> primal and basic decision in which He wills to be and actually is God, in the mystery of what takes place from and to all eternity within Himself, within His triune being, God is none other than the One who in His Son or Word elects Himself, and in and with Himself elects His people. In so far as God not only is love, but loves, in the act of love which determines His whole being God elects.[18]

We see in election that God does not simply enact election (and the salvation that follows from it), but that in Barth's actualistic account, this act is the primal self-determining act of God in which God is who God is. This differentiates the Christian understanding of God from all other false and abstract ideas of God.[19]

---

15. Hans Urs von Balthasar, *The Theology of Karl Barth: Exposition and Interpretation* (San Francisco, CA: Communio Books, Ignatius Press, 1992), 156. The following section is a summary of a section of a previously published chapter: Tom Greggs, *Barth, Origen, and Universal Salvation: Restoring Particularity* (Oxford: Oxford University Press, 2009). For greater detail of the significance of election to Barth's understanding of salvation, see chapters 2, 4, 5 and 7 of that book.

16. CD II/2, 116–17.

17. Herbert Hartwell, *The Theology of Karl Barth* (Bungay: Richard Clayton, 1964), is correct in asserting the Trinitarian nature of election, however: election takes place 'in obedience to the Word, spoken to Him by His Father within the inner Trinitarian life of God and accepted by Him as the Son in the mutual love of the Holy Spirit' (109).

18. CD II/2, 76.

19. Ibid., 5–7.

God is the electing God, and in the primal history of the covenant of God in the union of His Son with Jesus of Nazareth, one sees the gracious relating of God to humanity.[20] The will of God cannot be separated from the love of God:[21] Barth does not want to confront humanity with a God who might as well condemn people as save them, who might not be able to allow His deep Yes to overcome His No to sin. At the same time, the love of God cannot be separated from the will of God: God 'loves *in freedom*'.[22] Although election is an eternal decision, Barth wishes God's electing to remain a free decision in order to remain gracious: there must still be personhood and a centre of self-consciousness behind that loving in freedom,[23] a point much of neo-Protestantism had failed to realize.[24]

But what is this election like, and how does it relate to salvation? Barth asserts that the doctrine of election must be understood Christologically. It is Jesus Christ who is the Subject and object of election as electing God (*der erwählende Gott*) and elected human (*der erwählte Mensch*). The event of Jesus Christ is the first, truest and fullest reality of election that there can be. Jesus Christ is God in His movement towards and covenant with humanity.[25] In a radical departure from the tradition, the election of Jesus Christ is not passive and confined to His human nature, for Christ, according to Barth, is simultaneously electing God and elected human:[26] only in the active and passive election of the Son of God does humanity have the basis for its election.[27] Thus, God's election of all humanity is with and in Christ's own election.[28] Christ is the elected human, 'before all created reality, before all being and becoming in time, before time itself, in the pre-temporal eternity of God'.[29] There is no room for a prior decision of God to create, or elect and condemn before the decision to elect Jesus Christ (no *decretum absolutum*);[30]

---

20. Ibid., 8–9.
21. See Trevor Hart, 'Universalism: Two Distinct Types', in *Universalism and the Doctrine of Hell: Papers Presented at the Fourth Edinburgh Conference on Christian Dogmatics 1991*, ed. Nigel M. de S. Cameron (Carlisle: Paternoster, 1992), 1–34. Hart sees this desire not to separate the love and will of God as the heart of Christian universalism (15–16).
22. CD II/1, §28, emphasis added.
23. Ibid., 285–8.
24. Ibid., 288–97.
25. Ibid., 7.
26. Barth asserts that Aquinas overlooks this point (CD II/2, 107). He also states that he differs not in being Christocentric (which he considers Aquinas and indeed Calvin to be), but in seeing a continuity between the Christological centre and the *telos* of God's temporal works, as distinct from those who did not want to bring together the work of God and the eternal presupposition of that work (CD II/2, 149).
27. CD II/2, 104–5.
28. Ibid., 105–6. Barth cites scripture to buttress his beliefs: for example, in Jn 13.18 and 15.16 and 19, Jesus points to Himself as the one who elects His disciples.
29. CD II/2, 94.
30. See CD II/2, 127–45 in terms of Barth's discussion of supra- and post-lapsarianism. In this, Barth sides with supralapsarianism, but in a critical way which almost indicates that

instead, Jesus Christ is Himself the ultimate *decretum absolutum*.[31] This indicates a singularly positive turning towards humanity, in that it is eternally in Christ that God makes this movement and determines Himself for this covenant of grace. Indeed, in Barth's actualistic inner-logics,[32] it might even be stated that God is this movement and turning towards humanity: His economy and ontology cannot be separated.[33] Thus, for God who is love, election is the act of His love in its most glorious forms of condescension, patience, freedom and overflowing.[34] In self-electing, God brings the other upwards to Himself, so that He can never again be without it.[35] Election's nature is, therefore, Gospel.[36] Humanity continues to need to be rescued by God in its rejection of Him, but this is now considered in a wholly Christological way which brings together the Yes and No of God in the simultaneity of the elected and rejected Christ. It is He who demonstrates salvation as its originator and archetype. It is, therefore, in the humanity of the elected Christ that one needs to consider the destiny of human nature.[37]

Furthermore, in the election of Jesus Christ, God elects for Himself the negative part of predestination – perdition, death, rejection, exclusion and the No of God.[38] These are the things humanity deserves, and yet God decides in His freedom to suffer them on the cross in His self-election in Jesus Christ. Predestination

---

the doctrine itself does not go far enough. He rethinks the matter in terms of his own theme of Jesus as the particular Subject and object of election. The 'prior' willing of God is not *homo labilis* for the fall, but humanity's 'uplifting and restitution by an act of divine power; the demonstration in time, in the creaturely sphere, of His eternal self-differentiation' (142). Cf. Hartwell, *The Theology of Karl Barth*, 106–8 and 139–41; J. C. McDowell, *Hope in Barth's Eschatology: Interrogations and Transformations Beyond Tragedy* (Aldershot: Ashgate, 2000), 141; Jeannine M. Graham, *Representation and Substitution in the Atonement Theologies of Dorothee Sölle, John Macquarrie and Karl Barth* (New York: Peter Lang, 2005), 388.

31. CD II/2, 100–1. On the *decretum absolutum*, see Colin Gunton, 'Karl Barth's Doctrine of Election as Part of His Doctrine of God', *Journal of Theological Studies* 25, no. 2 (1974): 382. On Christ as *decretum concretum*, see G. C. Berkouwer, *Triumph of Grace in the Theology of Karl Barth* (London: Paternoster, 1956), 103.

32. On actualism, see Bruce L. McCormack, 'Grace and Being: The Role of God's Gracious Election in Karl Barth's Theological Ontology', in *Cambridge Companion to Karl Barth*, ed. John Webster (Cambridge: Cambridge University Press, 2000), 98–101; and Paul T. Nimmo, *Being in Action: The Theological Shape of Barth's Ethical Vision* (London: T&T Clark, 2007), esp. 4–12. A different account is given by Hunsinger, *How to Read Karl Barth*, esp. 30–2.

33. This point is, however, protected by Barth's continual and emphatic insistence throughout CD on the 'mystery' of God. See, for example, CD I/1, 320–1.

34. CD II/2, 9–10.

35. Ibid., 10.

36. Ibid., 13–14.

37. Ibid., 118; cf. 13.

38. Ibid., 166.

becomes, therefore, not one *modus* of salvation but *the modus* of the divine work of redemption, indeed of all of God's works *ad extra*.[39] In it, Christ has willed to take to Himself rejection in order that rejection can never again become the portion of humanity: 'He is *the* Rejected, as and because He is *the* Elect. In view of His election, there is no other rejected but Himself.'[40] It is this which makes the election of humanity in Christ so radical. Barth posits the integrity of election and rejection and yet unites these in the person of Jesus Christ in a chiastic move in which the elected of God (Jesus Christ) elects rejection in order that the rejected (sinful humanity) may be elect in His election of rejection: Christ suffers rejection on the cross and elects this in order that humanity may be elect even in its rejection of God.

The effects of this on soteriology cannot be underestimated. The election of the community and individuals occurs only in the prior election of Jesus Christ and cannot be abstractly separated from this. Included in Christ's election is the election of the other – the many 'whom electing God meets on this way'.[41] Since Barth's account of what it means to be 'in Christ' is so objectivist, to be 'in Christ' cannot be instrumentalized in relation to the resultant identity of Christ with each member of humanity.[42] As Barth writes about Christ's work of salvation: 'He really accomplished both His own and our justification and glorification. ... Death could not hold Him, and therefore it cannot hold us.'[43]

The Doctrine of Reconciliation

Barth expounds the outworking of his doctrine of election within volume IV of his *Church Dogmatics*: 'The Doctrine of Reconciliation'. This is a work of four part-volumes and around three thousand pages. Volumes I–III were completed, but volume IV on the ethical material of the doctrine remained incomplete and further fragments were published posthumously. In his preface to the doctrine, Barth asserts that to fail in his articulation of salvation would be to fail everywhere:[44] the reconciling work of God stands at the centre of the church's message with creation and redemption as its circumference but the covenant fulfilled in the atonement at its centre.[45] Barth wrote to his son that he awoke from a dream at 2.00 am with the structure of his doctrine of reconciliation in place and found himself scribbling

---

39. Ibid., 191.
40. Ibid., 353, emphasis Barth's.
41. Ibid., 195.
42. CD III/2, 133.
43. CD II/2, 558.
44. CD IV/1, ix.
45. Ibid., 3.

the details down.[46] Certainly the layers, interwoven complexity and elegance of volume IV make it exceptional even within the *Church Dogmatics*.

The structure of the three completed part-volumes is formed around the *munus triplex* of Christ as Priest, King and Prophet, but this is developed in an exciting and innovative way related to the Christological confession of Christ as very God, very human and ontologically one. Each section is then related to a particular aspect of human sinfulness that humans learn from knowing Christ (pride, sloth and falsehood). And an aspect of the knowledge of the event of reconciliation is explained (justification, sanctification and calling) and related to the work of the Holy Spirit in the community (gathering, upbuilding and sending), and the being of the Christian (faith, love and hope).[47] In discussing this event of reconciliation, what Barth believes we will find is 'the temporal happening of atonement God's eternal covenant with man, His eternal choice of this creature, His eternal faithfulness to Himself and to it'.[48] In discovering this reality, we find in the event of reconciliation:

> that its eternity and inflexibility are those of His free grace, and that the glory which He willed to maintain and defend is that of His mercy – His covenant a covenant of grace and His election an election of grace; so that conversely the atonement made in Jesus Christ will be seen to be wholly an act of the grace of God and therefore an act of sovereignty which cannot be understood in all its profundity except from the fact that God is this God and a God of this kind.[49]

The complex architectonics which Barth uses to describe the event of reconciliation are designed to offer us knowledge of the grace of God in which we come to knowledge of the God of salvation.

Barth's account begins, therefore, with the strictly Christological: the governing narrative is that true God truly became true human in the incarnation. *Church Dogmatics* IV/1 is orientated on Christ as truly God and the condescension of the Son of God to humanity. It is through this that we are to understand the priestly act of the Son in His substitutionary bearing of the human rejection of and by God: Jesus becomes the 'judge judged in our place'.[50] This, according to Barth, is the humiliation of God, and through this humiliation, the sin of human pride is overcome. Pride, for Barth, is 'the opposite of what God does for us in Jesus Christ in condescending to us, in humbling Himself, in becoming a servant to take to

---

46. Eberhard Busch, *Karl Barth: His Life from Letters and Autobiographical Texts* (London: SCM, 1976), 377.

47. An outline of the structure of volume IV is offered in CD IV/1, §58.

48. CD IV/1, 80. For a summary of the individual part-volumes of CD, see Daniel W. Hardy, 'Karl Barth', in *The Modern Theologians: An Introduction to Christian Theology since 1918*, ed. David F. Ford with Rachel Muers, 3rd edn (Oxford: Blackwell, 2005), 21–42.

49. CD IV/1, 80.

50. Ibid., §59.2.

Himself and away from us our guilt and sickness'.[51] In this act of the condescension of the Son of God to death upon even the cross, we are able to understand what it is for God to justify the proud sinner:

> Justification definitely means the sentence executed and revealed in Jesus Christ and His death and resurrection, the No and the Yes with which God vindicates Himself in relation to covenant-breaking man, with which He converts him to Himself and therefore reconciles him with Himself. He does it by the destruction of the old and the creation of a new man.[52]

The objective work of justification finds its subjective terminus in the life of the community and the individual, albeit that Barth believes that this rests in a very secondary and subjugated place. He approaches this theme in an ordered way, considering first the community and then the individual: salvation is the salvation of the individual in the community. This community is the historical community of the church that the Holy Spirit awakens as the power of the Word spoken by the Lord who became servant to judge and justify sinners.[53] Only in light of the community can the individual be considered. In terms of this act of justification of individual sinners, it must be noted that for Barth, justification is not a process in which humans become less sinful and more justified; instead, in justification humans are completely and fully both justified and sinner simultaneously (*simul iustus et peccator*).[54] Nevertheless, for Barth, 'the question of the subjective apprehension of atonement by the individual man is absolutely indispensable'.[55] Under this, Barth considers the faith of the individual Christian.

The same basic structure of argument is found in *Church Dogmatics* IV/2. Whereas IV/1 begins from the perspective of the true divinity of Christ, IV/2 begins from the perspective of the true humanity of Christ. Through the humiliation and condescension of God in Christ, humanity is exalted:

> As in Him God became like man, so too in Him man has become like God. As in Him God was bound, so too in Him man is made free. As in Him the Lord became a servant, so too in Him the servant has become a Lord. That is the atonement made in Jesus Christ in its second aspect. In Him humanity is exalted humanity, just as Godhead is humiliated Godhead. And humanity is exalted in Him by the humiliation of Godhead.[56]

---

51. Ibid., 142.
52. Ibid., 96.
53. Ibid., 151.
54. On this point, and generally on justification, see Trevor A. Hart, *Regarding Barth: Essays toward a Reading of His Theology* (Carlisle: Paternoster, 1999), chap. 3.
55. CD IV/1, 150.
56. Ibid., 131.

For Barth, however, these two aspects of the person and work of Christ cannot be divided into two separate or distinctive moments: they are one work which constitutes His person in its twofold form.[57] This exaltation is the kingly aspect of Christ by which he brings about the sanctification of humankind through His upward movement of the exaltation of humanity in response to the sin of human sloth. Sanctification cannot be thought of as a second or separated moment of reconciliation brought about by the action of individual believers. Instead, it must be thought of objectively in the first instance in relation to Jesus Christ:

> The sanctification of man which has taken place in this One is their sanctification. But originally and properly it is the sanctification of Him and not of them. Their sanctification is originally and properly His and not theirs. For it was in the existence of this One, in Jesus Christ, that it really came about, and is and will be, that God Himself became man, that the Son of God became also the Son of Man, in order to accomplish in His own person the conversion of man to Himself, his exaltation from the depth of His transgression and consequent misery, his liberation from his unholy being for service in the covenant, and therefore his sanctification.[58]

Sanctification thus comes to all humanity *de iure*. However, it takes place *de facto* in the lives of believers in the community, and by this the community is built up through the work of the Holy Spirit in order to give a provisional representation of the sanctification of all humanity through the event of the life, death and resurrection of Jesus Christ. In relation to the individual, this sanctification is considered in relation to Christian love as God raises humans up to correspond to His love.

Barth's most daring (and perhaps original) discussion of reconciliation comes in *Church Dogmatics* IV/3, a volume broken into two halves to be published because of its length. Having explored the divinity and humanity of Christ in relation to humiliation and exaltation, respectively, Barth engages with what it means to say that Christ is one. This is Barth's exploration of the prophetic office of Christ. While the priestly work of the Son of God involves a movement of God from above to below, and the kingly work of the Son of Man from below to above, the prophetic work involves a movement through time, space and history. This movement and work responds to the human sin of falsehood. Jesus Christ instead makes Himself the 'guarantor of the reality of that which has been done by Him as servant and Lord in that movement from above downwards and below upwards, of the fact that in Jesus Christ God has made Himself the witness of the truth of the atonement'.[59] It is under this office of Christ as Prophet that the sending of the community is considered. Barth writes:

---

57. Ibid., 133.
58. CD IV/2, 514.
59. CD IV/1, 143.

The Holy Spirit as the Spirit of Jesus Christ is the enlightening power of Him who as very God and very man is the Guarantor of the truth of the atonement made in Him-and therefore the summoning power of the promise given in Him to sinful man. When the promise is heard by men, inwardly and outwardly these men are together ordained to be the community sent out as a witness in the world and to the world. The historical reality and inward upbuilding of this community are not ends in themselves.[60]

This is a witness to the whole world of the objective reality of the work of Christ's atonement. Because of this reality, the work of the Holy Spirit in the believer enables the believer to be one who is enlightened in hope. By this, Barth means that the believer is able to move towards her final destiny with an 'immediate hope' in Christ.[61]

These three volumes are supplemented with an incomplete part-volume published by Barth (*Church Dogmatics* IV/4) on the ethics of reconciliation. The fragment that was published concerns baptism and is offered as an account of human faithfulness to God in response to God's constant faithfulness to humanity. Again, priority is given to the objective work of God in baptism by the Spirit before the consideration to subjective aspect of water baptism. This was to be followed by an account of the Christian life in relation to the Lord's prayer. Lecture fragments of this aspect of Barth's work were published posthumously as *The Christian Life*. For Barth, ethics can never be prised apart from dogmatics: the account of reconciliation requires an account of human action in correspondence to the divine event of salvation.

The life of faith and the scope of salvation

The issue for Barth of human response to God's work of salvation is one which requires further comment. His unprecedentedly strong account of soteriological objectivism could be understood to remove the significance of any human response or existential soteriology. Certainly, it is correct to say that humanity does not contribute anything to salvation. There is no creaturely cooperation in salvation for Barth, since salvation is singularly an act of the grace of God; human response does not condition God into fulfilling salvation for them. However, this does not mean that the existential aspect of salvation and the response of faith are unimportant for Barth. Yes, Barth wants to state: 'The work of atonement, the conversion of man to God, was done for all. The Word of God is spoken to all. God's verdict and direction and promise have been pronounced over all. To that extent, objectively, all are justified, sanctified and called.'[62] The conversion of

---

60. Ibid., 152.
61. CD IV/3, 902.
62. CD IV/1, 148.

humanity to God takes place on the cross – in the death and resurrection of Jesus Christ. However, Barth qualifies this immediately by stating:

> But the hand of God has not touched all in such a way that they can see and hear, perceive and accept and receive all that God is for all and therefore for them, how therefore they can exist and think and live. To those who have not been touched in this way by the hand of God the axiom that Jesus Christ is the Victor is as such unknown. It is a Christian and not a general axiom; valid generally, but not generally observed and acknowledged. Similarly, they do not know their sin or even what sin is, since it can be known only in the light of that axiom.[63]

Although Barth's account of salvation is orientated strongly towards objective soteriology, there is a place for the life of faith and for Christian particularity.[64] It is a work of God the Holy Spirit to relate this moment of salvation to the life of the community and the believer.

Indeed, the motif of being 'in Christ' which is so central to Barth's account of the atonement is helpful here. Certainly, Barth is clear that all of history and creation is enclosed within Christ, but he is also clear that 'in Christ' there are different ways of being participants. On the one hand, there is *de iure*, objective or passive participation in Christ; on the other hand, there is *de facto*, subjective or active participation in Christ.[65] The former is the grounds for the latter. It is not that Barth believes that faith effects our participation in Christ's work of salvation, or that we are unable to participate without Christ; it is rather that faith allows active participation in a reality in which we are already insiders regardless of whether we recognize ourselves to be or not.[66] This reality meets us in our present and contingent situation by the work of the Spirit within the community and the individual who is enabled by God to engage actively in the life of faith, love and hope in Christ. In this form, Christians are provisional representatives for the world of the reality of God's event of salvation. There is a life of obedience and correspondence to Christ's work of salvation. This is the conversion Barth speaks about: not a singular moment of decision, but a life of faith which begins anew each day, as the human being in Christ actively shares in His humanity as that which is orientated upon God and upon other humans.[67] This is why election and reconciliation require consideration of their ethical implications for Barth.

---

63. Ibid.
64. I have explored this theme in detail in *Barth, Origen, and Universal Salvation*.
65. See Adam Neder, *Participation in Christ: An Entry into Karl Barth's Church Dogmatics* (Louisville, KY: Westminster John Knox, 2009), esp. chap. 2.
66. See George Hunsinger, 'A Tale of Two Simultaneities: Justification and Sanctification in Calvin and Barth', in *Conversing with Barth*, ed. John C. McDowell and Mike Higton (Aldershot: Ashgate, 2004), 77.
67. E.g. CD IV/2, 560–3.

The theme of human response and its particular role within Barth's corpus is one which immediately raises a further question – that of the extent of salvation for Barth. His soteriological objectivism determines that what takes place in Jesus Christ takes place for all. As Hunsinger puts it:

> Perhaps no theologian of the church since Athanasius, in whom the same strong association of 'in Christ' with 'for all' is constantly present has so consistently tried to do direct justice to the universalistic aspects of the New Testament witness to Jesus Christ as has Barth. He simply refuses to qualify this aspect for the sake of a tidier conceptual outcome.[68]

Does this amount to universalism for Barth?[69] Barth's description of active and passive, *de facto* and *de iure* do not make the question a straightforward one. Perhaps reflective of the New Testament itself with the Pauline emphasis on the universal and the Matthean emphasis on decision and choice, Barth's account of salvation contains both universalist and exclusivist statements. Although the logic of Barth's theology clearly seems to point in a universalist direction,[70] Barth himself at various points in his theology emphatically denied that he was a universalist.[71] Nevertheless, it is difficult to deny that Barth's theology tends very strongly in a

---

68. Hunsinger, *How to Read Karl Barth*, 108.
69. This is a question I have tackled in detail elsewhere. While a summary is offered here, the reader is directed to Chapter 5 in this volume, 'Jesus is Victor'. For a more detailed engagement, the reader is directed to my *Barth, Origen, and Universal Salvation*; and *Theology against Religion: Constructive Dialogues with Bonhoeffer and Barth* (London: T&T Clark, 2011), chap. 5. For further discussion of this theme, Berkouwer, *Triumph of Grace*; Joseph D. Bettis, 'Is Karl Barth a Universalist?' *Scottish Journal of Theology* 20, no. 4 (1967), 423–36; Oliver Crisp, 'On Barth's Denial of Universalism', *Themelios* 29, no. 1 (2003); J. C. McDowell, 'Learning Where to Place One's Hope: The Eschatological Significance of Election in Barth', *Scottish Journal of Theology* 53, no. 3 (2000), 305–24; Hart, *Regarding Barth*, chap. 6, esp. 137–8; George Hunsinger, *Disruptive Grace: Studies in the Theology of Karl Barth* (Grand Rapids, MI: Eerdmans, 2000), chap. 10; John Colwell, 'The Contemporaneity of Divine Decision: Reflections on Barth's Denial of Universalism', in *Universalism and the Doctrine of Hell*; Paul T. Nimmo, 'Election and Evangelical Thinking: Challenging Our Way of Conceiving the Doctrine of God', in *New Perspectives for Evangelical Theology: Engaging with God, Scripture and the World*, ed. Tom Greggs (Abingdon: Routledge, 2010), 34–5; and Oliver Crisp, 'I Do Teach It, but I Also Do Not Teach It: The Universalism of Karl Barth (1886–1968)', in *'All Shall Be Well': Explorations in Universal Salvation and Christian Theology, from Origen to Moltmann*, ed. Gregory MacDonald (Eugene, OR: Cascade Books, 2011), 305–24.
70. On the logical outcome of Barth's position, see Berkouwer, *Triumph of Grace*; Crisp, 'On Barth's Denial of Universalism' and 'I Do Teach It'.
71. For example, CD II/2, 417, 476–7; and CD IV/3, §70.3; 'The Condemnation of Man'.

universalist direction, and he certainly did not display the anxiety that many other theologians display about the doctrine of universal salvation.[72]

To end where this chapter began, one way to think about this tension is to consider Barth's rejection of the category of 'universal salvation' as a rejection of any approach to theology in which a principle (universal salvation) replaces Christ as a person: Barth makes clear that while he cannot affirm universalism as a doctrine, he feels he must affirm that 'Jesus Is Victor'.[73] Barth's rejection of universalism is a rejection of any approach to salvation that does not have at its centre the particularity of Jesus Christ – a particularity that cannot be gained from a principle, not even that of grace. Furthermore, this emphasis on the particularity of salvation in Jesus Christ ensures that the sovereignty of God is in no way depreciated by the universal election of all humanity: God is under no obligation to elect, and in Jesus Christ, one is able to see the mysterious sovereign *will* of God. God is not bound to creation by a principle of universal salvation but chooses to bind Himself to creation in the particular person of Jesus Christ. That Barth rejects dogmatic universalism on occasion does not mean that Barth posits a limitation of the friendliness of Jesus Christ. Rather, Barth's rejection of universalism posits a limitation of the problems that can arise from such a universal scope for salvation in relation to the freedom and grace of God and the significance of the life of faith. Salvation, for Barth, is a gift of the God of salvation, the God who eternally self-determines to be God in a particular way, to be God in Jesus Christ; the Christian in faith, love and hope is a proleptic anticipation in time who witnesses to this eternal reality.

Conclusion

It is, indeed, the related themes of election, eternity and the scope of salvation in Barth's theology to which this book now turns. Who Jesus Christ, who is the same yesterday, today and forever, is as the one who was slain before the foundation of the world (Rev. 13.8) comprises a question which requires an unpacking in terms of the account of eternity as it relates to time. Furthermore, in relation to this, the constancy of that one Jesus Christ as the elect of God who bears our rejection requires a discussion of the impact of Barth's account of Jesus Christ on the scope of salvation, and – indeed – the impact of these issues on questions relating to the purpose of continued history, the battle between good and evil, and the life of faith. In the next two chapters, the framework for Barth's soteriology is offered in discussion of Barth's account of eternity, and the impact of Barth's account of salvation is considered in relation to the question of universalism.

---

72. See, for example, Karl Barth, 'Humanity of God', in Karl Barth, *God, Grace and Gospel*, trans. James Strathearn McNab (Edinburgh: Oliver & Boyd, 1959), 49–50.

73. See Chapter 5 in this volume, 'Jesus is Victor'.

Chapter 4

BARTH ON ETERNITY

This chapter seeks to draw out the distinctive and revolutionary contribution of Karl Barth to the doctrine of God's eternity, and seeks especially to consider how eternity, according to Barth, relates to creaturely temporality. Space does not allow a thoroughgoing examination of why this is an important thing to do (except in its own terms), but suffice it to say that the doctrine of eternity provides the Christologically determined metaphysics for Barth's radical redescription of the doctrine of election – a redescription that Bruce McCormack has said would take the theological community a hundred years to see its significance and originality.[1] Barth's discussion of eternity immediately precedes his radical material on election and provides the framework within which Barth's speech about the eternal election of Jesus Christ is meaningful. Barth's mature development of the doctrine of election arose from following the instincts of the work of Peter Barth presented at the 1936 *Congrès international de théologie calviniste* and the work of Pierre Maury. These perspectives laid the foundations for Karl Barth's own reworking of the doctrine of predestination,[2] but they also took place before Barth's reworking of his account of eternity in *Church Dogmatics* II/1: in one sense, the material on eternity dovetails precisely into the radical redescription of election and predestination in II/2. If the function of the doctrine of election is, as Barth states, 'to bear basic testimony to eternal, free and unchanging grace as the beginning of all the ways and works of God', then the doctrine of the triune eternity unpacks the dogmatic content of the descriptor 'eternal'.[3] It is for this reason that this chapter is sandwiched between a discussion of Barth on salvation on the one side and the scope of salvation (especially as it relates to the here and now) on the other.

This chapter will examine the material content of the doctrine of eternity in Barth's theology, especially the specific way in which he develops the Boethian description of eternity as *interminabilis vitae tota simul et perfecta possessio*. The

---

1. See Bruce L. McCormack, 'Grace and Being: The Role of God's Gracious Election in Karl Barth's Theological Ontology', in *The Cambridge Companion to Karl Barth*, ed. John Webster (Cambridge: Cambridge University Press, 2000), 92.

2. On this, see Bruce L. McCormack, *Karl Barth's Critically Realistic Dialectical Theology* (Oxford: Clarendon Press, 1995), 22.

3. CD II/2, 3.

first section of this chapter will outline Boethius's description of eternity and its appropriation in the centuries leading up to Barth's own time, highlighting the distinctive manner in which Boethius was appropriated by subsequent generations of theologians. The second and most substantive section seeks to offer a careful examination of Barth's own account of eternity in relation to Boethius. It is argued here that Barth engages in *ressourcement* of Boethius, drawing out distinctive features not attended to in the general appropriation of Boethius in theology, and that Barth adds to Boethius's *simul* by filling out just what is understood to be *simul* within the simultaneity. One way to describe this is that Barth adds order and movement to his account of the eternity of God, drawing upon the inner Trinitarian relations of God and the incarnation of the Son to offer content for his description of divine eternity. His comparison of eternity to time is not a negative one but a positive one, in which material content is gained for understanding time in relation to eternity, and vice versa. The third section offers a brief discussion of the description of time that Barth offers in CD I/2 and III/2 in relation to the Christological form that his account of the relation of time and eternity takes. Here, particular attention is paid to the material content of the subsistence of time within the eternal election of the second person of the trinity to be human in Jesus Christ. There is, we may suggest, an *enhypostatic* temporality within the divine eternal life; this displays a significant development in dogmatic accounts of eternity, comparable to the revolutionary development Barth offers in his account of election.

The Boethian foundation: Aeternitas est interminabilis vitae tota simul et perfecta possessio

Boethius's account of eternity as 'the simultaneous and complete [or perfect] possession of infinite [or unending] life'[4] is one which famously has captured the theological imagination of subsequent generations, and which tends to be the account to which lip service is paid in dogmatic accounts of eternity. However, the full potential of this account has rarely been fully exploited within systematics.[5] Boethius's account draws on the Plotinian conceptualization of the relationship between time and eternity. For Plotinus eternity was the presence of all of life as a whole – not as a sequential ordering but as perfect and whole.[6] Thus, eternity is not the opposite of time in Plotinus; rather eternity is the means of understanding time. This is different from the other major philosophical account of eternity which has influenced Christian theology, namely that of Plato. Plato's approach makes

---

4. Boethius, *de Consolatione Philosophiae*, prose VI.
5. CD II/1, 610–13.
6. For a discussion of this, see Wolfhart Pannenberg, *Metaphysics and the Idea of God* (Grand Rapids, MI: Eerdmans, 1990), 75ff.; and Michael Chase, 'Time and Eternity from Plotinus and Boethius to Einstein', in ΣΧΟΛΗ 8, no. 1 (2014): 68–110.

eternity timeless: for Plato, the eternity of ideas and the deity in its changelessness are the opposite of the changing nature of the temporal as it is subjected to change and flow.[7] Plato, it seems, has generally won the day within classical dogmatics. Augustine, for example, tended to follow the Platonic opposition of time and eternity: time is a creation of God and thus must be entirely separated from divine eternity; there is no time in the divine life, since eternity does not include time, is not present to time and is not the condition of the unity of time. Augustine related time to movement, and for him there was thus no movement before the movement of bodies in creatures.[8] Time is, for him, therefore, the antithesis of eternity: God's eternity is timeless.

Boethius, on the other hand, does not oppose time and eternity, but he does compare time and eternity. Compared to eternity, time *moves* for Boethius: we pass through from past to future, through changing passing moments. But, the *key* distinctive between time and eternity for Boethius is that time does not embrace the whole *simultaneously* as eternity does. He writes:

> What we should rightly call eternal is that which grasps and possesses wholly and simultaneously the fullness of unending life, which lacks naught of the future, and has lost naught of the fleeting past; and as such an existence must be ever present in itself to control and aid itself, and also must keep present with itself the infinity of changing time.[9]

This issue of the infinity of change in time is one which is important for Boethius's further unpacking of his definition. Through this definition of eternity's relationship to time, Boethius relates the eternity of God to God's 'own *single* nature'. This nature is contrasted by Boethius to 'the infinite changing of temporal things' which try but fail to imitate the 'simultaneous immutability of God's life'. Time fails to imitate eternity precisely because it moves. Although time mirrors eternity in that a single moment may exist forever, time nevertheless in comparison to the eternal life and its immutable form 'sinks … into change' and 'falls from the single directness of the present into an infinite space of future and past'.[10] By contrast, God is 'the eternal present', a 'never failing constancy in the present'. Boethius follows this discussion by relating these relatively brief observations to providence, election and free will. How does divine foreknowledge (if eternity is God's simultaneous perfect possession of unlimited time) not undermine the integrity of creaturely temporality, removing the individual qualities of given moments? For Boethius, the answer is as follows: 'Without doubt, then, all things that God foreknows do come to pass, but some of them proceed from free will; and though they result by coming into existence, yet they do not lose their own nature, because before they

---

7. See Plato, *Phaedo*, 97d, 80a f.
8. See, for example, *de Civitate Dei*, 11.6 and 12.15.2.
9. Boethius, *de Consolatione Philosophiae*, prose VI.
10. Ibid.

came to pass they could also not have come to pass.'[11] In what is essentially only a page or two, Boethius outlines his account of divine eternity and its relation to time and uses this as a basis for his account of providence and free will. Simultaneity is the key concept for him in relation to divine eternity, but this simultaneity lies in contrast to movement and stems from the simplicity and immutability of the divine life.

It is this aspect of eternity – its simplicity and immutability in contrast to movement – which Thomas Aquinas picks up in relation to his application of Aristotle's philosophy to the Boethian account. In his affirmation of Boethius's definition of eternity as the 'simultaneously-whole [sic] and perfect possession of interminable life', Thomas draws out two points. Firstly, eternity is interminable in that it has no beginning and no end. Secondly, eternity has no succession as it is simultaneously whole.[12] Furthermore, Thomas also states that knowledge of eternity comes for him by way of contrasting it to time. In his description of eternity, therefore, he seems to bring together both the Augustinian and Boethian accounts. By virtue of this contrast of eternity to time, simultaneity is understood as lacking succession or movement. Thus, he writes that time

> is nothing but the numbering of movement by *before* and *after*. For since succession occurs in every movement, and one part comes after another, the fact that we reckon before and after in movement, makes us apprehend time, which is nothing else but the before and after in movement. Now in a thing bereft of movement, which is always the same, there is no before and after.[13]

The lack of movement as a basis for the *simul*, pointed towards but not explicitly expanded upon in Boethius, is identified strongly in Thomas. So, too, is interminable life described as simultaneous because it lacks succession or order: 'whatever is wholly immutable can have no succession, so it has no beginning and no end.'[14] Although the latter point holds, the lack of succession in immutability rests on a preceding metaphysics of simplicity in a particular Aristotelian form. Indeed, Thomas makes it clear in the second article of question 10 that eternity follows from immutability. The question might arise, in relation to Thomas's use of Boethius, of how an unmoved and unordered account of the divine life can be such that we can understand there to be a *simul* in relation to unending life in any meaningful way. Put otherwise, what is it that is *simul* other than a tautological simultaneity which is simultaneous? How coherent is this account with an account of the *simul*? Or what meaning does *simul* have? Does this mean that Boethius's account, rather than seeking to offer a positive account of time and eternity's relation, ends up in

11. Ibid.
12. ST 1.1 q.10a.
13. Ibid.
14. Ibid.

the philosophical realms of timelessness?[15] Certainly, the account Thomas offers of Boethius when he revisits the matter in the fourth article of question 10 of *Summa* 1 suggests so. Here, eternity is contrasted to time, as time has a before and an after: Boethius's conceptualization is used to point to the difference between a permanent being and the movement of measured time. The *simul* is central, but almost stands in univocally for the simple – effectively denoting the same thing as timelessness.

The Thomist perspective on Boethius seems to find bedfellows in as different theologians as Louis Berkhof and Friedrich Schleiermacher. For Schleiermacher, eternity is the 'absolutely timeless causality of God'.[16] He relates both Augustine and Boethius to one another (like Thomas) in order to state: 'The divine causality, since time itself is conditioned by it, must so much the more be thought of as utterly timeless'.[17] For Berkhof, God's eternity is 'a timeless existence, an eternal presence'.[18] In light of this general appropriation of Boethius's work in a manner that makes eternity timeless, what does it mean, then, to say, in the words of Pannenberg: 'Materially Barth's theses are close to Plotinus's philosophy of time, which stands behind the definition of Boethius that Barth rated so highly'?[19] Given the use of Boethius in the subsequent tradition in relation to Aristotelian accounts of number and movement, in what sense does Barth draw upon Boethius? In what ways does he recover a pre-Thomistic account of Boethius? And in what ways does he develop Boethius's thought in his own formative work? It is to these issues that this chapter now turns in examining Barth on eternity.

Barth on Eternity

Barth takes up this definition of eternity which Boethius offers but develops it in distinct and marked direction which explicitly attends to the form of the description of eternity presented within Boethius;[20] he does this in contrast to those

---

15. Brian Leftow has argued this way. See his *Time and Eternity* (Ithaca, NY: Cornell University Press, 1991), chap. 6; and 'Boethius on Eternity', in *History of Philosophy Quarterly* 7, no. 2 (1990): 123–42.

16. Friedrich Schleiermacher, *The Christian Faith* (Edinburgh: T&T Clark, 1968), 203.

17. Ibid., 204; cf. §§53.1-2.

18. Louis Berkof, *Systematic Theology* (Grand Rapids, MI: Eerdmans, 1938), 131.

19. Wolfhart Pannenberg, *Systematic Theology*, vol. 1 (Grand Rapids, MI: Eerdmans, 2010), 406.

20. This is a reflection on the mature version of the doctrine as found in CD. Barth's earlier treatment of the dialectic between time and eternity, extremely important in his *The Epistle to the Romans* (Oxford: Oxford University Press, 1968) and *The Resurrection of the Dead* (Eugene, OR: Wipf and Stock, 2003), essentially made eternity into timelessness. See Bruce L. McCormack, *Karl Barth's Critically Realistic Dialectical Theology: Its Genesis and Development, 1909-1936* (Oxford: Clarendon Press, 1995), 262–6. There is a shift in Barth's presentation in relation to the mature theology. In relating the material on eternity

theologians who combine it with either Platonic or Aristotelian concerns.[21] Barth bemoans the reality that the content of Boethius's work on eternity has not entered fully into Christian dogmatics and not received the due attention it deserves. Clearly, Boethius's work has been used significantly, but Barth's presentation of it suggests some degree of *ressourcement* is required if he is to utilize Boethius's description of eternity effectively. But even in this re-examination of Boethius's work on eternity, Barth defines the Boethian approach in a particular way: his account of Boethius on eternity, in relation to his own dogmatic description of the eternal life of God, is one which does not repeat Boethius, but responds to and enhances his work. Whereas Aquinas – through whom the Boethian account has come down to most people – emphasizes eternity's simultaneity in relation to divine simplicity and immutability, *Barth reconsiders what it is that is simul*. For Barth, this results in an account which seeks to draw out that simultaneity points towards order and movement in eternity – rather than simplicity and immobility, perhaps in their particular Aristotelian forms.

---

to Boethius and because of the limitations of space, this chapter has had to limit discussion to the presentation of eternity in CD II/2.

21. The relationship between Barth's use of the Bible and philosophy is complex. Clearly, Barth brings certain presuppositions to the texts he uses. He discusses the relationship between philosophy and biblical exegesis in forming dogmatics in CD I/2, 727–40. Barth is clear that philosophy is crucial in exegesis as servant but not master. He asserts here that one cannot replace philosophy with a 'dictatorial, absolute and exclusive theology' and that theology must not forget that in itself and apart from its object it is a hypothetical form of philosophy (CD I/2, 734). For Barth, to write a biblically grounded dogmatics is to be aware of 'essential distance between the determinative thought of Scripture and our own imitative thought determined as it is by our philosophy' (ibid., 730). Nevertheless, Barth admits: 'In attempting to reflect on what is said to us in the biblical text, we must first make use of the system of thought we bring with us, that is, of some philosophy or other' (ibid., 729). See here: Andrew Louth, 'Barth and the Problem of Natural Theology', *Downside Review* 87, no. 288 (1969): 276; and Colin Gunton, 'No Other Foundation: One Englishman's Reading of *Church Dogmatics* Chapter V', in *Reckoning with Barth: Essays in Commemoration of the Centenary of Karl Barth's Birth*, ed. Nigel Biggar (London: Mowbray, 1988), 64–7, which argues Barth is still tainted with the syndrome of the Enlightenment for all of his seeming opposition to it. However, as much as philosophy may be a servant in helping Barth to understand what underlies everything, it is such only as it is servant to the master of the Bible from which Barth claims to draw his doctrines. It is worth observing, moreover, that Bruce McCormack seems correct in observing that Barth's anti-metaphysical stance is a rejection of a particular 'way' of knowing concerned with observing the phenomena around one and deducing or inducing a first cause. Knowledge of God could come only in terms of God's Self-disclosure in Christ (*Karl Barth's Critically Realistic Dialectical Theology*, 246). However, the 'first cause' of this Self-disclosure is election. It is in this way that one might hazard to speak of election fulfilling the role of metaphysics for Barth.

4. Barth on Eternity

In this section of the chapter, I wish to draw attention especially to Barth's initial moves in terms of the relating of time to eternity, and will dwell more on the opening section of the sub-paragraph of Barth's work on eternity than most commentators, who tend more to focus on the threefold form of eternal life. The reason for my own focus is that this threefold form itself arises from a redescription of divine eternity which recognizes the need for an *ordered simul* in terms of the eternal life of the triune God who is alive. It is also this part of the sub-paragraph which is most significant in terms of the taking up of time in all its creaturely integrity into the divine life in the incarnation of the Christ.

Barth considers divine eternity under the attributes of divine freedom, and links eternity to divine glory: because God is in and of Godself eternal, God is glorious. For Barth, being eternal is the unity of the beginning, middle and end as one and not three: it is a simultaneity.[22] But even here, it is noticeable that Barth places order in the account of the simultaneity: eternity is not just a simultaneous presence to time, but a simultaneity to the order that is innate within time: 'beginning, middle and end' is sequential and God is present to these three as one. It is in that way Barth speaks of what it means for eternity to involve 'pure duration'. It is important here to note what it is exactly that Barth says: 'Eternity is the simultaneity of beginning, middle and end, and *to that extent it is pure duration*.'[23] Pure duration is defined not as an unmoved *nunc stans* but as a simultaneous existence to temporal order. But in the same breath eternity is, for Barth, clearly differentiated from time. Eternity is not time – which is of course a creation or a form of the creation of God – since time has a beginning, middle and end that are distinct, whereas in the triune life these are one. Nor can eternity be confused with that which is everlasting: eternity is not an infinite extension of time backwards and forwards as, writes Barth, 'time can have nothing to do with God'.[24] There is a distinction in eternity and time which is the distinction that there is between Creator and creature.[25] It must be remembered that God is *free* and unchangeable in this duration. His eternity is the place where one can place one's trust, as God is constant. Eternity must be understood in relation to God's other perfections of freedom and is a way of expressing God's freedom inwards: 'As the eternal One, He is constant and He is also the One who omnipotently knows and wills.'[26] God's eternity is a perfection of the God who is unaffected by creation and constant in Godself: in eternity, God is omnipotent in His relation to time, and this secures God's constancy.

However, in stating and securing the eternity of God as an attribute of divine freedom, Barth also goes on to state that he thinks that it is poor and short-sighted

---

22. CD II/1, 608.
23. Ibid., emphasis added.
24. Ibid.
25. Barth refers to the following biblical texts for this: Isa. 43.10; Pss. 90.2-4; cf. 2 Pet. 3.8; Pss. 102.25-8 (CD II/1, 608–9).
26. CD II/1, 609.

only to understand God's eternity as the negation of all time: eternity is, instead, true duration as Barth has outlined it.[27] For Barth, the Bible is interested in the *positive* quality of eternity in the first instance, and only secondarily (if at all) in its non-temporality. There is in scripture an *order* in the way in which eternity is described: eternity is generally ascribed to God in terms of beginning, middle and end. It is at this point that Barth draws directly on Boethius's definition of eternity as *interminabilis vitae tota simul et perfecta possessio*.[28] For Barth, this definition goes farther and deeper than the work of Augustine and Anselm, who are, for him, far too occupied with the confrontation of time and eternity. However, it is of note that the discussion of Boethius's conceptualization arises in the context of God's relation to the sequence and order of time. Barth is happy to state (classically) that total possession of unlimited life is eternal life, but he goes on to explain that this is only so long as the eternity of God is prior, above, after and under all being, and not the eternity of *being* as such. It is insufficient to compare simply the *nunc fluens* of creaturely time to the *nunc stans* of the divine life, according description of the one by virtue of the other. In fact, Barth criticizes Boethius in his *De Trinitate* for doing just this. He writes: 'If an unmoving, persistent present is distinguished from our fluid and fleeting present, which can be understood only as a mathematical point, this distinction rightly describes the problem of our concept of time, but it does not rightly describe the concept of eternity in so far as this is to be understood as the *possessio vitae*.'[29] For Barth, God's eternity is without question the '*now*', the *nunc*, which he defines as 'the total simultaneous and complete present of His life'.[30] But this now is *both* a concept of the now which must be defined with reference to our problematic concept of the creaturely now (with its instability in its passing form owing to the *fluere* of creaturely temporality) as *stare*, and a concept which must not be defined as an abstract non-temporality: 'The concept of the divine *nunc* must not exclude the times prior to and after the "now," the past and the future, nor may it exclude the *fluere*.'[31] To have a genuine *simul* in relation to unending life involves for Barth a need for order to which the *simul* is indexed in the divine life.

One way to put this relation of the *stare* and the *fluere* is to say that Barth's concern in his discussion of eternity is that dogmatics must not treat eternity as if there were no time. Neither can dogmatics treat time as if it were not a creation of the eternal God who becomes incarnate in time. Eternity simply cannot be the negation of time: we know eternity by the knowledge of God as *possessor interminabilis vitae*. God's eternal life (eternal now) is both *stare and fluere* – but not *fluere* in the instability of creaturely times – and *fluere and stare* – but without the inability to become that belongs to all creaturely *stare*. As Barth puts it with characteristic polemic and panache: 'The theological concept of eternity must be

27. Ibid., 610.
28. Ibid.
29. CD II/1, 611.
30. Ibid.
31. Ibid.

set free from the Babylonian captivity of an abstract opposite to the concept of time.'[32] Eternity has, instead, a positive relation to time.

For Barth, therefore, eternity is the simultaneous and perfect possession of everlasting life, and as such the eternity of God involves beginning, succession and end simultaneously, which is to say, in ordered simultaneity. Barth is free to write, therefore, that 'God has time' because by this he means 'God has time because and as He has eternity.'[33] The basis on which Barth is able to state that God has time is revelation. God has time for creation; this is the time of revelation, the time of Jesus Christ.[34] This Christocentric shift at this point gives some indication of where Barth again develops the tradition he receives, or deviates from its starting points in relation to eternity. Barth does not (as with Thomas) wish to use a principle of simplicity (stemming from a foundation in divine aseity) in order to derive and specify the nature of divine eternity. He wishes instead to point to the perfect and superabundant *aliveness* of the God of salvation,[35] not the simplicity of God the unmoved mover, to unpack what it means to speak of divine eternity. Since God is alive, for Barth, God's unity includes multiplicity, and constancy includes movement. Allow me to quote Barth here at length:

> God does not first create multiplicity and movement, but He is one and simple, He is constant, in such a way that all multiplicity and movement have their prototype and pre-existence in Himself. Time, too, pre-exists in this way in Him, in His eternity, as His creation, i.e., with space, the form of His creation. The form of creation is the being of God for a reality distinct from Himself. But the form of God's being for us and our world is space and time. The proto-types in God's being in Himself which correspond to this form are His omnipresence in regard to space, and His eternity in regard to time. If God in Himself is the living God, this prototype, too, is in Himself identical with His eternity. The fact that He is the enduring God, duration itself, does not prevent God from being origin, movement, and goal in and for Himself.[36]

For Barth, what distinguishes God's eternity from temporality is not the order of origin, movement and goal, or of past, present and future, but that God's eternity has no opposition, conflict or competition between these orders. Again, in Barth's words: 'In Him all these things are *simul*, held together by the omnipotence of His knowing and willing, a totality without gap or rift, free from the threat of

---

32. Ibid.
33. Ibid.
34. Ibid., 612.
35. This supremely *living* character of God is, interestingly, a quality Barth commends Hegel as having rightly emphasized. See Karl Barth, *Protestant Theology in the Nineteenth Century: Its Background and History* (Grand Rapids, MI: Eerdmans, 2002), chap. 10. It may be, at this point in Barth's argument, that we see Barth enacting his 'bit of Hegeling'.
36. CD II/1, 612.

death under which time, our time, stands.'[37] For Barth, these distinctions in order exist in divine eternity, but they are distinctions innate to the *simul* and the *perfect possession of unending life*, and they do not exist in contradiction to divine eternity. Just as God's omnipresence is not the negation of our space but is first and foremost God's space and therefore real space, so too God's eternity is not the negation of our time but first and foremost God's time and therefore real time. There is a need for a positive sense of the concept of eternity on which the main emphasis of *sempiternitas* (eternity) must fall.

Thus, there is no space for a negative theology in relation to the divine perfection of eternity. As the eternal One, God is the One who has absolutely real time, and this does not sublate order or remove the integrity of each moment of time or its order within eternity. God's eternity for Barth is not 'timeless but supremely temporal'.[38] In this way, Barth wishes to demarcate his theology from what he sees as Roman Catholic theological perspectives (read here, I suspect, in terms of Cajetan and Suarez's interpretations of Thomas). For Barth, Roman Catholicism spends too little time on God's time and too much time on created time. Roman Catholic theologians fail to recognize fully the fact that God really knows and wills the temporal from eternity. This is not, for Barth, to imply that created things coexist with God in God's eternity.[39] But it is to say that God wills and ordains them in and to their temporally ordered integrity, and that God is present to them. In this way, there is a 'part truth' (to use Barth's phrase) in the Augustinian approach to eternity: this is the freedom of God in relation to our time. Time and eternity still differ, but this does not mean that their relationship is one of opposition. Barth goes on to demonstrate this in relation to two loci: firstly, triunity and secondly, Christology.

Firstly, for Barth, the positive understanding of eternity becomes clear when one recognizes that one is dealing not with an abstract atemporal god or with an idol moved by created whims and actions but with the triune God revealed in scripture, with the God who is unbegotten, begotten and succession, which is to say, with Father, Son and Spirit. Barth indexes the nature of eternity to the unity and simultaneity of eternal inner Trinitarian relations. This triune life is the eternal life of the eternal God, the God of the eternal now which cannot come into being or pass away. Yet, in this, there is order and succession: eternal begetting, eternal begottenness and eternal succession or spiration. Again, Barth's concern in relation to the *simul* is to consider the content of it and to demonstrate that there is order and movement here. He writes:

> For this 'all' is pure duration, free from all the fleetingness and the separations of what we call time, the *nunc aeternitas* which cannot come into being or pass away, which is conditioned by no distinctions, which is not disturbed and

---

37. Ibid.
38. CD II/1, 614.
39. Ibid.

interrupted but established and confirmed in its unity by its trinity, by the inner movement of the begetting of the Father, the being begotten of the Son and the procession of the Spirit from both. *Yet in it there is order and succession. The unity is in movement. There is a before and an after.* God is once and again and a third time, without dissolving the once-for-allness, without destroying the persons or their special relations to one another, without anything arbitrary in this relationship or the possibility of its reversal.[40]

Contrary to the form we find in Thomas, Barth's description of eternity does not arise from an account of simplicity or non-movement. For Barth, the eternal subsistent relations in the divine life indicate succession and order, which retain their integrity within the *simul*, and which are required for the *simul*: simultaneity requires order and succession in order to be simultaneous. This means that for Barth, there is order within the divine eternity, movement (but not a movement such that anything passes away) and succession (but succession which 'in itself is also beginning and end'). Lest anyone should object, Barth also makes it clear that it is not enough to distinguish the *principium ordinis* from the *principium temporis*: these are, for him, identical in God.

Secondly, the positive relation of eternity to time is further unpacked in relation to the divine economy. For Barth, the only way in which it is possible to get a positive account of the eternality of God is in relation to an account of the economy of grace – the covenant of fellowship between the eternal God and the temporal creature. This covenant means that a Christian account of eternity must be considered from the perspective of Christology, beginning with the incarnation of the eternal God in temporal creation.[41] For Barth, the incarnation of Jesus Christ means concretely that without ceasing to be eternity and with its power, eternity became time. This is not just about God granting creation time as its form (though of course, it is this as well), it is more that in Jesus Christ God takes time to Godself. In the eternal One's becoming temporal, God submits Godself to time and permits created time to become and be the form of God's eternity; this is not just a sovereign ruling over time, but an eternity which is capacious enough (without losing the form of eternity) to incorporate creaturely time and its forms. This does not mean God ceases to be who God is in God's own superiority. There is no lessening of God's deity here, but a display of the full power of deity. In this act of God, we learn what it means to speak of God as eternal, and Jesus Christ's name is enough to be a refutation of the idea of God as only timeless.[42] The incarnation means that God is not only eternally present to all time but temporal in His eternity in the act of the epiphany of the Messiah, and again in every act of faith in Him. To describe eternity, one must look at the revealed eternity of God in which Jesus was able to be temporal; this is the power of true eternity. True

---

40. CD II/1, 615, emphasis added.
41. Ibid., 616.
42. Ibid.

eternity does not have to be opposed to temporality, but speech about eternity in this form does have to ensure it does not reduce God to the level of being a creature.[43] One way to consider this, in light of the Boethian conceptualization, is to say that this is *perfect* possession of unending life – including in the incarnation the genuine contingencies of human creaturely existence, but *perfectly* possessed. There is no necessity here on the part of God's relation to time: God's readiness for eternity to bear the form of time and be subjected to it is a gracious form which eternity eternally takes, one which arises from the eternal willing of the God who is simultaneously present to all of time to be God in Jesus Christ.[44] God's eternity is not in itself time, but the absolute basis of time and the absolute readiness for it. This is an asymmetrical relationship, however, and we cannot reverse the above principle of eternity's relation to time in order to make time an eternal coexistence with God.

It might be worth, here, unpacking further the doctrine of *enhypostasia*, though Barth does not, and generally makes less use of this concept than his commentators seem to suggest. Incarnation makes it possible only to speak of a readiness for time in the eternal triune life. God is not bound to take time to God: to be incarnate is all an act of free grace in creation and reconciliation, but also an act to which God is simultaneously present throughout all eternity. The implication of this readiness for time in eternity, however, is that God's eternity is more than the unity of all times with the goal and purpose of His will; eternity is not exhausted by this description. God's eternity is rather the presupposition of the unity.[45] Again, this presupposition suggests the significance of order in the way in which Barth speaks of the *simul* of divine eternal life.

It is, indeed, at this point in his argument that Barth rehearses the better known aspect of his account of eternity in identifying the pre-temporality, super-temporality and post-temporality of the divine eternal life. I have written in more detail about this before and will rehearse the argument in only a brief form here.[46] Barth asserts that this threefold distinction in eternity is a biblical distinction within the unity of eternity in which it is possible to see eternity's positive relationship to time since in it God has the power to exist before, through and after time.[47] Firstly, God's pre-temporality means God's existence precedes our existence and the existence of all things.[48] It is in this that one can begin to understand the direct relationship between eternity and the doctrine of election. Emphatic in his belief in *creatio ex nihilo*, Barth reminds the theologian that creation is not eternal, and yet he claims its time was decided and determined before time: to

---

43. CD II/1, 617.

44. For Barth's detailed discussion, see CD II/1, 618.

45. CD II/1, 619.

46. See my *Barth, Origen, and Universal Salvation: Restoring Particularity* (Oxford: Oxford University Press, 2009), 35–41.

47. CD II/1, 619.

48. Ibid., 621.

reconcile the world to Godself, God decided that the world should be. Because of Jesus Christ's central position in this, one must say that all of this was determined beforehand by and in God: 'To say that everything is predestined, that everything comes from God's free, eternal love which penetrates and rules time from eternity, is just the same as to say simply that everything is determined in Jesus Christ. ... We have to recognize that eternity itself bears the name Jesus Christ.'[49] Thus, God's eternal decision to elect takes precedence even over creation, and results in the work of salvation being the 'first' (rather than a subsequent) decision of God in the ordered simultaneity of God's eternity. Secondly, recalling that eternity is the simultaneous possession of all times, this pre-temporality cannot be separated from supra-temporality. God's eternity goes with time, moves with it:[50] 'eternity assumes the form of a temporal present, all time, without ceasing to be time, is no more empty time, or without eternity'.[51] Thirdly, God's eternity, furthermore, is also post-temporal.[52] God is when time will be no more. This is the sense of God's being 'all in all' (1 Cor. 15.28). Again, one should not think of this as a linear procession: God is already 'all in all' supra- and pre-temporally.[53] Nevertheless, there is in eternity a direction which is irreversible, since all humanity is led towards God's post-temporal eternity.[54] Again, the *simul* of eternal life is one which for Barth is ordered and involves movement, but is such as a genuine *simul* and thereby without creaturely time's passing form.

To summarize, we can see, therefore, that for Barth, the Boethian description is revived in its original Plotinian form and developed in relation to the material content of what the *simul* might mean in relation to the complete and perfect possession of unending life – Plotinus with a bit of Barth's fondness for 'a bit of Hegeling'.[55]

---

49. Ibid., 622, justified on the basis of Jn 8.58; Eph. 1.4-5; and 1 Pet. 1.18-19.

50. See John Colwell, 'The Contemporaneity of Divine Decision: Reflections on Barth's Denial of Universalism', in *Universalism and the Doctrine of Hell: Papers Presented at the Fourth Edinburgh Conference on Christian Dogmatics 1991*, ed. Nigel M. de S. Cameron (Carlisle: Paternoster, 1992), 151–3; Gerhart Sauter, 'Why Is Karl Barth's Church Dogmatics Not a "Theology of Hope"? Some Observations on Barth's Understanding of Eschatology', *Scottish Journal of Theology* 52, no. 4 (1999): 420–2; John Thompson, 'The Humanity of God in the Theology of Karl Barth', *Scottish Journal of Theology* 29, no. 3 (1976): 258–60. On the historical development of this idea in Barth's thought, see McCormack, *Karl Barth's Critically Realistic Dialectical Theology*, 371–4.

51. CD II/1, 626.

52. John C. McDowell, *Hope in Barth's Eschatology: Interrogations and Transformations Beyond Tragedy* (Aldershot: Ashgate, 2001) correctly re-emphasizes this aspect of Barth's thought.

53. CD II/1, 630.

54. Ibid., 639.

55. Eberhard Busch, *Karl Barth: His Life from Letters and Autobiographical Texts* (London: SCM, 1976), 387.

Barth on time

In order to understand further the concrete meaning of this positive relationship of eternity to time, it is necessary not only to consider Barth's account of eternity but also the accounts of time which underpin and flow from this account.[56] For many commentators, Barth's account of eternity appears to suggest that there is a dissolution of time and history – given the emphasis on simultaneity.[57] This critique fails, however, to appreciate the careful relationship of time to eternity for Barth and to see the importance of simultaneity (in the form described above) in Barth's thought. Time is central to Barth's theology. Indeed, Barth discusses time on two separate occasions in his *Church Dogmatics*, and in both what we see is a determinately Christocentric account – *Church Dogmatics* I/2, 'The Time of Revelation' and *Church Dogmatics* III/2, 'Man in His Time'.

In the discussion in *Church Dogmatics* I/2, various moments and forms of time are accounted for. However, in relation to the account of divine eternity offered by Barth in the subsequent volume, this discussion – particularly of the narrower understanding within the paragraph of the time of revelation – adds material to

---

56. The centrality of this relationship cannot be over-emphasized in CD. Indeed, Ford sees CD as 'standing like a massive, unfinished, but formally simple and consistent sculpture – a spiral round and round the self-expression of God *in time*' (David F. Ford, 'Conclusion: Assessing Barth', in *Karl Barth: Studies of his Theological Method*, ed. S. W. Sykes [Oxford: Clarendon Press, 1979], 201). On time and eternity, see the informative but unsatisfactory Robert Jenson, *God after God: The God of the Past and the God of the Future, Seen in the Work of Karl Barth* (Indianapolis, IN: Bobbs-Merrill, 1969), esp. chap. 8. Cf. George Hunsinger, *How to Read Karl Barth: The Shape of His Theology* (Oxford: Oxford University Press, 1991), 15–19; and on the 'scandal of particularity', David F. Ford, 'Barth's Interpretation of the Bible', in *Karl Barth*, ed. Sykes, 61–2; Trevor A. Hart, *Regarding Barth: Essays toward a Reading of His Theology* (Carlisle: Paternoster, 1999), 56ff.; Richard H. Roberts, 'Karl Barth's Doctrine of Time: Its Nature and Implications', in *Karl Barth*, ed. Sykes, 88–146; and Richard H. Roberts, *A Theology on Its Way? Essays on Karl Barth* (Edinburgh: T&T Clark, 1991), esp. chap. 1. Cf. B. D. Marshall, 'Review of Richard Roberts, *A Theology on Its Way? Essays on Karl Barth*', *Journal of Theological Studies* 44, no. 1 (1993): 453–8; McDowell, *Hope in Barth's Eschatology*, 41–5, 123–6; Hart, *Regarding Barth*, chap. 1.

57. For the most thorough discussion of this, see Roberts, *A Theology on its Way*, chap. 1. In this, Roberts engages in a thorough and fierce criticism of Barth on time, concluding that Barth is ultimately 'ambiguous' and seeing the dissolution of time by eternity in Barth's theory. For Roberts, there is an overly strong influence of Hegel and Kant on Barth that leads him along the path of idealism and the resulting destruction of real human time. I have addressed this criticism in *Barth, Origen, and Universal Salvation*, 38-41. See also here, G. C. Berkouwer, *The Triumph of Grace in the Theology of Karl Barth* (London: Paternoster, 1956), and Barth's own response to him in CD IV/3, 173–84. Also of note is McCormack, 'Grace and Being'; and Hunsinger, *How to Read Karl Barth*, 12–15.

the preceding discussion in which God's relation to time is understood in relation to *real* time, that is, the time of revelation: the Christological determinant for the account of the relationship of time and eternity is unpacked in terms of the meaning of time in and for the event of revelation. For Barth, it is crucial that in relation to the time of revelation, revelation is the 'event' of God in which God can become cognizable by us by analogy with other forms known to us.

This form is a human being like us who, at a definite point in time and space, lives and dies, and in Him God's Word is revealed: it is the human form of Jesus Christ.[58] As Barth writes, 'the event of the incarnation of the Word, of the *unio hypostatica*, is to be understood as a *completed* event, but also as a completed *event*.'[59] This event of incarnation reveals 'God's time' to (and for) humanity. This is the time of revelation, which is real and fulfilled time since in this time 'God has time for us.'[60] We see here language to which Barth returns in *Church Dogmatics* II/1 in defining what it means for God to live in eternal life. For Barth, God's time is not our time but God's.[61] In its form, the incarnation is still an *historical* event (though not historically [*historisch*] demonstrable).[62] However, this revelation does not simply take place in our time because in this revelation time, the Word of God lives forever (Isa. 40.8), just as the Word became flesh and remains so after resurrection.[63] In Barth's account of revelation time, one is dealing with – in what might seem to be a contradiction in terms – 'eternal time', since eternity is not apart from time as there is a temporal presence in the Word of God becoming flesh which means revelation is not timeless.[64] Revelation must be temporal or else it is not revelation – and, in that much, the idea of 'myth' as an account of the Christian narrative is rejected by Barth.[65] Revelation time is a genuine present time, which is also a genuine perfect and future since Jesus is Lord of time – real, fulfilled time.[66] While the incarnation happened in history, it has not happened in the same way as the rest of history since in it there is no continuation, completion, pointing beyond itself, striving after a goal, addition or subtraction, as is the case with other historical occurrence: 'Its form cannot be changed. It has happened as self-moved being in the stream of becoming. It has happened as completed event, fulfilled in time, in the sea of the incomplete and changeable and self-changing.'[67] Here, we see Barth changing language of 'unmoved' to 'self-moved' in terms of

---

58. CD I/2, 36.
59. Ibid., 165.
60. Ibid., 48.
61. Ibid., 49.
62. Ibid., 325.
63. There is perhaps here the beginnings of a pointing towards where Barth will go in CD II/2 in relation to the eternal election of Jesus Christ.
64. CD I/2, 50.
65. Ibid., 51.
66. Ibid., 52.
67. Ibid., 116.

God's relation of time to eternity, seeing the movement of God to the world in Jesus Christ as being an event in which we begin to comprehend the eternal time of God. Again, as with his account of eternity, there is an account here which involves movement in the divine life. For Barth, the eternal willing of God cannot be separated from the event of revelation in fulfilled time. Barth's understanding of time demonstrates that God's eternal act and being cannot be separated in the event of incarnation. He writes: 'In the reality of revelation He is, in His assumed humanity, the Son of God from eternity, and we, for His sake, are by grace the children of God from eternity.'[68]

Indeed, in the event of incarnation, Barth sees an accomplished reality that came true in the fullness of time, which is given its ontological reference by being an objective fact, namely, the fact of the man Jesus in space time. Thus, there is a unity between the *Logos incarnatus* in the form of the Church's recollection of Christ, and the *Logos incarnandus* in the form in which the Logos existed for the time of expectation.[69] Barth's trading on the Boethian concept of eternity as the perfect and simultaneous possession of unending life is again significant in the order and movement that is introduced into the account of the *simul*. In determining Himself to be the *Logos incarnandus* the Word of God not only 'has time for us' but has willed this for all eternity such that (as Barth was to write in later years) 'in the mirror of this humanity of Jesus Christ is revealed the humanity of God which is included in His divinity'.[70]

The theme of the supreme and perfect temporal nature of eternal life is further used in Barth's reflections on time in his anthropology, which come after his writings on eternity. In *Church Dogmatics* III/2, Barth is once again concerned to point out that there is true time in the divine living. He writes: 'Even the eternal God does not live without time. He is supremely temporal. For His eternity is authentic temporality, and therefore the source of all time.'[71] The basis Barth gives for this is the hypostatic union of the true God with the true human Jesus. Barth is at pains to point out that Jesus lives in genuine human, creaturely time as the Eternal Son of God. Thus, Barth states:

> The eternal content of His life must not cause us to miss or to forget or to depreciate this form, separating the content from it and discarding the form, as though we could see and have the content without it. ... If we abstract Him from His time, we also lose this content of His life. If we retain the content, we must needs retain the form as well, and therefore His temporality.[72]

---

68. Ibid., 238.
69. Ibid., 165.
70. Karl Barth, 'The Humanity of God', in *God, Grace and Gospel* (Edinburgh: Oliver and Boyd, 1959), 42.
71. CD III/2, 437.
72. CD III/2, 440; cf. Thomas F. Torrance, *Space, Time and Resurrection* (Edinburgh: T&T Clark, 1998), 95.

But that is not the end of the significance of the incarnation for the eternity of God. It is not simply that the Eternal One unites Himself in time with time. Rather the significance is that this is the basis for all existing time: because of the eternal covenant of God with humanity in Jesus Christ, there is time in the divine eternity. In an interesting reflection on Jn 1's account of the Logos, Barth states that 'the Prologue [to John's Gospel] is not speaking of an eternal Son or divine Logos *in abstracto*, but of a Son and Logos who is one with the man Jesus'.[73] Barth expands exegetically on this claim in the following radical way:

> 'The same was in the beginning with God.' The *houtos* here refers to the incarnate Logos. It is He who was 'in the beginning.' And not only that, but even before this beginning He was with God and was Himself God, participating in the divine being and nature, before created time began, in the eternity of God. This eternity includes not only the present and future, but also the past. God's eternity does not invalidate past, present and future, and therefore time; it legitimates them ... The man Jesus is in this genuine and real yesterday of God's eternity, which is anterior to all other yesterdays, including the yesterday of creation.[74]

The *simul* of Boethius is once more developed to give content to the *simul* in relation to the acts and events of God in time, acts and events which derive from God's singular act to be God in the person of Jesus Christ in the election of Jesus Christ which is the beginning of all God's ways.[75] Eternity in its ordered simultaneity has a form, and that form is the life of the incarnate, crucified and resurrected Jesus Christ, who was and is to come. There is a subsistence of time in the eternal willing of God to be God in Jesus Christ: time in all its givenness and in the – albeit perfected – creaturely form it takes in Jesus Christ subsists in the divine life eternally. This Christological content cashes out what it means for eternal life to be *interminabilis vitae tota simul et perfecta possessio*. For eternity to involve the *simul* and the *perfecta* determines that in relation to time, eternity is not the negation but the basis on which time might exist. This is a truth won, not through any analogy of the being with God to the being of creation but through the eternal willing of the Son of God to be for creation in the person of Jesus Christ.

Conclusion

Barth's account of eternity develops a tradition which stems from Boethius. He recovers Boethius's Plotinian propensities from their Aristotelian and Platonic

---

73. CD III/2, 483.
74. CD III/2, 484.
75. Note the 'singularis' here. CD III/2, 484f.: 'A thing which is resolved from all eternity necessarily has the character of absolute singularity. At this last and highest stage, the pre-existence of the man Jesus coincides with His eternal predestination and election.'

perversions through a *ressourcement* of Boethius' account. However, such a *ressourcement* is not one of repetition but one of creative dogmatic appropriation of the material content of Boethius. Not only does Barth follow his instincts that Christian theology does not describe an abstract deity but the triune God of salvation, such that the account of eternity we engage in offering has to be one which understands the dynamic relationality of the triune life and the positive relationship of the eternal God to history as the external working of the covenant of God with humanity: there is order and movement in simultaneity. But also his recognition of the temporality of the human Jesus and the power of the resurrection adds further material content to the integrity of the temporal, which is supremely real as it subsists in eternal life of God in the *Logos incarnandus*, who is present in the willing of time, with the progression of time, and after time, and who is supremely temporal in the event of God's salvation in the incarnation. Time bears the name of Jesus Christ, and exists because of Him. Eternity, we might say, is the eternal life of the One whose identity, as Calvin realized, defines God as eternal – the same yesterday, today and forever: the one who is that which he is; who will be that which he will be; who was that which he will be; and who will be that which he was. God is alive, perfectly, totally and in a moving and ordered simultaneity.[76] It is to the question of what this might mean to accounts of Barth's understanding of the scope of salvation to which this book now turns.

---

76. John Calvin, *Institutes of Christian Religion* (Philadelphia, PA: Westminster, 1960), I.10.2. Calvin realized the divine eternity is contained in the name YHWH: 'let us observe that his eternity and self-existence are announced in that wonderful name twice repeated.'

Chapter 5

JESUS IS VICTOR!

Barth once stated with characteristic wit: 'There is a certain merit to an unfinished dogmatics; it points to the eschatological nature of theology!'[1] Nevertheless, the incomplete nature of *Church Dogmatics* has led to a litany of speculation on what his doctrine of redemption might have looked like, taking its lead from Barth that the answers are to be found within the thirteen volumes already written.[2] We are left to wonder and are charged with the task both of addressing ourselves to the clues left in the existent volumes and of constructing a dogmatics of Christian eschatology in keeping with the ground Barth has already cleared.

This chapter is an exercise in the former of these tasks. It seeks to consider the much discussed question of Barth's attitude towards universalism. There seems at times here to be an impasse. While the tenor of Barth's soteriology clearly points in a universalist direction, Barth on a number of occasions specifically and emphatically rejects the doctrine of universalism or *apokatastasis*.[3] This denial has been seized upon by a variety of commentators, desirous of defending Barth against his opponents from what is a definite charge of universalism.[4] Scholarly and sympathetic as these are, they miss at times the exciting, radical newness of Barth's work, bringing Barth so far away from the door of universalism on which it appears he has been knocking that one is left to wonder why the charge was ever

---

1. Recorded by John D. Godsey, 'Barth as a Teacher', in *For the Sake of the World: Karl Barth and the Future of Ecclesial Theology*, ed. George Hunsinger (Grand Rapids, MI: Eerdmans, 2004), 214.

2. Eberhard Busch, *Karl Barth: His Life from Letters and Autobiographical Texts* (London: SCM Press, 1976), 487.

3. See CD II/2, 417 and 476–8; and also CD IV/3, §70.3, 'The Condemnation of Man'. For the history of the word *apokatastasis* in the New Testament and antiquity, see Morwenna Ludlow, *Universal Salvation Eschatology in the Thought of Gregory of Nyssa and Karl Rahner* (Oxford: Oxford University Press, 2000), 39–44.

4. See the excellent pieces by Joseph D. Bettis, 'Is Karl Barth a Universalist?', *Scottish Journal of Theology* 20, no. 4 (1967): 423–36, https://doi.org/10.1017/S003693060005314X; John Colwell, 'The Contemporaneity of Divine Decision: Reflections on Barth's Denial of Universalism', in *Universalism and the Doctrine of Hell*, ed. Nigel M. de S. Cameron (Carlisle: Paternoster, 1992), 139–60.

brought before him. Certainly, the tone of some such pieces does not reflect that of Barth's theology. Bettis's defence of Barth, for example, does not seem satisfactory when he states, '[Barth] rejects universalism because the future of all men is uncertain. Rather than ask whether Barth attributes too much to Christ's work, the question is whether Barth attributes enough to Christ's work.'[5] Similarly, Colwell (perceptive as he is on the relationship between Barth's understanding of eternity and election) states the need to be cautious in creating too simple a relationship between the ontological definition of the election of all humanity in Christ and the actual election of the individual. The church must proclaim the election of Jesus Christ on behalf of all humanity, but this does not imply ultimate salvation for all individuals as its consequence.[6] Better are studies which recognize not only this tension in Barth but also the extremely optimistic and hopeful direction in which he tends with regard to the issue of the salvation of all humanity.[7] However, even the best of these only recognize the 'tension' as being the key to understanding the issue, presenting Barth's position on universalism as 'reverent agnosticism'[8] and 'holy silence'.[9] Such views are correct in asserting the danger of saying too much on either side;[10] just as they are also correct in recognizing the biblical foundations for such inconsistencies.[11]

However, there is a danger in such studies that Barth is almost perceived as neutral on the issue, and that election becomes no news rather than good news. Although unwilling to judge on the plight of individuals (and therefore all),[12] to say that Barth 'points' in the direction of universalism is not the same as saying he is 'agnostic' or 'silent'.[13] Silence hardly seems appropriate to a theme which

5. Bettis, 'Is Karl Barth a Universalist?', 433.

6. Colwell, 'The Contemporaneity of Divine Decision', 148.

7. See John C. McDowell, *Hope in Barth's Eschatology: Interrogations and Transformations beyond Tragedy* (Aldershot: Ashgate, 2000); John C. McDowell, 'Learning Where to Place One's Hope: The Eschatological Significance of Election in Barth', *Scottish Journal of Theology* 53, no. 3 (2000): 316–38, https://doi.org/10.1017/S0036930600051012; and George Hunsinger, *How to Read Karl Barth: The Shape of His Theology* (New York: Oxford University Press, 1991), 128–35, in which he claims that Barth tends in a 'universalist direction' (132).

8. Hunsinger, *How to Read Karl Barth*, 134.

9. George Hunsinger, *Disruptive Grace: Studies in the Theology of Karl Barth* (Grand Rapids, MI: Eerdmans, 2000), 243.

10. Cf. CD II/2, 417 with 418; and CD IV/3, 477 with 478.

11. Hunsinger, *How to Read Karl Barth*, 132.

12. One should note well the order in which Barth addresses election: first Jesus Christ, then community and lastly the individual.

13. David Fergusson, 'Will the Love of God Finally Triumph?', in *Nothing Greater, Nothing Better: Theological Essays on the Love of God*, ed. Kevin J. Vanhoozer (Grand Rapids, MI: Eerdmans, 2001), 186–202, esp. 195n20. Fergusson correctly indicates, however, that the leaning of Barth's theology is clearly in a universalist direction and not simply at an equidistant point between limited atonement and universalism.

occurs not only in the doctrine of election but also throughout the doctrine of reconciliation. Furthermore, it does not seem to capture the wealth of material in Barth's occasional writings which point in the direction of universal salvation. There is an almost inexhaustible list of Barthian aphorisms on this: 'The dogma is that Hell exists, not that people are in it'[14] or 'We believers ... must always become what we are. ... The others are already what they are to become.'[15] Most powerfully, silence does not seem to give full weight to Barth's words regarding universalism:

> It would be well not to yield to that panic fright which this word seems to have a way of spreading around it, at least before one has come to an understanding with regard to its possible sense or nonsense. ...
>
> It would be well, in view of the 'danger' with which the expression is ever and again seen to be encompassed, to ask for a moment, whether on the whole the 'danger' from those theologians who are forever sceptically critical, who are again and again suspiciously questioning, because they are always fundamentally legalistic, and who are therefore in essentials sullen and dismal, is not in the meantime always more threatening among us than that of an unsuitably cheerful indifferentism or even antinomianism, to which one could in fact yield oneself on one definite understanding of that conception. One thing is sure, that there is no theological justification for setting any limits on our side to the friendliness of God toward man which appeared in Jesus Christ.[16]

Thus, it seems that there is an apparent impasse between a theology which seems to point in a universalist direction and one which simultaneously denies that charge.

This chapter seeks to argue that Barth's rejection of universalism or *apokatastasis* does not involve a limitation of God's ultimate salvific work as some of Barth's commentators seem to imply. Rather, it marks a dismissal of the problematic elements associated with universalism. I argue this specifically by considering what Barth does and does not reject when he claims he is dismissing universalism: outlining the origins of the so-called 'charge' of universalism; examining Barth's own response to the charge of universalism looking specifically at his dialogue with Berkouwer, and highlighting what precisely of Berkouwer Barth is rejecting and the implications of this; demonstrating that it is the replacement of the person of Jesus Christ with a principle, rather than any limitation of the salvific work of God, that Barth dismisses in rejecting *apokatastasis*; and concluding with a consideration of whether the matter should be rendered a 'charge' at all. It is hoped thereby to clear a path through the contradictory and mutually exclusive studies of Barth on this issue.

---

14. Busch, *Karl Barth*, 362.
15. Ibid., 446.
16. Karl Barth, 'The Humanity of God', in Karl Barth, *God, Grace and Gospel* (Edinburgh: Oliver and Boyd, 1959), 49–50.

The roots of the so-called 'charge': The doctrine of election

The roots of the charge of universalism lie within Barth's radical re-description of the doctrine of election.[17] Barth's departure from traditional understanding of the doctrine is most clearly seen in his assertion that the doctrine of election must be understood Christologically. Jesus Christ is the subject and object of election as electing God and elected human. Jesus Christ as God and human stands as a mediator: in him, God reveals himself to humanity and humanity knows God; in him, one sees the will, judgement, deliverance and gift of God.[18]

In seeing Christ as electing God, one sees who the 'Subject God' is,[19] and in the primal history of the covenant of God with humanity in the union of his Son with Jesus of Nazareth, one sees the gracious relating of this God to humanity.[20] A true doctrine of God must speak not only of God in himself but also of all his ways and works, and the way in which these have been determined – that is in his primary decision to be electing God in Jesus Christ. In this way, one can begin to present a doctrine of the graciousness of God in the beginning of all of these ways and works,[21] through which one sees the self-determination of the electing God: 'In so far as God not only is love, but loves, in the act of love which determines His whole being God elects.'[22] Throughout the doctrine of election, Barth's concern seems to be not to separate the will of God from the love of God as Calvinists traditionally had done. In his at times sermonic tone,[23] Barth does not want to confront humanity with a God who might as well condemn them as save them.

---

17. It should be noted, however, that Barth does see himself standing in line with scripture in his articulation of the doctrine, which is the reason he gives for departing strongly from the tradition (CD II/2, 3–4), and in some line of continuity with the positive elements of Augustine, Lombard, Aquinas, Isidore of Seville, Gottschalk and the Reformers (CD II/2, 16–24). Most especially, Barth sees himself as in line with what he finds in the Synod of Dort (CD II/2, 17–18).

18. CD II/2, 94.

19. Ibid., 5–7.

20. Ibid., 8.

21. Ibid., 99.

22. Ibid., 76. For a fuller description of the effect of the placing of election in the doctrine of God see Eberhard Jüngel, *God's Being Is in Becoming: The Trinitarian Being of God in the Theology of Karl Barth: A Paraphrase*, 2nd English edn (Edinburgh: T&T Clark, 2001). To test his statement that for Barth 'God's being is in becoming' he appeals to the doctrine of election (82–7). For Jüngel, 'God's being-in-act' means God is his decision, and that the primal decision which is made by and determines God is the election of grace. This leads to the 'free self-determination' of God (87).

23. For example, his movement into the second person (e.g. CD II/2, 322–3). Interestingly, Berkouwer cites pastoral concerns as at the heart of Barth's reworking of the doctrine of election. G. C. Berkouwer, *The Triumph of Grace in the Theology of Karl Barth* (London: Paternoster Press, 1956), 95–6.

Equally, the love of God cannot be separated from the will: for Barth, God 'loves in freedom'.[24] Although it is an eternal decision,[25] Barth wishes God's electing to remain a free decision in order to remain gracious. There must still be personhood and a centre of self-consciousness behind that loving in freedom.[26]

The nature of Christ's electing to be simultaneously the elected human in the pre-temporal eternity of God means that there is no room for a prior decision of God to create, or elect and condemn before the decision to elect Jesus Christ (no *decretum absolutum*); Jesus Christ is himself the ultimate *decretum absolutum*.[27] Indeed, in Barth's actualistic inner logics,[28] it might even be stated that God *is* this movement and turning towards humanity: his economy and ontology cannot be separated.[29]

What is most shocking and dangerous is that this election is a self-election to the negative part of predestination – perdition, death, rejection, exclusion and the No of God.[30] These are the things humanity deserves, and yet God decides in his freedom to suffer them in his self-election of Jesus Christ. This does not excuse human sinfulness, but in election God irreversibly takes its torment to himself.[31] Predestination becomes, therefore, not simply one *modus* of salvation but *the modus* of the divine work of redemption, indeed of all of God's works *ad extra*.[32] In it, Christ has willed to take to himself rejection in order that rejection can never again become the portion of humanity: 'He is *the* Rejected, as and because He is *the* Elect. In view of His election, there is no other rejected but Himself.'[33] It is this which makes the election of humanity in Christ so drastic and radical. Belief in the simultaneous nature of Christ as elected and elector sees the self-election of Christ bringing rejection into the sovereignty of God, that those who reject him

---

24. CD II/1, §28, emphasis added.

25. Here, one must be careful to remember Barth's particular understanding of eternity. See CD II/1, 608–40.

26. CD II/2, 174–8.

27. Ibid., 100–1. Barth asserts here as elsewhere that it is the election of God which is described in Jn 1.1-2 as the result of the repetition of οὗτος ἦν which he considers refers to Jesus being 'the same' who was. In CD IV/2, 33, Barth draws attention to the further use of this οὗτος ἦν in the proclamation of the Baptist in v. 15 referring to the incarnate Christ. He sees this incarnate one as the referent of the earlier οὗτος.

28. For a definition of 'actualism' see Hunsinger, *How to Read Karl Barth*, esp. 30–2. A different account is given by Bruce L. McCormack, 'Grace and Being: The Role of God's Gracious Election in Karl Barth's Theological Ontology', in *The Cambridge Companion to Karl Barth*, ed. John Webster (Cambridge: Cambridge University Press, 2000), 98–101.

29. This point must, however, be held in dialectic with Barth's continual and emphatic insistence throughout CD on the 'mystery' of God, for example, CD I/1, 321.

30. CD II/2, 166.

31. Ibid., 167.

32. Ibid., 191.

33. Ibid., 353.

are therefore simultaneously elected in him, since he has elected their rejection for himself. Barth goes, therefore, beyond the simple binary of Calvin's elected and rejected humanity,[34] by keeping the integrity of election and rejection and yet uniting these in the person of Jesus Christ in a chiasmic movement in which the elected of God elects rejection in order that the rejected may be elected. It is, therefore, in God's singularly positive turning towards humanity in the elected Jesus that one needs to consider the destiny of human nature.[35]

The soteriological implications of this cannot be over-estimated. The election of the community and individuals (who are elect only for the sake of the community[36]) comes to belong to the sphere of the simultaneous divine–human self-election in Christ. Human election occurs only in his prior election and cannot be abstractly separated from this:

> That which has been eternally determined in Jesus Christ is concretely determined for every individual man to the extent that in the form of the witness of Israel and of the Church it is also addressed to him and applies to him and comes to him, to the extent that in His Word the electing God enters with him into the relationship of Elector to elected, and by His Word makes Him an elected man.[37]

It is only 'in Christ' that this election of the community and individual has its meaning. One is able to see at work the dialectic of the particular and the universal. While the universal implications of the doctrine seem clear, the original election of Jesus Christ is what gives particular truth to individual election,[38] just as it is in witness to election that the particularity of church and Israel is maintained: both witness to the self-elected rejection in Christ that is seen in the self-electing of rejecting humanity in the church and Israel with respect to their positions pre- and post-crucifixion and resurrection.[39] Desirous to forward correct proclamation in

34. On the logic of binaries and triads, see Peter Ochs, *Peirce, Pragmatism, and the Logic of Scripture* (Cambridge: Cambridge University Press, 1998), esp. chap. 8.
35. CD II/2, 118.
36. 'It is not men as private persons in the singular or plural. It is these men as a fellowship elected by God in Jesus Christ and determined for all eternity for a particular service' (CD II/2, 196). For him, the 'other' involved in election is designated as community. This term covers both Israel and the church. See CD II/2, §34. It is important to note that this paragraph comes before §35, 'The Election of the Individual'.
37. CD II/2, 309–10.
38. Ibid., 310.
39. There is a second almost chiasmic movement in Barth: the particular elect of Israel reject and are thus rejected in order that the mercy of God may be revealed in his eternal promise to them despite their rejection (e.g. CD II/2, 305); just as the once rejected Gentiles elect and are elected in order that the universality of God's election can be witnessed (e.g. CD II/2, 238–41). These two communities must exist in simultaneity to indicate the simultaneous election and rejection of Christ and thus the simultaneous rejection and

the church about election, Barth instructs the preacher to exhort: 'In Jesus Christ, thou, too, art not rejected – for He has borne thy rejection – but elected.'[40] Election and rejection belong together in the primal decision of Christ to self-elect the rejection belonging to humanity.

Rather than simply instrumentalizing the 'in' under discussion of election 'in Christ', for Barth election is actual both in terms of the self-determination of God in his act in Jesus Christ and in the relationship that results from this between Christ and each member of humanity.[41] Barth summarizes this well: 'Nor does it mean only through Him, by means of that which He as elected man can be and do for them. "In Him" means in His person, in His will, in His own divine choice, in the very basic decision of God which He fulfils over against every man.'[42]

Jesus Christ elects humanity as electing God, 'electing them in His own humanity.'[43] While His election is unique, it must also be said that 'His election is the original and *all-inclusive* election; the election which is absolutely unique, but which in this uniqueness is *universally* meaningful and efficacious, because it is the election of Him who Himself elects.'[44] One can easily see where the charge of universalism in Barth stems from, if all of humanity is elected 'in Christ', even in their rejection of God (seen typologically in Israel), and, if this has its origins in pre-temporal eternity, it is difficult to find space logically for God's rejection of those who reject him. It is following such logic through that led to Berkouwer's monumental study *The Triumph of Grace in the Theology of Karl Barth*.[45] In this

election of humanity in him (CD II/2, 205–305). When one considers the date of this volume's publication (1942), the importance of Barth's writing of the church and Israel synecdochally as both elected and rejected cannot be underestimated. For more on Barth and the Jews, see Eberhard Busch, 'Indissoluble Unity: Barth's Position on the Jews during the Hitler Era', in *For the Sake of the World: Karl Barth and the Future of Ecclesial Theology*, ed. George Hunsinger (Grand Rapids, MI: Eerdmans, 2004), 53–79, along with Katherine Sonderegger's response, 80–8; Mark Lindsay, 'Dialectics of Communion: Dialectical Method and Barth's Defence of Israel', in *Karl Barth: A Future for Postmodern Theology?*, ed. Geoff Thompson and Christiaan Mostert (Hindmarsh, South Australia: Australian Theological Forum, 2000), 122–43; and Katherine Sonderegger, *That Jesus Christ Was Born a Jew: Karl Barth's 'Doctrine of Israel'* (University Park: Pennsylvania State University Press, 1992).

40. CD II/2, 322.

41. In his doctrine of creation, Barth states, 'A decision has been made concerning the being and nature of every man by the mere fact that with Him and among all other men He too has been a man' (CD III/2, 133).

42. CD II/2, 117.

43. Ibid.

44. Ibid., emphasis added.

45. Colin E. Gunton asserts that such a view of Barth is also evident in a different form in the work of David F. Ford: Colin E. Gunton, 'The Triune God and the Freedom of the Creature', in S. W. Sykes, *Karl Barth: Centenary Essays* (Cambridge: Cambridge University Press, 1989), 46–68. Certainly, Ford's excellent study of Barth's use of the character of Judas indicates such a position, in which the reality of the Gospels is swallowed up by a

work, Berkouwer believed that Barth's doctrine of election involved the eventual salvation of all, and that Barth was, therefore, being inconsistent in his rejection of universalism.[46]

Getting the matter straight: Not the 'triumph of grace' but 'Jesus is victor'

Given this charge by Berkouwer, it is my argument that the clearest sense of what Barth is rejecting in 'universalism' comes in his discussion of Berkouwer's work in CD IV/3. In examining this, therefore, one can truly understand whether Barth is positing a limitation on the ultimate salvation of all people. For all of Berkouwer's criticism of Barth, the great polemicist is extremely praising of Berkouwer's work. He observes that 'Berkouwer has undoubtedly laid his finger on an important point'.[47] Barth's concern is the book's title, which indicates that Christianity is for Barth an absolutely 'triumphant affair'.[48] One who has understood Barth so well (albeit critically) is criticized thus: 'If I am in a sense understood by its [*The Triumph of Grace*'s] clever and faithful author, yet in the last resort cannot think that I am genuinely understood for all his care and honesty, this is connected with the fact that he tries to understand me under this title.'[49] This title, Barth feels, should be replaced with 'Jesus is victor'.[50] Barth here reveals what he is rejecting in critiquing the thesis of Berkouwer, as well as what he is accepting. It is interesting to observe in this that Barth never overtly rejects (nor does he mention) universalism. What he rejects are some of the *implications* that Berkouwer draws from this, not the positively objective soteriology itself. This does not remove the emphatically positive ultimate message of the eternal election of Jesus Christ but clarifies the sense in which this is to be understood – most determinately *in Jesus Christ*. This is explained by Barth in four points.

Firstly, Barth accuses Berkouwer of presenting him as one whose work is underlined by a Christological principle.[51] There is nothing worse to Barth's

less realistic *Bildungsroman*. David Ford, *Barth and God's Story: Biblical Narrative and the Theological Method of Karl Barth in the 'Church Dogmatics'*, 2nd edn (Frankfurt am Main: Lang, 1985), 91–2.

46. For example, Berkouwer, *The Triumph of Grace in the Theology of Karl Barth*, 111.
47. CD IV/3, 173.
48. Ibid.
49. Ibid.
50. Ibid.
51. Gerhard Sauter is no doubt correct when, regarding a different issue, he writes: 'When Barth uses the word "principle", it connotes nothing less than the theological equivalent of a major industrial accident, if not a nuclear power plant explosion which can no longer be contained within tolerable limits', Gerhard Sauter, 'Why Is Karl Barth's Church Dogmatics Not a "Theology of Hope"? Some Observations on Barth's Understanding of Eschatology', *Scottish Journal of Theology* 52, no. 4 (1999): 407–29, https://doi.org/10.1017/S0036930600050468.

Nachdenken mode of theology.⁵² Thus, not even election can take priority over Jesus Christ because 'we are not dealing with a Christ-principle, but with Jesus Christ Himself as attested by Holy Scripture'.⁵³ By making Christ a principle, Berkouwer has wrongly understood Christ primarily to be the 'mighty executive organ of the divine will of grace',⁵⁴ giving truly Christological thinking only a secondary place. Thus, for Barth, one cannot even use grace as a principle: election takes place in Jesus, in a person and not in a principle that humanity is elected. The *Gnadenwahl* must be understood through the person of Christ, not the person through the *Gnadenwahl*.

Secondly, Barth asserts that in Jesus one deals with a free person and his free act that cannot simply be grasped 'in the sense of conceptual apprehension or control'.⁵⁵ He is not an *in abstracto* engaged in a battle with evil *in abstracto*. Jesus is a living person. And yet this is a person in whom one cannot have limited confidence. Barth concurs with Blumhardt that the superiority of Christ over his opponent can only end in Christ's triumph: this is decided from the very start because 'the One who is the First will also be the Last'.⁵⁶ However, again, this is not to replace *him* with a 'principle'. Principles could be doubted in terms of the biblical message: there might be room for other interpretations. There is no room for an interpretation of scripture which does not recognize that 'Jesus is victor'. It is not the principle but this man in whom humanity is elected.

This does not, thirdly, deny the reality of evil.⁵⁷ Barth defends his case regarding this. Berkouwer believed that all of history was sewn up in Barth's theology which determined that Barth had denied evil its reality. Barth continues to be emphatic in his assertion that it is only through 'Jesus is victor' that one can understand the nature and reality of evil. Admitting that he has taken his terms from outside scripture, Barth still claims he has used insights from the Bible in shaping his doctrine. In speaking of 'nothingness' (*Das Nichtige*),⁵⁸ Barth speaks of something which does not exist as God or his creatures do. Rather, he speaks of something which has no basis for its being. Yet, this does not deny its existence to which it has no right.⁵⁹ Evil has reality in the existence humans give it, but it is to be 'seen in Jesus Christ', and thus must be understood in its 'absolute inferiority'.⁶⁰

---

52. On *Nachdenken*, see David F. Ford, 'Barth's Interpretation of the Bible', in *Karl Barth, Studies of His Theological Method*, ed. Stephen Sykes (Oxford: Clarendon Press, 1979), 55–87, esp. 81–6.
53. CD IV/3, 174.
54. Ibid., 175.
55. Ibid., 176.
56. Ibid.
57. CD IV/3, 177.
58. See CD III/3, §50, 'God and Nothingness'.
59. CD IV/3, 178.
60. Ibid.

Fourthly, Barth addresses the charge that his work removes the historical encounter between God and evil.[61] Barth holds to his belief that '*from the very outset*' (which Berkouwer finds so distasteful) God is infinitely greater and stronger than evil. However, one is not to understand this as a principle which dissolves history. It is in the narrative of the life of Jesus in God's encounter with the world that this is seen. Rather than removing any sense of history, it is this which establishes it: only in the history of Jesus can humanity know God and evil, and the relationship of each to the other. And in narrating the life of Christ, one sees that there is no 'easy "triumph of grace."'[62] What is more, this is a history and a conflict in which humanity must engage. Since it is *his* conflict, neither an easy gain nor an uneasy pessimism can be its end:

> Only victory is to be expected in view of its commencement, in view of Jesus, who has already fought the battle. Yet we have this confidence only with the last and bitter seriousness enjoined and demanded by this commencement by Jesus. Neither hesitant qualifications nor rash and slothful assurance are possible at this point.[63]

It is from this that Barth moves into his discussion of the drama, war and history of reconciliation,[64] a history into which humanity is drawn.[65]

Beginning to pass the impasse

What, then, has this to say to the issue of universalism in general, and Barth's eschatology in particular? It will be argued that in rejecting universalism, Barth is not rejecting the final victory of Christ but rejecting a particular (and wrong) understanding of the *means* by which this is achieved. He is reinterpreting the matter, by carefully removing the negative charges involved with an ultimate salvation of all humanity, while still allowing for and pointing towards that ultimate salvation. Barth rejects universalism because 'universalism' itself can never be the victor: this victory is Jesus Christ's.

Firstly, the most notable feature to emphasize is the continued and sustained sense of being *in Christ*. Salvation is offered to humanity in its election *in* Christ – the Christ of whom it must be said 'Jesus is victor'. It is in the eternal decision, and the history and narrative of the life of the incarnate Christ that our election takes place. For this reason, those who criticize Barth's doctrine of election and objective soteriology on the grounds of there being no reason for the ongoing nature of

---

61. CD IV/3, 179.
62. Ibid.
63. CD IV/3, 180.
64. Ibid.
65. CD IV/3, 181-3.

history cannot be justified. The election of humanity in Christ means an election in a life, in a person. It is as a result of this that Barth's chapter on 'The Command of God' follows that on election. Since election is the election of a *person*, it is the determination of a person, and therefore the question arises of human self-determination which corresponds to *this* determination. Election in the *person* of Jesus allows the space for human freedom which a principle never can. Barth rejects universalism, therefore, as he is determined to keep the particularity of the person of Jesus Christ – a particularity which cannot be gained from a principle.[66] Here, John Webster is helpful in allowing one to recognize the room for human freedom this allows in his discussion of the ethical implications of *enhypostasis*.[67] Although *enhypostasis* is not a doctrine Barth uses overtly in his discussion of election, it is used clearly in Barth's thought both before and after the doctrine of election.[68] Because for Barth election is in the person of Jesus Christ, 'human reality, and therefore human agency, are "*enhypostatically* real", drawing their substance from the human reality of Jesus Christ'.[69] This is not to merge the two realities but to recognize that our humanity exists from and in his. Against the charge of Christomonism, Barth writes,

> It does not mean that Jesus Christ has merged into world-occurrence and world-occurrence into Him, so that we can no longer speak of them as separate things. This would be Christomonism in the base sense of that unlovely term. What it does mean is that according to the true insight of the people of God the twofold form of world history loses the appearance of autonomy and finality, the character of an irreconcilable contradiction and antithesis, which it always seems to have at a first glance.[70]

World occurrence and the history of humanity still continue after Jesus Christ,[71] but the contradiction and antithesis are ultimately removed. It is not that reality is dissolved into a greater reality, but rather that the very particularity of the person Jesus provides the basis for the very existence of the 'twofold form of world history', and in that way the very existence of all particularity. Barth's discussion of 'Jesus

---

66. Indeed, Barth cites his allergy to metaphysics as the reason for his rejection of *apokatastasis*: 'His [God's] election and calling do not give rise to any historical metaphysics, but only to the necessity of attesting them on the ground that they have taken place in Jesus Christ and His community', CD II/2, 417–18.

67. John Webster, *Barth's Moral Theology: Human Action in Barth's Thought* (Edinburgh: T&T Clark, 1998), 88–91.

68. On *an-* and *enhypostasis*, see CD I/2, 162–70, 216 (*anhypostasis* only); CD IV/2, 49–50. See also Jüngel, *God's Being Is in Becoming*, 96–7.

69. Webster, *Barth's Moral Theology*, 89.

70. CD IV/3, 713.

71. Ibid., 714.

is victor' allows the room for this in its consideration of the particularity of Jesus and the conflict with evil.

Secondly, the emphasis on the particularity of the person of Jesus Christ guards the freedom and sovereignty of God while still allowing for the salvation of all humanity. Emphasizing the *person* Jesus allows for a freedom which cannot be espoused in a principle. It is not that God is bound by the Christ-principle, but rather that in his sovereign freedom he *wills* to be this God in *self*-limitation – to be Jesus Christ. It is not that Jesus Christ replaces the *decretum absolutum* as a principle: it is that he crowds it out as a person. Barth is clear that God is under no obligation to elect.[72] In Jesus Christ, one is able to see the mysterious sovereign *will* of God, as Jesus is 'the Prophet who knows and proclaims the will of God which is done in His existence'.[73] While one might be concerned that a principle might bind the sovereignty of God in Barth's theology (especially the principle of universalism), the insistence on the will of God, found in the emphasis on the person of Jesus Christ, underscores God's sovereignty. This is a sovereignty God demonstrates in God's willed decision to be for humanity in the election of Jesus Christ.

Thirdly, related to both preceding points is the need for a full and proper sense of Barth's understanding of eternity and time, which means that there is no removal of time by eternity.[74] Suffice it to say, in Barth's theology, God's eternity is more than simply the unity of all times with the goal and purpose of his will. His eternity is not exhausted by this. God's eternity is rather the *presupposition* of this unity. For that reason, Barth speaks of pre-, supra- and post-temporal eternity, which he believes is a biblical distinction within the unity of eternity in which it is possible to see eternity's positive relationship to time since in it God has the power to exist before, above and after time.[75] All too often, commentators on Barth have failed to see the importance of this distinction and this *positive* relationship of eternity to time. God's eternity is the precondition of temporality rather than a simple dialectic of time over and against timelessness. Eternity does not obliterate time; it allows for it. The simultaneous possession of all time does

---

72. CD II/2, 101.

73. CD IV/3, 180.

74. In addition to the brief comments here, see Chapter 4 in this volume, 'Barth on Eternity', as well as CD II/1, §31.3; I/2, §14; and CD III/2, §47. For the most thorough discussion of this, see Richard H. Roberts, *A Theology on Its Way? Essays on Karl Barth* (Edinburgh: T&T Clark, 1991), esp. chap. 1. In this, Roberts engages in a thorough and fierce criticism of Barth on time, concluding that Barth is ultimately 'ambiguous' and seeing the dissolution of time by eternity in Barth's theory. While Roberts is undoubtedly correct in the emphasis he places on these concepts in Barth's theology and identifies the innermost logics of his work, his overall conclusions cannot be accepted. For a critique of Roberts, see Bruce D. Marshall, review of *A Theology on Its Way? Essays on Karl Barth* by Richard H. Roberts, *Journal of Theological Studies* 44, no. 1 (1993): 453–8.

75. CD II/1, 619.

not mean the dominance of any one time: pre-temporal eternity does not have priority over supra- or post-temporal eternity as many commentators would have us believe. Rather it is *simultaneous*. This does not remove the integrity of any one moment of time or of eternity but unites them. To suggest that in Barth all of time and history is sewn up by election is to fundamentally misunderstand both Barth's presentation of eternity and the election of Jesus Christ. Indeed, one should note well that §31 (in CD II/1) which ends with discussion of eternity and glory dovetails perfectly into §32 (in CD II/2) on election. The election of Jesus Christ is an election of time in the life and particularity of Jesus:

> Before all created reality, before all being and becoming in time, before time itself, in the pre-temporal eternity of God, the eternal divine decision as such has as its object and content the existence of this one created being the man Jesus of Nazareth, and the work of this man in His life and death, His humiliation and exaltation, His obedience and merit. It tells us further that in and with the existence of this man the eternal divine decision has as its object and content the execution of the divine covenant with man, the salvation of all men.[76]

One misses the radicality of this movement if one fails to see this particularity. To misunderstand eternity is to fail to grasp the particularity involved in the statement 'Jesus is victor' – a particularity that can never be involved in a principle. It is also to fail to see that there are few theologians who allow for so much time for humanity as Barth does. A principle may well dissolve or negate time; the life in time of a human person cannot. Barth rejects a universalism which removes temporality, but this in no way limits the ultimate victory of Christ.

Fourthly, the issue of ultimacy requires further comment. In dealing with the *eschaton*, one is dealing with that which is ultimate; in dealing with human history, one is faced with that which is penultimate. Each requires the other, and each is important, but the ultimate is always that – ultimate.[77] Barth finds room for the freedom of humanity and the continued existence of history and world occurrence through his use of this concept. He rejects a universalism which does not allow for this distinction, but he still allows what is ultimate to be ultimate. It is this way that one is to understand the existence of the Christian

> in the final manifestation of Jesus Christ. There can be no doubt, however, that in the liberation which comes to the Christian here and now, in that which is personally and specifically disclose and given him in and with his calling, the Christian himself is not the end of the ways of God but only the preliminary sign of this end.[78]

---

76. CD II/2, 116.

77. See Bonhoeffer's discussion of the relationship between the ultimate and the penultimate, DBWE 6, 146–70.

78. CD IV/3, 675.

Christianity and faith in the present are not an ultimate decisive factor but a 'preliminary sign of this end'. Moreover, this sign is one 'not only in anticipation of its own awaited completion but also in anticipation of what is truly and finally purposed in what God has done and revealed in Jesus Christ, namely, the liberation of all men'.[79] The Christian is a penultimate sign of the ultimate; and she is one who cannot be separated from the ultimate.[80] Faith, however, must never be seen as being ultimate: '[in] the recognition of faith we are speaking of most important penultimate things, but not of ultimate things'.[81] Penultimacy allows the room for human freedom in history. This is a history which is real and valid in its penultimacy. In it is the room for faith; just as in it is the room for rejection, condemnation and unbelief. But these are not ultimate. The ultimate is this: 'Jesus is victor'. Jesus' victory does not drown out but is the basis for human history – not simply through some single bang in a pre-temporal eternity which renders all notes in time meaningless.[82] This is the way in which one is to understand the discussion of rejection in Barth's doctrine of election.[83] The reality of rejection is there, indeed uncomfortably so.[84] As Berkouwer observes, this is a double predestination.[85] However, rejection is also elected *in* Christ. Yet this rejection is not ultimate: the verdict of the Father is seen in resurrection.[86] To deny that the penultimacy of rejection makes it unreal is tantamount to the suggestion that the penultimacy of the cross makes it unreal. Both are necessary in the correct order: neither undoes the reality of the other. So, too, for Barth's soteriology, the penultimacy of human rejection cannot undo the ultimacy of God's election; yet this does not undermine the reality of either. In Barth's discussion of judgement, condemnation and the threat of hell, rejection and the abyss, one deals with what is penultimate: the unbeliever is distinguished from the Christian in that she has the fear that these things are that which *is* ultimate.

79. Ibid.
80. CD IV/3, 351–2.
81. CD IV/1, 767.
82. Here, one should see the reason for Barth's emphatic use of the biblical term 'covenant'. God is a covenantal God – a God of history.
83. CD II/2, §35.2 and 4.
84. Lindsay draws attention to the fact that the lectures which provided the basis for most of the analysis of election (including its understanding of the rejection of Israel) were given in the winter semesters of 1939–40 and 1941–2 – at roughly the same time as the Wannsee Conference of 20 January 1942, Lindsay, 'Dialectics of Communion', 125.
85. For example, Berkouwer, *The Triumph of Grace in the Theology of Karl Barth*.
86. See CD IV/1, §59.3. For this connection, see also CD II/2, 558, as well as Barth's thesis at §39, 'He judges us as in His Son's death He condemns all our action as transgression, and by His Son's resurrection pronounces us righteous' (CD II/2, 733).

Conclusion

The emphatic sense of election *in* Christ and the reiterated point that 'Jesus is victor' determine that Barth's theology clearly points in a universalist direction. That Barth rejects *apokatastasis* is not because of a limitation of his hope for humanity or his belief in the all-encompassing nature of election and the objective nature of salvation. It is rather a rejection of a principle. In Barth's own words: 'I don't believe in universalism, but I do believe in Christ, the reconciler of all.'[87] As Webster puts it, 'We must not allow worries about the universal scope which Barth claims for the history of Jesus to crowd out that the most basic function of his presentation is to stress Jesus' *particularity* before his cosmic pertinence.'[88] The principle of universalism brings along with it certain dangers that the continued stress on salvation in the particular *person* of Jesus Christ can help to overcome. For Barth to place his faith in universalism would be to place his faith in something which was greater than Christ and undermined the sovereignty of God; to place his faith in 'Christ, the reconciler of all' and to proclaim 'Jesus is victor' is not to allow some a priori to govern God but properly to allow God to be the subject of salvation. This is truly what it is to be elected *in Jesus Christ*. In a way similar to his rejection of the word 'person' regarding the trinity,[89] Barth does not wish to be governed by a conceptual framework a word brings with it: in rejecting *apokatastasis*, he reveals an unease with the use of the word which might be an easy epithet with which to misconstrue his own particularist agenda in describing God's election; instead, he finds a *new* way to talk about such matters that this old word cannot convey. He does not wish to imply the charges so often brought against him regarding the meaningless of history or evil or rejection, which this term is insufficient in answering. If we are to charge Barth with universalism, we must be careful not to charge him with the universalism he so carefully and overtly denies and avoids. In Barth there is something new – not a limitation of the friendliness of Jesus Christ but a limitation of the problems that can arise from such a universal scope for salvation.

Indeed, perhaps the impasse regarding Barth on universalism stems from how radically new his steps are. What is certain is that this radicality is all too easily removed when we seek to defend Barth by taking him away from his advances on his *theologia viatorum* back to the safe and entrenched comfort zones of orthodoxy. Then, we become those whom Barth charges with seeing the 'danger'

---

87. Busch, *Karl Barth*, 394.

88. John Webster, 'The Grand Narrative of Jesus Christ: Barth's Christology', in *Karl Barth: A Future for Postmodern Theology?*, ed. Geoff Thompson and Christiaan Mostert (Hindmarsh, South Australia: Australian Theological Forum, 2000), 29–48, esp. 42.

89. On Barth's rejection of the word 'person', see Alan J. Torrance, *Persons in Communion: An Essay on Trinitarian Description and Human Participation with Special Reference to Volume One of Karl Barth's Church Dogmatics* (Edinburgh: T&T Clark, 1996).

out of legalism and indifference.⁹⁰ In an age of religious fundamentalism, it may well be that the danger lies on the other side. A positive message to humanity of salvation brought about by particularity (not the removal of it) and allowing for particularity is infinitely superior to the endless and dreadful dividing of humanity into categories.⁹¹ This leads to an attractively radical reformation in the agenda of preaching and ethics, necessary for an age which sees religious intolerance and the divisive use of unhelpful binaries in religious language. It is necessary to recognize, as Barth records he did while writing *Church Dogmatics* II, that as important as it is to say 'no', to say 'yes' is even more important and pressing.⁹² As Barth wrote regarding the atheism of Max Bense:

> I know the rather sinister figure of the 'atheist' very well, not only from books, but also because it lurks somewhere inside me too. But I believe I know even better the real God and the real man who is called Jesus Christ in the unity of both. He let the atheist depart once and for all and long ago, completely, and that goes for Max Bense as well as for me. Only in our bad dreams can we want to be 'atheists'.⁹³

What is important for Barth is that the Christian cannot view the non-Christian as anything other than the person for whom God elected, who is elected in Christ and whose rejection is all too well known by the reality of the faith community as well. If we are to charge Barth with universalism, it cannot be that universalism which has been articulated previously. What Barth cannot be charged with is a failure to recognize the monumentally and radically new situation of humanity eternally elected in Christ. Yes, Christ stands at the door and knocks, but in the power of his resurrection, he makes his way into locked rooms (cf. Jn 20).

But what of those others who are not Christians themselves? What can be said about their beliefs in relation to the all-encompassing uniqueness of Christ? What about the differentiation between the Christian and the non-Christian, and indeed the 'co-religionist' and the 'secularist'? Clearly, there is something significant for the church to learn from Barth's understanding of salvation for those outside of the church, but is this the end of the story? In an age which is complexly secular and pluralist, might Barth have anything to say about the genuine otherness of the secular or religious other? Building on the preceding insights from Barth, it is these issues which the subsequent two chapters on Barth consider.

---

90. Barth, 'The Humanity of God', 50. Although by no means universalist, Trevor Hart too states the danger of Christians who might feel disappointed should God choose to save all humanity, 'Universalism: Two Distinct Types', in *Universalism and the Doctrine of Hell*, ed. Nigel M. de S. Cameron (Carlisle: Paternoster, 1992), 1–34, esp. 34.

91. It was this which Barth saw as being at the root of his disagreements with pietism. See Busch, *Karl Barth*, 445.

92. Ibid., 284.

93. Karl Barth, *Fragments Grave and Gay*, ed. Martin Rumscheidt (London: Collins, 1971), 45–6.

Chapter 6

BRINGING BARTH ON RELIGION TO THE INTER-FAITH TABLE

Although he criticized Barth under the enigmatic phrase 'positivism of revelation',[1] Bonhoeffer saw Barth's criticism of religion as 'his really great merit'.[2] In the present age in which inter-faith dialogue has become more pressing than it has perhaps ever been before, theology can at times engage in two conversations which are not only separate but at worst self-contradictory: in its discussions with secular society, theology can engage in critical discussions about religion, drinking deeply from the well of criticism offered by the likes of Feuerbach, Nietzsche, Durkheim and Marx;[3] yet, in its discussions in inter-faith settings, the danger can arise that these critiques are thrown out altogether, or at least lie in abeyance. If we are truly to realize the potential Bonhoeffer glimpsed in Barth's critique of religion,[4]

---

1. See DBWE 8, letters of 30 April 1944 (364), 5 May 1944 (373) and 8 June 1944 (429).

2. DBWE 8, 5 May 1944. On the relationship between Barth and Bonhoeffer over the question of religion, see Andreas Pangritz, *Karl Barth in the Theology of Dietrich Bonhoeffer*, trans. B. and M. Rumscheidt (Grand Rapids, MI: Eerdmans, 1999), 71–114; Ralf K. Wüstenberg, *A Theology of Life: Dietrich Bonhoeffer's Religionless Christianity*, trans. Doug Stott (Grand Rapids, MI: Eerdmans, 1998). Wüstenberg argues correctly that Barth and Bonhoeffer are seeking to achieve different things: Barth offers a critique of religion but never a religionless Christianity.

3. As these names indicate, this is a specifically modern European conceptual development which cannot claim to be relevant for every religion in each part of the world.

4. CD I/2 §17, 'The Revelation of God as the Abolition [*Aufhebung*] of Religion'. References to further criticisms Barth cites against religion can be found in Garrett Green, 'Challenging the Religious Studies Canon: Karl Barth's Theory of Religion', *Journal of Religion* 75 (1995): 473–86. The present chapter does not address directly Barth's discussion of the secular parables of the kingdom and the lights of creation, except to make points for conceptual clarity or in order not to misrepresent Barth. The reader is, however, directed to CD IV/3 §69.2; George Hunsinger, *How to Read Karl Barth: The Shape of His Theology* (New York: Oxford University Press, 1991), 234–80; Geoff Thompson, 'Religious Diversity, Christian Doctrine and Karl Barth', *International Journal of Systematic Theology* 8, no. 1 (2006), esp. 10–18; and Glenn A. Chestnut, 'The Secular Parables of the Kingdom', presented at the Society for the Study of Theology, Leeds, 2006.

it is my contention that we must not leave this important piece of theology aside as we enter dialogue with members of other faith communities. Moreover, to engage in two separate conversations in almost completely different languages betrays the danger of becoming a two-faced monster, and of failing to recognize our own particularity not simply as Christians but Christians *in the twenty-first century*. Such an approach of separate conversations – while it may be the simpler to follow – fails to recognize that each tradition is simultaneously engaged in an interface with secular culture *and* an interface with other faiths as well.[5] It holds the danger of creating a conversation with faith partners in which the real – albeit complex – dynamics of each faith are reduced to a unidirectional discussion which lacks the complexity of each faith's relations in and with the world.

To look to Karl Barth, and especially to his paragraph on religion, for help with this may not at first seem a sensible or apparent possible solution.[6] Barth lived in an age in which his concerns as a Christian were far more focused on the secular culture around him, and for all of his criticism of religion, he is prepared to conclude

---

5. There exists a vast wealth of material on the concept of religion and the secular. At a broad level, 'secular' (from the Latin *saeculum*) refers to an increased focus on this age or the world as opposed to a focus on the divine. This has had various effects and developed in various forms, which one is ill advised to see as a single movement or unified whole. On varieties of secularism and secularization, see David Martin, *The Religious and the Secular: Studies in Secularization* (London: Routledge & Kegan Paul, 1969), chaps. 1 and 4; and David Martin, *Reflections on Sociology and Theology* (Oxford: Clarendon Press, 1997), chap. 14. See also Timothy Jenkins and Ben Quash, 'The Cambridge Interfaith Programme: Academic Profile', 22 August 2006, https://www.interfaith.cam.ac.uk/resources/journalarticlesandbookchapters/cipacademicprofile, 2–3, in their differentiation between secularism as 'a set of minimal rules or dispositions that allow the working together of the various religious intensities in some sort of political unit for some sort of collective good' and as 'a rival form, seeking to displace all these various forms of intensity (designated collectively as "religion")'. This latter view of secularism as a doctrine is also discussed in Talal Asad, *Formations of the Secular: Christianity, Islam, Modernity* (Stanford, CA: Stanford University Press, 2003), chap. 1. Asad also remarks, however, that one should note of particular worth that 'because the secular is so much a part of our public life, it is not easy to grasp it directly' (16). In a sense following Asad, for the purpose of this chapter, in addressing Barth's own critique of religion, reference to the illusive concept of the secular will be understood in very general terms as taking a critical stance towards religion. Through examining Barth's understanding of religion (itself influenced by the modern Western secular critiques of religion), this chapter seeks to demonstrate what it is to internalize that critique to the Christian faith, and how that may itself help to underscore the practice of inter-faith dialogue by warning the Christian of the dangers of idolatry.

6. Indeed, Thompson advocates that CD §17 may be more problematic than helpful as a resource for contemporary discussions, and that one should ground a theology of the religions elsewhere in Barth. Thompson, 'Religious Diversity, Christian Doctrine and Karl Barth', 3, 6–10.

his paragraph by speaking of the church as the locus of 'True Religion'.[7] With the exception of the particular question of the relationship of Christianity to Jewish people, Barth did not betray an interest in inter-faith issues.[8] His approach to Islam was highly polemical, seeing it, for example, as a paganized form of Judaism,[9] and Mohammed as comparable to Sabellius.[10] Sadly, this betrays the fact that Barth was very much a man of his times – struggling with the questions of his own age. While his generation's questions clearly concerned Christianity's relationship with the Jewish people, his primary concern was not people of *other* religions but those secularists of *no* religion. His target was 'the critical turn against religion'.[11] However, Barth's clear concern with the issues of his own day charges the present-day theologian with a task not simply to repeat Barth's own theology, but to seek direction from the one whose tremendous theological acumen should critically be brought to bear on the pressing issues of today's generation. What from his thought can one extract to assist us in our present theological needs?

It has often struck me that one can find an unusual parallel between Barth and the landscape gardener Capability Brown. Like Brown, Barth's theology forms a landscape which will take a century to realize its 'capabilities'. The task for students of Barth is neither to clear the land altogether, which will only bring us back to the starting point, nor to allow the garden to grow wildly without any pruning or care, which will leave no thing of beauty at all. Rather, it is to tend to this landscape, to nurture it, to prune it and allow it to grow, bringing in new features which are in keeping with it and ever improving the ground work that was carried out with such foresight. It is the task of today's theologian to prepare the garden in different theological seasons, with the concerns and issues that the march of time brings about.

In order to keep to the above hermeneutical approach to Barth, this chapter will not offer a detailed exegesis of §17. This has been done extremely well elsewhere and does not require addressing here.[12] Instead, it will seek to apply Barth's theology to an area where it may have unexpected fruit – the inter-faith table – and

---

7. CD I/2, §17.3.

8. See Eberhard Busch, 'Indissoluble Unity: Barth's Position on the Jews during the Hitler Era', in *For the Sake of the World: Karl Barth and the Future of Ecclesial Theology*, ed. George Hunsinger (Grand Rapids, MI: Eerdmans, 2004), 53–79; Mark Lindsay, 'Dialectics of Communion: Dialectical Method and Barth's Defence of Israel', in *Karl Barth: A Future for Postmodern Theology?*, ed. Geoff Thompson and Christiaan Mostert (Hindmarsh, South Australia: Australian Theological Forum, 2000), 122–43.

9. CD III/3, 28.

10. CD I/1, 365. For a more detailed and sensitive discussion of Barth's relationship with Islam, see Carys Moseley, 'Karl Barth's Theology of Religion: Interpreting Religious Change Yesterday and Today', presented at the Society for the Study of Theology, Leeds, 2006.

11. CD I/2, 323.

12. Green, 'Challenging the Religious Studies Canon', 473–86; Karl Barth, *On Religion: The Revelation of God as the Sublimation of Religion*, trans. and intro. Garrett Green (London: T&T Clark, 2007); and J. A. Di Noia, 'Religion and the Religions', in

to ask the question of what this looks like in an inter-faith setting.¹³ While Barth does not address inter-faith issues, his paragraph on religion can highlight issues that arise in approaching and sitting at an inter-faith table, which must necessarily (given the concerns of the faiths) be one on which secular-religious concerns also lie. Barth's own approach to religion as a general category is influenced heavily by the modern Western critique of religion as found especially in Feuerbach.¹⁴ However, as will be seen, Barth's version of this critique is grounded in a Christian specific form of that critique, which means that not only is religion itself sublated by revelation but so too is his notion of religion.¹⁵ He gives a Christianized view of the critique of religion that offers an interpretation of the category of 'religion' that is still in reference to thought that may be considered 'secularist'. Furthermore, it will be argued that in this endeavour Barth's paragraph provides tools with which to approach inter-faith dialogue while still retaining one's own particularity. The chapter will offer a vision of future inter-faith dialogue centred around the concerns of Barth's critique of religion and seek to discover what such dialogue might aim to achieve.

This chapter offers a programmatic theory for inter-faith dialogue centred around this paragraph of Barth, rather than primarily a reflection on practice with all the human complexity that this involves. However, it is hoped that this theory

---

Cambridge Companion to Karl Barth, ed. John Webster (Cambridge: Cambridge University Press, 2000), 243–57.

13. To that end, this chapter was circulated and discussed by Muslims, Jews and Christians in Cambridge and London interested in inter-faith matters to seek to discover how such ideas are perceived by those actively engaged in this work, and to attempt to gain the view of these thoughts from the perspective of the other gathered around the table.

14. Although only a few references to Feuerbach exist in CD I/2 §17, one sees his influence on Barth in Barth's introductory essay to Ludwig Feuerbach, *The Essence of Christianity*, trans. George Eliot (New York: Harper & Row, 1957), x–xxxii. Barth states, for example, that 'the attitude of the anti-theologian Feuerbach was more theological than that of many theologians' (x); and 'so long as the talk about "God in man" is not cut out at the roots, we have no cause to criticize Feuerbach, but are with him "the true children of *his* century"' (xxx). Therefore, while little direct discussion of the notion of the 'secular' will take place in the body of this chapter, it is believed that Barth's own understanding of religion in §17 is underscored by such secular critiques of religion from the nineteenth century. For a consideration of Barth's engagement with Feuerbach, see John Glasse, 'Barth on Feuerbach', *Harvard Theological Review* 57, no. 2 (1964), 69–96.

15. This point is made (albeit critically) by Thompson when he states, 'the very argument about religion which Barth resisted had already internalized the "religions" within Christian discourse on the basis of a putatively universal category of religion of which the religions were specific instances'. However, Thompson goes on to state: 'This is not to deny a priori the legitimacy of a Christian, theological interpretation of what have come to be designated "the religions"'. See Thompson, 'Religious Diversity, Christian Doctrine and Karl Barth', 8.

may provide avenues for practice, particularly for those who construct their own theology in dialogue with the great Basel professor.[16]

Some honesty about some difficult issues

Barth's placing revelation in a position of primacy over religion, when taken out of context, can confront one with the dangerous creature of exclusivism.[17] A deeper reading makes it quite clear that this cannot be maintained, and instantaneously, one would have to agree with D'Costa that 'Barth overturns these categories by being both an exclusivist, inclusivist and universalist.'[18] However, the exclusivist tones of Barth's work cannot be ignored. The church is singled out as the 'locus of true religion'.[19] While revelation denies that any religion *is* true in and of itself, the Christian religion *becomes* true from without in close analogy to the way in which the sinner is justified.[20] Within this analogy, Barth writes that 'we have no hesitation

---

16. CD §17 marks only one point of entry into inter-faith dialogue for one utilizing the theology of Barth. If the critique of religion is seen to be too negative, perhaps more positive assessments can be found in the likes of Barth's doctrines of providence, witness and the Holy Spirit.

17. It is useful here to differentiate between types of exclusivism that may be confused by readers of Barth: (a) there is a Christological exclusivism; (b) related to this, there is revelational exclusivism; (c) there is eschatological exclusivism which denies salvation to the non-Christian. While there can be no doubt that (a) is a proper and appropriate form of exclusivism for Barth's theology, I have argued elsewhere that this does not lead to (c) but quite the opposite: see Chapter 6 in this volume, '"Jesus is victor"'. With regard to (b), the situation is more complex. Certainly, it cannot be separated from the one event of (a), which means that pluralism must necessarily be rejected as there can be no sources of revelation outside of Jesus Christ. There is, thus, an exclusivity that exists in scripture and (at least in the early volumes of CD) church proclamation as it attests to the one revelation of God in Jesus Christ (see CD I/1 §4 on the threefold nature of the world of God). However, this exists in the dialectical tension that comes with also realizing that the one Word of Jesus Christ relativizes *all* human words, and that can be seen in Barth's later work on truth *extra muros ecclesiae* (CD IV/3 §69). See Hunsinger, *How to Read Karl Barth*, 245–7. Hunsinger summarizes Barth's position nicely in the aphorism '*exclusivism without triumphalism* or *inclusivism without compromise*' (280). It may well be, therefore, that the form of Christological exclusivism which Barth presents is the least dangerous form of exclusivism one can have while still retaining a proper level of internal coherence with basic expressions of belief for Christianity (as seen, e.g. in Nicaea and Chalcedon).

18. Gavin D'Costa, 'Theology of Religions', in *The Modern Theologians: An Introduction to Christian Theology in the Twentieth Century*, ed. David F. Ford, 2nd edn (Oxford: Blackwell, 1997), 630.

19. CD I/2, 280 and 298–9.

20. Ibid., 325–6.

in saying that the Christian religion is the true religion'.[21] In the Hegelian dialectical terminology Barth employs, religion is (to use Green's language) 'sublated' or (as he later prefers) 'sublimated' by revelation.[22] In singling Christian revelation out in this way, it is clear that Barth, in one sense at least, sees the Christian religion as unique from his insider perspective as a Christian. That this perspective belongs to Barth's insider view as a Christian is underlined by his grounding this claim in terms of the Holy Spirit and the church. He writes that the true religion 'is an event in the out-pouring of the Holy Spirit. To be even more precise, it is an event in the existence of the church and the children of God. The existence of the church of God and the children of God means that true religion exists even in the world of human religion.'[23] This may seem a bold and arrogant claim. Moreover, Barth condemns theology that has lost its proper object and turned to religion rather than revelation 'in all its uniqueness'.[24] He is, furthermore, concerned with mission, speaking of Christianity's authority as a 'missionary religion' with the authority 'to confront the world of religions as the one true religion, with absolute self-confidence to invite and to challenge it to abandon its way and to start on the Christian way'.[25] For Barth, the ultimate distinction between Christianity and the other religions lies emphatically in the name of Jesus Christ in whom the Christian religion is created,[26] elected,[27] justified[28] and sanctified.[29] The ultimate and unshakeable distinction between religions and the 'true religion' can be seen 'only in Him, in the name of Jesus Christ, i.e., in the revelation and reconciliation achieved in Jesus Christ. Nowhere else, but genuinely so in Him.'[30] For Barth, this revelation and reconciliation are inseparably identical with the person of Jesus Christ: reconciliation is the content of revelation, and revelation the only direct and overt means by which reconciliation may be known (albeit there may be incognito forms).[31] Both revelation and reconciliation are identical with the person ('the name') of Jesus Christ. They are, thus, an event (a history) before they are a body of ideas. In this event, the Jesus Christ of history who lived and died for us in the first century CE in Palestine is present and effectual in the here and now.

21. Ibid., 326.
22. See Green, 'Challenging the Religious Studies Canon', 477–86. Green traced the development of his terminology in 'Barth on Religion', presented at the Society for the Study of Theology, Leeds, 2006. It is the word 'sublimated' that he now prefers for *Aufhebung* and uses in his new translation.
23. CD I/2, 344.
24. Ibid., 294.
25. Ibid., 357.
26. Ibid., 346–8.
27. Ibid., 348–52.
28. Ibid., 352–7.
29. Ibid., 357–9.
30. Ibid., 346.
31. Discussed in CD IV/3, §69.2.

Such an exposition of the paragraph leaves one wondering whether Barth's revelational model can provide any hope for inter-faith discussion at all. At worst, he may seem intolerant; at best, he stands so far within his tradition, it is difficult for him to see the other, let alone engage in dialogue with her. This type of interpretation, as it is hoped the following sections of this chapter will show, is in some ways to build a straw man in the place of Barth in order to knock him down. But it is worth acknowledging that clear difficulties exist in Barth's presentation of the critique of religion, and it is not difficult to see how some readers may take away the impression that Barth is a somewhat bigoted Christian who seeks apologetically to establish the uniqueness of Christianity over and against any other faith position. Crude as such a presentation is, it does, however, highlight certain issues that the Christian theologian engaging in inter-faith dialogue must confront.

For all of Barth's suggested exclusivism (at least on a Christological level if not on a soteriological one), one is forced to ask the question in confrontation and dialogue with other religions: is he right? Does Christianity contain elements of exclusivity, an element of which is no doubt found in all faiths? There is a very real danger that, in speaking to other faith communities about Christianity, what is brought to the table for discussion is not actually Christianity as known and practised at all. Indeed, the same may well be true of the Muslim, the Jew, the Hindu and others: desirous not to cause hurt or offense, many of us often leave the exclusivist elements of our faith at the door before entering into dialogue with those of other faiths. Barth is surely right to assert, 'The Christian religion is the predicate to the subject of the name of Jesus Christ. Without Him it is not merely something different. It is nothing at all, a fact which cannot be hidden for long.'[32] Only Christianity knows this name in its significance, in spite of everything, for what it is. To sit at the inter-faith table without this fact, painful as it may be in face of the other, is to engage in a dishonest dialogue dishonestly. Our very need to sit together is grounded not only in what we share but – and herein lies the rub – in the differences we have. A very real danger can arise from a number of quarters if this is ignored. There is, firstly, the danger that we sit down not as the other but as the same and thus do not sit down as religious people wishing to engage in dialogue at all. By this is meant that if we gather together around shared values (perhaps associated with one of many shades of social liberalism), we do not gather together *primarily* identifying as people of particular faiths but only *secondarily* so: we can run the danger of actually gathering together as people who are united by a (for all of the vagueness of this term) liberal agenda, through which we then see our own faith. Thus, for example, the Christian engaging in dialogue with the Muslim (who is thereby simultaneously engaging in dialogue with the Christian) finds it easier to see herself in the Muslim who will engage in such dialogue than the fundamentalist of her own faith who will not. The dynamics of identity are complex. Without facing up to the difficult and painful forms of

---

32. CD I/2, 347.

exclusivity all faiths possess (whether in terms of the revelation of Jesus Christ or the Qur'an or the Abrahamic covenant), we run the danger of people meeting *primarily* not from the shared position of being members of different faiths or religions but from a shared secular world view of some neutral space in which to mediate conflict in which faith is only expressed secondarily.

This leads to a second danger. This is that we do not engage in dialogue but in mutual agreement and 'head nodding'. Without confronting the painful reality of the exclusive ultimates that we have (however inclusive these may be),[33] we run the risk of entering into the kind of universalizing that modernity has engaged in its understanding of religion – seeing ourselves as all the same, and not therefore presenting the at times problematic elements of the coexistence of our faiths in the religiously and socially heterogeneous communities of which we are a part. Underscoring this is the descriptive inadequacy of sameness which can logically leave one wondering why one is a Christian rather than a Muslim, Hindu, Buddhist, Jew or Sikh. Part of the difficulty and pain in coming to the inter-faith table is that we arrive as representatives (or better, members) of one religion, and thereby not as representatives (or members) of another. But if we do not come as ourselves in all our rainbow-like differences, we can never engage in dialogue, and certainly not inter-faith dialogue. Uncomfortable as Barth's theology of religion often is, it reminds us of how uncomfortable those seats at the inter-faith table not only are but – if we are to be internally coherent and be present as members of our own faiths – have to be. This is not to engage in something unloving; quite the opposite, it is to bear that discomfort out of love for the other. Surely that sacrificial love is an even greater virtue than that of tolerance:[34] while tolerance

---

33. Since, as has been stated, both revelation and reconciliation are identical with the person of Jesus Christ and are, therefore, an event before they are a proposition, Barth makes clear in a later stage of his dogmatics that the Jesus Christ who died for us in history is present and effectual here and now even *extra muros ecclesiae*:

> As the reconciliation of the world to God, the justification and sanctification of man, is the reality, and indeed the living and present reality in Jesus Christ the true Witness of its truth, ... not only *intra* but *extra muros ecclesiae* there are also lights in the darkness, clarities in confusion, constants in the oscillating dialectic of our existence, orders in disorder, certainties in the great sea of doubt, genuine speaking and hearing even in the labyrinth of human speech. They are all very wonderful and unexpected and unforeseen. (CD IV/3, 476)

There is, therefore, a radical inclusivity to be found in Barth's radical Christological exclusivity. On the relationship between Barth's exclusivist Christology and recognizing truth in non-Christian sources, see George Hunsinger, 'Epilogue: Secular Parables of the Truth', in *How to Read Karl Barth*, 234–80. See also, expressing this in terms of ethics and natural theology, Stanley Hauerwas, *With the Grain of the Universe: The Church's Witness and Natural Theology* (London: SCM, 2002), 197–204.

34. Note, however, Barth's own theological defence of tolerance. See CD I/2, 299.

pertains principally to ideas, love pertains to persons, and in sitting with those who believe different things than we do, we do not simply play with ideas but engage in love for the other.

Arriving at the table primarily critiquing oneself and not the other

If elements of Barth's revelational exclusivism cause modern liberal sensibilities to feel uneasy at times, far more comforting is Barth's recognition of the inclusive elements of the category of 'religion'. Barth's critique of religion is not aimed at other faiths. Indeed, his general lack of engagement in inter-faith dialogue should surely remind us of this. The Christian religion is one form of the subject 'religion' of which there are other forms.[35] Christianity, too, therefore, stands under the critique of religion as *Unglaube* (faithlessness). What is more, the Christian religion stands under this judgement above all religions. Far from revelation raising the status of the Christian religion above all other religions to a position of superiority, it reveals to the Christian her religion as unbelief.[36] Indeed, Barth spends the first nineteen pages of his section on 'True Religion' setting provisos for the way in which the Christian must never construe her religion as true. The Christian religion cannot engage in heightening its position through the judgement of revelation over and against religion; instead, 'it is our business as Christians to apply this judgement first and most acutely to ourselves: and to others, the non-Christians, only in so far as we recognize ourselves in them'.[37] Similarly, he writes: 'The Christian religion … too, stands under the judgment that religion is unbelief, and that it is not acquitted by any inwards worthiness.'[38] For all that the category of religion is negative for Barth, Christianity is included in this category as the religion standing most firmly under the judgement of God. From the great polemicist, there is the clear assertion that the criticism of religion and speech about Christianity as the 'true religion' can never be engaged in 'as preliminary polemic against the non-Christian'.[39] Even in achieving their goal, the religion of the church of Christ is viewed negatively. Barth is able to speak of 'knowledge and worship of God and a corresponding human activity', but goes on to describe this in the following terms: 'We can only say of them that they are *corrupt*. They are an attempt born of *lying* and *wrong* and committed to *futile means*. And yet we have also to say of them that (*in their corruption*) they do reach their goals.'[40]

Such an approach to the Christian religion has a number of beneficial practices to bring to the inter-faith table. The first is the clear need for humility in

---

35. CD I/2, 281.
36. Ibid., 326.
37. Ibid., 327.
38. Ibid.
39. CD I/2, 326.
40. Ibid., 344, emphasis added.

approaching other faiths. Any sense of human superiority whatsoever is excluded by Barth in his description of how Christianity is the 'true religion': Christianity only becomes true through a complete act of grace on God's behalf.[41] It is true only as the religion standing most firmly under the judgement revelation offers to religion – faithlessness. This is not to say that Christianity is to lack confidence in God's gracious act towards it, but that it is dialectically to recognize the way in which it is 'true religion' (grounded in the fact that God has elected to reveal himself in the religious form of Christianity) only as within the thesis of 'Religion as Unbelief'. Standing most sharply judged under this thesis, the Christian cannot come to the inter-faith table with any sense of a privileged position, nor even as an equal, but only as one who is the most guilty of idolatry and self-righteousness, even in the quest to purge herself of these things. Christianity's solidarity with the other is never as *primus inter pares* but only as the religion to whom God's 'No' is most sharply spoken in its search and quest for God. It is this sharpest 'No' spoken to the Christian church that Barth is concerned with – never an intolerant attitude towards other faiths or an unloving one towards members of those faiths. Barth teaches the Christian engaging in inter-faith dialogue that judgement does indeed begin in Christianity's own house.

Secondly, Barth emphasizes that we cannot separate the church from other religions on the basis of a concept of 'religion'.[42] This means that the Christian religion stands in solidarity with other religions. It is clearly part of a category to which other forms of religion belong. The connexion is evident, and it is only a short step from here to speak of the need to engage with the other forms of this phenomenon. However, for all that Barth sees solidarity between faiths, he is correct to realize that there is still difference and uniqueness: the flaw of naïve pluralism is clear to Barth, and he stands firm in the belief that Christianity needs Jesus Christ. In solidarity with the other, one must be truly concerned with *other* religions.

This need primarily to critique oneself brings with it the third implication of never confusing God or revelation with the human form of religion. Revelation stands over and against religion; it contradicts it rather than stemming from it, or returning to it.[43] Religion is not revelation. Nor is religion God. Religion seeks to

---

41.

> The confession of Jesus Christ as the one Word of God, says Barth, has nothing to do with an arbitrary self-glorification of Christianity, the church, or the Christian. It is a strictly christological statement. … As such it does not entail any exaltation of the Christian over the non-Christian, but rather an important bond between them. For the statement confronts Christian and non-Christian alike with 'the one truth superior' to them both. (Hunsinger, *How to Read Karl Barth*, 244)

42. CD I/2, 298. In this way, as in secular critiques of religion, Barth does not see the uniqueness of any one religion (even his own) qua religion.

43. CD I/2, 303.

be both of these things and fails because it is idolatrous. This distinction is helpful when one dares to assume at the inter-faith table the position of one's own God, whoever that unique God may be conceived to be for whichever faith. A solidarity which mediates our differences around this point helps one truly to engage in dialogue – not denying our particularities but also able within our particularity not to have to close our ears to the words of the other. Gathering at the table as people of our own 'religion' is not the same as sitting in judgement as if we were our God. Turning the critique of religion back primarily on ourselves as Barth does helps to accentuate this point and prevents us from engaging in the blasphemy of playing God.

A critique of universals and the need for particulars

Early in the paragraph on religion, Barth very helpfully observes a relationship between universals and particulars: 'The revelation of God is actually the presence of God and therefore the hiddenness of God in the world of human religion. By God's revealing of Himself the divine particular is hidden in a human universal, the divine content in a human form, and therefore that which is divinely unique in something which is humanly only singular.'[44] Leaving aside the question of the hidden-revealed dialectic found throughout Barth's works, within the universal of human 'religion', Barth recognizes the divine particularity. That this particularity of the divine revelation is found within something which is humanly universal (i.e. religion) means that Christianity must be spoken of as something which is *humanly* only singular (or remarkable) and not unique. This suggests a complex dynamic between faiths. Not only is religion perceived to be a human universal (as had been the case in nascent studies and critiques of religion), but within

---

44. Ibid., 282. This passage is a difficult one to translate. Green's new translation puts it thus: 'God's revelation is in fact God's presence and thus God's hiddenness in the world of human religion. Because God reveals himself, the divine particular is hidden in a human universal, the divine content in a human form, and thus the divinely unique in something merely humanly remarkable'. Green, *Barth on Religion: The Revelation of God as the Sublimation of Religion*, 35. Clearly, 'universals' and 'particulars' have special connotations philosophically, especially to what might be broadly spoken of as post-modern thought, and one must be careful not to directly associate such usage with Barth for all of the lines one might draw between his thought and post-modernism. For more on Barth and post-modernism, see Thompson and Mostert, *Karl Barth*. The following reflections on this quotation seek – in keeping with the hermeneutical approach to Barth outlined in the introduction – to broaden out Barth's specific discussion here, applying his thought on the critique of Christianity's religion and its relation to the uniqueness of revelation to the broader question of Christianity's claim of uniqueness and its relation to other faiths. To do this, the inner logics of Barth's thought have been sought and expressed in a manner which perhaps at times is more philosophical than Barth himself may have intended.

that recognized universal, Barth suggests, Christianity must perceive its unique revelation of the particular hidden God within its specific human form. Given this relation of the particular to the universal, that which is 'divinely unique' is present in something which is 'humanly only singular'. A sensitivity to this relationship between the universal and the particular is the way in which Barth can speak both of the relationship of Christianity to all other religions and of it as the 'true religion'.

Implicit to this speech about religions as singular, in comparison to the divine particularity found in 'revelation' and the human universal found in 'religion', comes a way of mediating dialogue with the other truly as the other while still recognizing the need to speak to each other at all grounded in the universal of 'religion'. In the movement away from universals and overarching theories of religion, this may seem rather outmoded, and certainly, for Barth this human universal does not suggest God's direct revelation is present in other religions.[45] However, this dynamic really does explain something of the desire to sit at an inter-faith table at all. It recognizes a relationship between religions in terms of the human existence of 'religion' and yet the singularity of each religion from their own perspective of divine particularity: one does not have to surrender one's uniqueness in order to recognize one's relationship to other forms of religion. It is clear that in gathering around a table with Muslims, Hindus, Sikhs, Jews and so on, the Christian is doing something different than in gathering around a table with Marxists, economists, milkmen and jugglers. Yet, in gathering with people from other religions, the Christian must also recognize that he is gathering not only with people of religion but also with people of *other* religions.

The desire to say that the other is really like me lacks any form of adequacy in description either of myself or of that other. And while without a certain level of dissimilarity dialogue would neither be necessary nor interesting, if the other is so dissimilar to me, the grounds for shared dialogue are extraordinarily difficult. Inter-faith dialogue falls between these two positions of seeing the other as the same as me, or as so alien to me that I do not have any shared language or identity to dialogue with them at. Inter-faith dialogue recognizes the other truly as *other* to itself, but also truly as other *to itself*. While there may be little pressing need for Christianity as Christianity to sit at the table with a group of jugglers as jugglers, the otherness of other religions is an otherness in which the Christian can perceive *her* otherness *to* those other religions. Barth's lengthiest discussion of another religion (with the exception of Judaism) comes in terms of his engagement with two forms of Pure Land Buddhism.[46] While he recognizes in them the traits of Protestantism as a religion of grace, Barth still recognizes the otherness of these

---

45. Here, one again sees a connection between Barth and the secular critique of religion. The grouping together of all religions (regardless of their various particularities) under the title 'religion' is very much related to the modern view of religion that underlies secular critiques of 'religion' as a universal phenomenon. This has been sharply criticized. See, for example, Martin, *The Religious and the Secular*, 14–15.

46. CD I/2, 340–4.

forms of religion *to* Christianity, and of Christianity's otherness to them. Sitting at the table with someone one perceives as oneself requires no tolerance, never mind the higher virtue of love: indeed, respect for the otherness of the other is essential to a hermeneutics of *apage*. To listen to another and only hear oneself is not to listen at all. Yes, there is a need for a recognition of the universal of religion (or else we fail to see the particularity of religion as compared to those with no religion), but around the inter-faith table we gather in our singularities.

The need to listen and the need to speak

Part of Barth's sharpest critique of religion lies in its self-centredness. Even in its attempt to overcome idolatry and self-righteousness in the forms of atheism and mysticism, it remains idolatrous and self-righteous, and Barth asserts: 'Even in these two supposedly higher and apparently inimical forms, whether in good or evil, in failure or success, religion is still thoroughly self-centred.'[47] The turn in towards the self in which man claims faith in himself is at the heart of Barth's criticism of what is wrong with religion.[48] It is perhaps a way of speaking of religions under the Lutheran epithet *cor incurvatum in se*. To be thoroughly self-centred seems to be the worst possible of sins, on a par even with idolatry and self-righteousness. Even for the Christian who believes hers is the 'true religion', this danger is never far away. What is condemned by Barth is

> our Christian concepts of God and the things of God, our Christian theology, our Christian worship, our forms of Christian fellowship and order, our Christian morals, poetry and art, our attempts to give individual and social form to the Christian life, our strategy and tactics in the interest of our Christian cause, in short our Christianity, to the extent that it is *our* Christianity.[49]

Inasmuch as Christianity is turned towards itself and the Christian towards herself, Christianity stands under God's judgement.

Such a criticism surely marks the need to recognize the other. For Barth, this other is clearly Jesus Christ. But this, too, provides possibility for speaking to the other in dialogue. Barth famously characterized Christ both as the man for God and as the man for other humans.[50] For the Christian to be centred on Christ, rather than herself, means that she should be one centred both on God and on other human beings. While religion might simply point one back to oneself, Christ orientates the Christian outwards to God and to the world. The radical inclusivity of this is clearly evident within Barth's work: 'If we see Him, we see with and

---

47. Ibid., 314–15.
48. Ibid., 314.
49. Ibid., 327.
50. CD III/2, § §44.1, 45.1.

around Him in ever widening circles His disciples, His people, His enemies and the countless millions who have not yet heard His name. We see Him as theirs, determined by them and for them, belonging to each and every one of them.'[51] Part of this radical outwardness and orientation on the other must surely include those of other faiths to whose humanity Christ belongs. The Christian church must never be a merely inwards looking entity. If it is such, it ceases to be the *Christ*ian church by Barth's description. The radical criticism of religion does not point the Christian away from the religion of others; it points towards them.

In this movement away from self-centredness in religion, there is a need to listen to the other. Barth criticizes religion for seeking to 'grasp at God'.[52] Within the context of discussing revelation, Barth criticizes the need of man to speak in religion instead of listening.[53] For Barth, this is clearly the need to listen to revelation rather than to presume to speak for God. The inter-faith table is not what he is picturing in speaking about this. But, again, what does it look like bringing this perspective on Christian faith to that table? The danger of speaking too quickly, and presuming to speak for God, is surely a useful concern to have in sitting with people from other religions. Moreover, with that clear danger of speaking must simultaneously come the need to listen. The opposite danger to failing to recognize the otherness of the other at the table is the danger of seeing the other as one to whom we must only speak, put right and help to understand ourselves. Such a failure leads us directly back to the problem of self-centredness: in the dialogue we feel we need the first and last word, or else we seek to set its agenda on our own terms. In short, we can fail to listen properly. Barth's critique of religion leads the person of faith to recognize the need to listen. For the person of faith at the inter-faith table, there are two positive respects to this. Firstly, she must listen to God's unique revelation to Christianity properly and carefully as it critiques her religion, rather than seeking to speak from her religion, recognizing that revelation is not her own but God's and belongs only as much to her as to any 'religion'. Secondly, as a result of this, she must be aware of the dangers of speaking too quickly, and the need to listen to the other. For the Christian, these two cannot be separated. Jesus not only talked to but he talked *with* people; he conversed. While (understandably) the gospel narratives focus on his speaking, they also remind us of his listening.[54]

Is this to say that the Christian engaging in inter-faith dialogue should never speak? Clearly, no; or else it would be no dialogue at all, or a dialogue from which we are removed. To cease to engage, to be so fearful of speaking and to abandon the

---

51. Ibid., 216.

52. CD I/2, 302.

53. Ibid.

54. One may see this, for example, in the likes of Jn 4.1-41 in which Jesus engages in genuine dialogue with the Samaritan woman (notably, a woman of a different faith from orthodox Second Temple Judaism). Rather than simply lecture or preach at the woman, Jesus asks and answers questions, and discusses a major religious divide of his age – worship at Mount Gerizim. Other examples of Jesus listening or engaging in dialogue can be found in Mk 7.24-30 and Mt. 8.5-13.

desire to form a conception of God leads only to the worst of all dangers – to the path towards atheism or mysticism, which is itself a return to self-centredness.[55] Instead, Christianity must engage in a dialogue held in the dialectical tension of speaking simultaneously of religion as unbelief and of a true religion. How, then, are we to speak and listen? It is to this that it is now necessary to turn.

What do we seek to gain from inter-faith dialogue?
Gathering around the critique of religion

Dialogue is not simply an academic exercise. To employ German terms, there is not only a sense in which dialogue involves *wissen*; there is a sense in which it also involves *kennen*. It is not a religious studies lecture or textbook in which we seek to learn empirical facts about the other – to know about festivals, rites of passage, community formation, holy books and so on. Important as these may be, they are only a precursor to dialogue. To gather around the inter-faith table involves facing the other. In that way, it is not only educational but also formative. It is not simply bidirectional (I speak and you listen) but complexly multidirectional (I speak, you listen, we learn, you speak, I listen, I rethink, I speak again, etc.). It brings with it all the complexity of human relations and interaction, and the fact that we are shaped by those around us. Barth's critique of religion reminds us, while still retaining the position of an insider to one singular faith, that no religion is an island. In that way, it has something quite distinct to offer to the inter-faith setting. This distinct thing is its critical approach to the nature of religion in *any* form. In bringing this to the table, one must note how we are shaped by inter-religious dialogue, and we are engaged in the process of shaping: not simply writing books to the other which are there in black and white with the final full stop in place but engaging in ever-ongoing conversation.

Barth's critique of religion has an important shaping role to inter-faith dialogue. Speaking as a Christian about the Christian struggle with religion can help the Christian and possibly the other to identify also those elements of their religion with which they struggle. For the Christian to identify how her own religion is unhelpfully at times 'conditioned by nature and climate, by blood and soil, by the economic, cultural, political, in short, historical circumstances in which [s]he lives' enables her in inter-faith dialogue to recognize the historical penultimates of their religions which have been made the ultimates of practitioners.[56] It is to recognize that all religions are continually engaged in a choice between evolving in their historical form or preserving their present (or past) natures. It is to help and support the other in that and to recognize that God should not be confused with such penultimates.[57] To come humbly to the table recognizing these problems

---

55. CD I/2, 317–25.
56. Ibid., 316.
57. It is here, again, where the secular critique of religion in its Barthian theological form proves helpful: in accepting their criticism of religion, the religious person is enabled to

is to arrive at the table truly as we are – struggling with not only our place among the religions but also our place in an ever-changing and developing world. It is to recognize the problems that come along with these changes – problems all too well known and variously violently expressed in a host of fundamentalisms. Sometimes it is only in seeing the other that we truly see ourselves. If the Christian is truly to engage in dialogue, this critique (of her religion) is what she must bring to and (all the more importantly) take from the inter-faith table in the hope that it will enable us all to begin to realize the cultural determinants of our different religions, which so often (confused with revelation) we wrongly see as the different eternal decrees we each believe are uniquely given to our particular religions. Perhaps it is this way that the Christian engaging in inter-faith dialogue is to understand the aforementioned passages in Barth about mission, which may seem to her most challenging in her inter-faith setting: the mission with which to attend the inter-faith table is a mission to recognize religion for what it is and to help to mediate against confusing it with God or revelation in all of their uniqueness – from each of our perspectives – to each of us.[58] This is in itself a particularist (or singular) agenda which revolves around a Christian-specific interpretation of the critique of religion as espoused from certain secular criticisms of religion. While the Christian cannot assume that other religionists will accept this critique (though sometimes they might), the necessity of attendance at the inter-faith table is for the good of the Christian herself who, in dialogue with the other, may be enabled to engage more easily in this self-critique, which might also be modelled for others.[59]

The Christian should not simply believe she is engaged in shaping; in dialogue she is simultaneously being shaped. The other must also help her to identify more sharply the confusions she has between religion and revelation, or religion and God. Gathering around this critique or struggle with religion with the other can highlight this more than with those who are like us. I was struck by this at the 2006

---

distinguish between the penultimate nature of her human religion (which is normally the critique offered to her) and the ultimacy of God (albeit, whom secular critics often confuse with religion).

58. This is not an expression of some form of pluralism. It makes no suggestion that the 'Gods' different faiths speak of are the same one God expressed differently, nor that their revelations are different expressions of the one reality. Instead, this recognizes the unique (and at times exclusive) truth claims of each faith, but also the way in which these are corrupted through each faith's attempts at human expressions of this in their religion in a manner which allows room for both unity and uniqueness. It recognizes that each faith is in its own struggle with religion and can learn from other faiths with the same problems about the danger of confusing ultimate truth claims with religion. An example of this is given in the next paragraph.

59. Alasdair MacIntyre states that shared problems do not provide traditions with 'a neutral standard in terms of which the irrespective achievements can be measured. Some problems are indeed shared. But what importance each particular problem has varies from tradition to tradition, and so do the effects of failing to arrive at a solution.' *Whose Justice? Which Rationality?* (London: Duckworth, 1988), 348.

Society for the Study of Theology conference in Leeds, England. In an extremely moving and (in a rarely appropriate use of the word) holy paper, Aref Nayed placed 'God' on the conference agenda in a way in which Christian (and indeed Jewish) scholars had – perhaps for being too similar to the others in this predominately Christian conference – been unable or unwilling to do.[60] In a conference which had addressed 'Theology and the Religions', God seemed at times to be quietly absent from the discourse. This is no comment on the other excellent and stimulating papers, but it is to say that in the Muslim other's entirely Muslim and in many ways confessional paper, the conference was not reminded but, rather, moved to remember God in our dialogues and discussions. In a presentation singularly regarding his own faith, the implications of Nayed's interpretation of Muslim thought to Islam made clear to the ears of the Christian and Jewish participants the need to reform Christian and Jewish theology in a way similar to the manner in which Nayed had seemed to articulate Muslim theology, not in a way that would make these theologies more 'Muslim' or 'pluralist' but in a way necessary to make these theologies more Christian and Jewish, respectively, reminding Christians and Jews of the need to have the nature of God (however uniquely God may be conceived to a faith) as central to any discussion of the theology of religions and salvation. The other in speaking about herself can convict us to recognize the need to reform ourselves. As the other, she can have a shaping effect upon us. In Barth's terms, they can help us recognize our own *Unglaube* in our religion and remind us to turn the critique of religion back primarily onto ourselves. The other can help us approach the revelation offered to us in fresh and dynamic ways and with critical eyes turned towards ourselves insofar as we make it our revelation and confuse it with our religion. The other can help us to recognize in the penultimate in which we all dwell the ultimacy of God.

Conclusion

It is hoped this short attempt at an application of Barth's critique of religion to the pressing question of inter-faith dialogue has pointed to the creative fruit Barth's work might bear on this topic. Taken from the perspective of Christian faith, it is hoped that it helps us to understand the way in which we can gather together holding to the veracity of our own faith (as others will with theirs) and, therefore, truly as members of our faith, simultaneously recognizing our solidarity with the other under the term 'religion'. Indeed, it is perhaps under this title that we recognize the need most clearly to speak to each other. Against the simple universalizing tendencies of modernity, it is necessary to recognize the connected singularities of each religion and the complexity with which we engage in speaking to the other. The dangers of modernity in seeing us all as the 'same' must be

---

60. Aref Nayed, 'Al-Rahman: God the Compassionate', presented at the Society for the Study of Theology, Leeds, 2006.

countered along with the reactionary elements of our own traditions which see the other religion as insurmountably alien and – at worst – the enemy.

In recognizing this need to remember the critique of religion as a religious person (or more specifically, as a Christian), one sees the great value of meeting around Barth. To end where we began, it stops us from having two separate, dissimilar and (ultimately) internally incoherent conversations which ignore each other. We are forced to remember the complex dynamics of inter-faith and secular-faith conversations and to bring to each an awareness of the other.[61] This is the true mediation the practitioner of inter-faith dialogue is engaged in: in the secular-faith setting, reminding the secular powers of the particularities of faith communities and ourselves of the critique of 'religion', and in the inter-faith setting, reminding ourselves and the other of the way in which secular modernity has shaped (often by reaction) forms of our own faiths, and reforming ourselves accordingly.[62] So often, our mediation is between faith and non-faith in both settings. These are matters which are best done together and easier to come to clarity over in dialogue with the other. Gathering around a critique of religion can help us offer something formative; it stops inter-faith dialogue being something proper and fitting that we engage in and helps it to become essential for the good of our own existence. To gather in this way begins to give proper place to the complex dynamic and dynamic complexity of gathering around a table together as simultaneously members of different faith communities and as members of late-modern society.[63]

61. Ford states that 'the world is not simply religious and not simply secular but is complexly both religious and secular, with all sorts of constantly shifting interactions and balances'. David F. Ford, 'Gospel in Context: Among Many Faiths', presented at the Fulcrum Conference, Islington, 2006. See also David F. Ford, 'Abrahamic Dialogue: Towards Respect and Understanding in Our Life Together', presented at the inauguration of the Society for Dialogue and Action, Cambridge, 2006.

62. To quote Ford once more: 'The pathologies of the religions are of course made worse by their mirror opposites in the secular sphere, as the extremes reinforce each other. Unwise, fundamentalist religious dogmatisms feed off unwise, fundamentalist secular ideologies, and vice versa'. David F. Ford, 'God and Our Public Life: A Scriptural Wisdom', *International Journal of Public Theology* 1 (2007): 78.

63. As was the case with Barth's ecumenical involvement, no doubt Barth's own approach to inter-faith dialogue would have been more ad hoc than this chapter may suggest: his approach would have at once been more decided and also more open (and hence dialectical) than my own. The chapter's purpose throughout has been to think from Barth rather than towards him, to push at Barth rather than to repeat his findings. It has proceeded, therefore, in the belief that the present political climate of the West demands sustained and ongoing commitment to inter-faith dialogue in order that the conversations between faiths can be kept going. An element of this was perhaps recognized by Barth in his acceptance of Marquardt's critique and his admittance that he had attended more to biblical Israel than contemporary Judaism: see Letter 260 to Dr Friedrich-Wilhelm Marquardt (5 September 1967) in Karl Barth *Letters, 1961–1968*, ed. Jürgen Fangmeier and Hinrich Stoevesandt, trans. Geoffrey W. Bromiley (Edinburgh: T&T Clark, 1981), 261–3. Also of note on this point is Katherine Sonderegger, 'Response to Eberhard Busch', in Hunsinger, ed., *For the Sake of the World*, 80–7.

Chapter 7

THE LORD OF ALL

The humility advocated in the preceding chapter in terms of Christianity's self-awareness of its own religious failings and in terms of its approach, therefore, to the religious and secular other is a helpful springboard from which to consider the themes present in the current chapter. This humility should be driven, moreover, not only by the sense of the limitations and temptations of our religious speech but also because systematic theology should be the humblest of all disciplines in the theological enterprise. Its role is to engage in second-order statements about the Christian faith which might aid the reading of scripture in the preparation of sermons which proclaim the good news of the Kingdom of God to the people of faith. And having listened to this proclamation, systematic theology must rethink its own propositions in light of the command of God in the word heard through the proclamation that arises from scripture. The so-called system can never be static or completed, therefore, but must be dynamic and responsive to the call of God and to the endless depths of the Bible. The system cannot succumb to becoming a religion itself!

However, given its role within the hermeneutical cycle, informing the reading of scripture and the sermons that arise from that reading, and then being informed by the sermons and led back to scripture, systematic theology must recognize that its own speech has a determining role in informing the preaching of the church, and thereby in shaping the church and society of which the church is a part. Systematic theology has, therefore, both a descriptive role, as it arises from within a tradition, and a prescriptive role, as it seeks to shape and form that tradition. In its prescriptive role, systematic theology must be alert to the effects it has on the church and society. Systematic theology should never exist, therefore, as if it were simply an intellectual game separated from its relationship to, and impact upon, the church and society; nor should it understand its relationship to the church as being singularly creative: it is in arising from its descriptive enterprise that its prescriptive has a place, because the context of the prescription is in response to the preaching of the church, in light of the reading of scripture. The prescriptive work of systematic theology is, while always provisional, directed towards the context from which the description has arisen, with the desire to make that description truer to scripture.

At a time when the place of religion and the religions are very much on the national and international stage, there is a responsibility for theologians to consider how to understand the place of the religious other in their theological systems.[1] As a people who are called by scripture to 'seek the peace of the city' (Jer. 29.7), systematic theologians must engage in their own way in protecting and creating peace in the complexly secular and religious societies in which the church exists.[2] Theology must attend to areas in Christian self-description which might offer the potential for hospitality and peace towards the religious other, through forming from Christian self-description the potential for future sermons which are true to that genuine Christian identity and which offer a hospitable place for the other. In offering a light framework with which to read scripture, systematic theology should seek to articulate the doctrinal and theological rationale for the potential of such hospitality.

No single chapter (or indeed volume) could hope to achieve this in and of itself. The present chapter cannot be, therefore, a piece of regular dogmatics in that there is not the space to engage in the various interconnections of individual doctrines in their relations to each other. Building from the preceding chapter in its discussion of the critique of religion, this piece is a work of irregular dogmatics[3] that seeks to identify and engage one major doctrine of the Christian church, that of providence, and to seek to identify from it what might be gained from attending carefully to it for the broader theme of exclusion and religion.[4]

The method of seeking to identify one central doctrine which is particularly and exclusively Christian and working on that doctrine might seem an odd one in terms of preventing exclusion. However, if systematic theology has a formative role in shaping communities through its simultaneous being informed and informing of Christian preaching, and if systematic theology can identify areas of Christian proclamation that might help with the propagation of peace (or at least the prevention of exclusion), then it will have practical implications for the church and society by aiding the reading of scripture for the preachers who are confronted regularly with congregations comprising members of society. That this discussion takes place singularly within the context of the Christian community does not undermine its desire to prevent wrong forms of exclusion. It is not the place of the Christian to offer dictates or even advice to the religious other. To do

---

1. See my 'Legitimizing and Necessitating Inter-faith Dialogue: The Dynamics of Inter-faith for Individual Faith Communities', *International Journal of Public Theology* 4, no. 2 (2010), as well as Chapter 9 in this volume.

2. The term 'complexly religious and secular' is borrowed from David F. Ford, 'Gospel in Context: Among Many Faiths', presented at the Fulcrum Conference, Islington, 28 April 2006.

3. Cf. CD I/1, 275–8.

4. This is a method which has been used in Christian theology in J. A. DiNoia, OP, *The Diversity of Religions: A Christian Perspective* (Washington, DC: Catholic University of America Press, 1992).

so is a version of inclusion that includes by doing violence to the otherness of the other: it includes by making the 'other' the 'same'. To limit with humility the focus of the discussion and potential implications is not an engagement in exclusion, but a recognition of the various exclusivisms in operation in theological speech. Limiting the remit of the piece guards against the presumption of speaking on behalf of, or to changing, those who are members of other faiths or none, but only those who are members of my own community.[5] In concrete terms, therefore, this chapter seeks to influence the preaching of evangelical Christians in terms of the issue of exclusion of the religious other, by attending to one motif of Christian theology that reminds the preacher of the universality of God's grace. It is in this way that, as well as addressing theoretical questions about exclusion, this chapter seeks to have practical implications for the life of the church in the world. Through a dialogical approach with Barth this essay seeks to articulate a theology of providence which can serve the church and world in this time of religious conflict,[6] a conflict often undergirded by separationist and exclusivist approaches to the religious other preached from pulpits of (among others) the evangelicals of my own ecclesial community.[7]

A strong doctrine of providence

For all of Barth's seeming religious exclusivity, his *Doctrine of Creation* presents a tremendously strong doctrine of providence. Indeed, it is necessary to remember that while Calvinist theology has traditionally taught double predestination, the doctrine of election has always been articulated alongside a strong doctrine of the providential guiding of all of history by God. The sense of this providential preservation and guiding cannot be limited. For Barth, the depth of this is almost unfathomable:

> Everything was open and present to Him: everything in its own time and within its own limits; but everything open and present to Him. Similarly, everything that is, as well as everything that was, is open and present to Him, within its own limits. And everything that will be, as well as everything that was and is, will be open and present to Him, within its own limits. And one day-to speak in temporal terms-when the totality of everything that was and is and will be will only have been, then in the totality of its temporal duration it will still be open

---

5. For further on this, see my 'Legitimizing and Necessitating Inter-faith'.
6. For exegetical discussion of Barth on providence, see Kathryn Tanner, 'Creation and Providence', in *The Cambridge Companion to Karl Barth*, ed. John Webster (Cambridge: Cambridge University Press, 2000), 111–26; and George Hunsinger, *How to Read Karl Barth* (Oxford: Oxford University Press, 1991), 185–224.
7. See my *Barth, Origen, and Universal Salvation: Restoring Particularity* (Oxford: Oxford University Press, 2009), vii–xv.

and present to Him, and therefore preserved: eternally preserved; revealed in all its greatness and littleness; judged according to its rightness or wrongness, its value or lack of value; but revealed in its participation in the love which He Himself has directed towards it. Therefore nothing will escape Him: no aspect of the great game of creation; no moment of human life; no thinking thought; no word spoken; no secret or insignificant enterprise or deed or omission with all its interaction and effects; no suffering or joy; no sincerity or lie; no secret event in heaven or too well-known event on earth; no ray of sunlight; no note which has ever sounded; no colour which has ever been revealed, possibly in the darkness of oceanic depths where the eye of man has never perceived it; no wing-beat of the day-fly in far-flung epochs of geological time.[8]

God's involvement in every aspect of creation is a reality that can neither be suspended nor removed, as it is grounded in the very ontology of God in the second mode of His Being: 'In Jesus Christ God gave to the creature far too high a dignity, and God bound Himself to the creature far too seriously and unreservedly, for Him to be able to repent and to desire to be in isolation and apart from the creature.'[9] Clearly, all things are not held to be equal by God: everything will need to be judged, 'judged according to its rightness or wrongness, its value or lack of value'.[10] But God's involvement in His creation, His guiding and preservation is universal and eternal for creation.

This strong doctrine of providence does not determine, however, that God can be confused with world-events. Barth is emphatic that the God who providentially guides the world is the King of Israel.[11] However, Barth posits a connection between the events of scripture and the belief in God as being the ruler of the world. On the one hand, the basis of this is in scripture:

To apprehend and affirm the idea we have to think of definite periods in human history as this name leads us. And we have to think of definite places – the land of Canaan, Egypt, the wilderness of Sinai, Canaan again, the land on the two sides of Jordan, Jerusalem, Samaria, the towns and villages of Judaea and Galilee, the various places beyond in Syria, Asia Minor and Greece, and finally Rome. We have to think of definite events and series of events which according to the witness of the Old and New Testaments actually took place at these periods and in these places, relating them always to the spoken and actualised 'I am'. And

---

8. CD III/3, 89–90.
9. Ibid., 89. Cf. on election, my *Barth, Origen, and Universal Salvation*, chap. 2; and Paul Nimmo, 'Election and Evangelical Thinking: Challenges to our Way of Conceiving the Doctrine of God', in *New Perspectives for Evangelical Theology: Engaging God, Scripture and the World*, ed. Tom Greggs (London: Routledge, 2009), 29–43.
10. CD III/3, 89.
11. See, for example, ibid., 176.

then necessarily we have to think of the concrete Scripture which bears witness to these events, the text of the Old and New Testaments.[12]

But, on the other, the scriptures teach a God who is Lord of *all* things: 'For the Subject who speaks and actualizes the "I am" in these events, the King of Israel, *is the God who rules the world*.'[13] Put otherwise, Barth posits a total salvation which includes all things in the victory of Christ:

> He is not only the way and the truth; He is also the life, the resurrection and the life. If He were not the Saviour in this total sense, He would not be the Saviour at all in the New Testament sense. It is a serious matter that all the Western as opposed to the Eastern Church has invariably succeeded in minimising and devaluating, and still does so to-day, this New Testament emphasis. And Protestantism especially has always been far too moralistic and spiritualistic, and has thus been blind to this aspect of the Gospel. In this respect we have every cause to pay more attention rather than less. We certainly cannot afford to make arbitrary demarcations, and therefore not to see, or not to want to see, the total Saviour of the New Testament.[14]

The breadth of the providential sustenance of God is difficult to limit for Barth.

Clearly, there are things in creation which are contrary to God's will and providential guidance; Barth discusses these things in the very same volume as his doctrine of providence under the title 'Nothingness'.[15] However, it is clear that God's involvement in every tiny detail of creation and history includes to some degree the existence of other religions: they do not count simply as 'Nothingness'. Barth expounds this through a discussion of 1 Cor. 13.12, about which he writes:

> What does it mean for an understanding of creaturely occurrence that it takes place in this co-ordination under the divine rule? We venture to answer, as we may well do in the light of 1 Corinthians 13:12, that creaturely occurrence acquires in this co-ordination the character of a mirror. The distinction and inter-connexion of the two historical sequences are both brought out in this comparison. The original, God's primary working, is the divinely ruled history of the covenant. The mirror has nothing to add to this. In it the history of the creature as such cannot play any role. The mirror can confront it only as a reflector. It cannot repeat it, or imitate its occurrence. It can only reflect it. And as it does so it reverses it, the right being shown as the left and *vice versa*. Yet the fact remains that it gives us a correspondence and likeness.[16]

---

12. CD III/3, 177.
13. Ibid., emphasis added.
14. CD III/3, 311.
15. Ibid., §50.
16. Ibid., 49.

However, applying these themes to religion does not determine that there is an easy liberal notion of the historical relativity of all religions as reflections of the real thing but not the real thing itself. Barth questions the existence of other religions through a discussion under this theme of Israel:

> How strange it is that there is still a people Israel, and that this people is so brightly spotlighted in our own day! Nor is there lacking the phenomenon of gods and their worship, of sacrifices, prayers and the like, of religious history. We must be careful not to identify the reflection with the original, the history of the creature with the true history of salvation. For reasons which have nothing to do with its creatureliness, the former is one long history of the very opposite of salvation, as emerges even more clearly in religious history, and in what is known as 'Israel' in world history. But we cannot overlook or deny the fact that creaturely history is still similar in every respect to the history of salvation, as a reflection resembles the original.[17]

While the assessment here of the typological category of 'Israel' seems on first reading to be rather negative – not confusing the continued existence of the religious creature with the *Heilsgeschichte* – there is nonetheless a sense in which there is genuine reflection of the history of salvation in these others: 'Its occurrence is calculated to reflect and illustrate and echo these acts of God.'[18]

Differentiated exclusivisms

It is necessary now to be a little clearer in terms of what Barth is doing with regard to the providential work of God and its relationship to other religions. As we have seen already, all that Barth states about providence arises out of specifically Christian speech and the basis of the Christian tradition, grounded supremely in scripture. For Barth, the subject of providence must be discussed and undertaken 'from a Christian standpoint and with Christian material',[19] but its subject is the universal lordship of God. In this, Barth is radically inclusive of all creation, but radically exclusive in terms of the basis for the claims he makes. It is as the result of the special history of God with his particular people that one may know the providential power of God in general world-occurrence. Only the radical exclusivity of the former can be the basis for any speech about the latter:

> That world history in its totality is the history in which God executes His will of grace must thus be taken to mean that in its totality it belongs to this special history; that its lines can have no other starting-point or goal than the one divine

---

17. Ibid., 50.
18. Ibid.
19. CD III/3, 33.

will of grace; that they must converge on this one thin line and finally run in its direction. This is the theme of the doctrine of providence. It has to do with the history of the covenant, with the one thin line as such. Or rather, it has to do with it only to the extent that it for its part is undoubtedly one among the many other lines of general world-occurrence, and that these many other lines of general world-occurrence have their ontic and noetic basis in the fact that the God from whom they come and to whom they return pursues on this one line the special work which the creature must serve on these other lines. The doctrine of providence must not level down the special history of the covenant, grace and salvation; it must not reduce it to the common denominator of a doctrine of general world occurrence. In so doing it would lose sight of the starting-point and therefore of its concept of the subject. And then it would no longer be speaking of the world dominion of God revealed in His Word. This God is the Father of Jesus Christ, the God of Abraham, Isaac and Jacob, the God of the prophets and apostles, the God who pursues His special work on this special line of world-occurrence. The doctrine of providence presupposes that this special history is exalted above all other history.[20]

This is no doubt a part of the radical inclusivity and exclusivity that is required of monotheism: there (exclusively) is only one God, who is (inclusively) the God of all the world. Barth puts it thus: 'There is no other meaning or purpose in history. For there is no other God.'[21] While knowledge of God and God's special work is known only through the salvation history of the Judaeo-Christian tradition, that exclusivity does not mean that God is not the God who in His providence guides all the world as well: 'There is only one God – the God of Jesus Christ – and God is *that* God in all God's dealings with creatures.'[22]

I want to refer to this theological manoeuvre as a move of 'differentiated exclusivisms'. By this is meant that the exclusive knowledge of providence arises from the special revelation of God to his people in Israel and the church (exclusively), that it is (exclusively) the Christian God who is the ruler of all creation, *but* that this God is (in a radically inclusive way) the God of all the world.

To understand this divine governance, one must understand the twofold rule of divine governance. Firstly, it is necessary to look at world events in general outwards from the particular (and exclusive) events attested in the Bible and the covenant of grace executed in Israel and the community of Jesus.[23] Secondly, one must look back from world events of nature and history to events attested in Bible from the promise which initiated it to the final fulfilment.[24] For Barth, it is true that

---

20. Ibid., 36–7.
21. Ibid., 36; cf. 176.
22. Tanner, 'Creation and Providence', 114.
23. CD III/3, 183.
24. Ibid., 183–4.

'general events have their meaning in the particular'.²⁵ Without this relationship to the particularity of the Judaeo-Christian tradition, the providential sustaining of the world would become little more than the 'activity of a chief Monad'.²⁶ In this way, Barth differentiates the God of Christian theology from other expressions of the divine:

> In most religious and philosophical systems there is some conception of a relationship between a higher and lower principle, an absolute, infinite, unconditioned or heavenly being and an earthly, spirit and matter, nature and reason, and of the superiority and even dominion in this relationship of the first and higher element over the second. ... But the relationship between Creator and creature with which we have to do in the Christian belief in providence stands outside this debate. The question whether there is in this relationship a Lord, and who this Lord is, is settled before it is asked. This alone shows us that the belief does not belong to the same category as religious and philosophical systems.²⁷

Barth is conscious here of the danger of deducing God or confusing God with history.²⁸ The key aspect for providence is that the Christian sees God *first*, the God who then illuminates this history for the Christian. This helps humans to see in the creation, in all of its multiplicity and confusion, a divine 'Nevertheless'. Crucially, this is only possible in *first* knowing God's providence. The Nevertheless 'is grounded in a supremely illuminating Therefore'.²⁹ Christian faith enables the Christian to see the world in a different way, identifying (albeit without transparency) the providential guidance of God in the world.

However, this providence is grounded in the person of God and cannot be confused with a *principle* of providence. Not only is this the case for panentheism and pantheism, but it is also true for Barth of Christianity's brother religions of Islam and Judaism. He writes:

> Its [Rabbinic Judaism's] God and Ruler of the world has necessarily a strangely obscure and hidden character. The devout Jew is never wholly clear as to His love or wrath, His grace or judgment. And His obscure character is projected into His government of the world, which the devout Jew follows, but only with anxious and hypercritical concern to justify it, and not with the childlike confidence of the clear presupposition that He the Lord will always be in the right. Where it is not known that God has already done the right in a fulfilled history of salvation, it is impossible to attain to this presupposition in respect of

---

25. Ibid., 184.
26. Ibid., 191.
27. Ibid., 27.
28. Cf. ibid., 123–4.
29. Ibid., 44.

His rule of the world. And in Islam this obscurity of God and His rule has been made a principle and therefore a caricature.[30]

This is a deeply painful and difficult claim on Barth's part, and no doubt we would not wish to express these matters thus today. However, it is worth noting that the primary distinction here between the Christians and their Abrahamic brethren is exclusive *knowledge* of this reality: for Barth, the Jewish person is never 'wholly clear as to His [God's] love or wrath, His grace or judgement'; and the concern with Islam is the making into a principle of God's obscurity and rule. Barth never, it is worth noting, considers that this is not God (in the sense of the proper noun); rather his concern is the *perception* and degree of *knowledge* of the One God. Here, we may see a further level of differentiated exclusivisms: Judaism is differentiated as closer to Christianity than Islam, which is in turn – as the passage above unfolds – differentiated from pantheism and polytheism.[31] The revelation of God, even in His hiddenness, is the basis for the Christian doctrine of providence, not the general history itself. In this way, the Christian doctrine of providence is differentiated from all other expressions of providence. However, this does not limit God's providential guidance only to that which is Christian. The Christian is called in recognition of the providential power of God to recognize 'the revealed God in His hiddenness' and as a child of the Father to 'find his way about the House of the Father'.[32] Through the doctrine of providence, the Christian is called in exclusivity to recognize the universal lordship of God: from the particular expression of her faith, she is led to the universal extent of God's providential reach.

Differentiated participation

These differentiated exclusivisms do not end simply with issues of epistemology (at least in terms of modernist understandings of 'knowledge'). The exclusive capacity of Christian doctrine to offer a true recognition of the universal lordship of God also determines a differentiated participation in history and providence for the Christian in contra-distinction to all others. This does not determine that those outside of the Christian faith are not part of God's providential purpose; rather it determines that the response to providence will be distinctive. We might identify this distinctive participation in God's providence in terms of the active participation of the Christian compared to the passive participation of the non-Christian.[33]

---

30. Ibid., 28.
31. Ibid.
32. CD III/3, 251.
33. See Jeannine M. Graham, *Representation and Substitution in the Atonement Theologies of Dorothee Sölle, John Macquarrie and Karl Barth* (New York: Peter Lang, 2005), 318–20,

Barth arrestingly puts this as follows: 'Of all creatures the Christian is the one which not merely is a creature, but actually says Yes to being a creature.'[34] This is because the Christian recognizes in her existence alongside all others the genuine universal lordship of God in history. As Barth puts it with regard to the Christian:

> In virtue of what he (and only he) can see, the Christian is the one who has a true knowledge in this matter of the providence and universal lordship of God. This providence and lordship affect him as they do all other creatures, but he participates in them differently from all other creatures. He participates in them from within. Of all creatures he is the one who while he simply experiences the providence and lordship of God also consents to it, having a kind of 'understanding' – if we may put it in this way – with the overruling God and Creator.[35]

This does not mean, however, that the Christian has insight into the mysteries of existence but is rather the only one 'who knows that there is no value in any of the master-keys which man has thought to discover and possess.'[36] This closing down also involves, therefore, an opening up, grounded in the very mystery of God because the active participation that the Christian has in providence is in the *universal* lordship of God. Providence and the universal lordship of God are 'actual to the Christian in faith, in obedience, and in prayer.'[37] It is these which are the forms of the Christian attitude, notably an attitude which is marked by dynamism.[38] Faith, therefore, does not lead the Christian inwards simply – into the community or even the religious self. Instead, writes Barth: 'It is as he participates in Jesus Christ in faith that the Christian participates in the divine providence and universal lordship. The same Holy Spirit who first led him into the narrower and central sphere now leads him out over its periphery into the wider circle.'[39] Participation in the universal lordship of Christ determines an outwards and open perspective on creation. In obedience and by the power of the Spirit, the Christian is called to participate in the more general sphere of God's providence. In this the church is obedient to its calling. This calling is the calling 'obediently to participate in the lordship of God in this more general sphere, and therefore – and this is the real problem of obedience – to participate in it actively, justifying by his conduct that which God Himself is doing in this sphere.'[40] To be a Christian is, therefore, to

396; cf. George Hunsinger, 'A Tale of Two Simultaneities: Justification and Sanctification in Calvin and Barth', in *Conversing with Barth*, ed. John C. McDowell and Mike Higton (Aldershot: Ashgate, 2004), 76–9.
   34. CD III/3, 240.
   35. Ibid., 242.
   36. Ibid.
   37. CD III/3, 245.
   38. Ibid.
   39. CD III/3, 248.
   40. Ibid., 257.

be obedient to God's purposes *in the world* and not to form an isolated community separated from world occurrence. Furthermore, it is in this way that one is to understand Christian prayer: 'The asking community stands together with its Lord before God on behalf of all creation.'[41] The service of prayer in the church community is not for religious self-preservation but for the world more broadly.

Thus for Barth, while God's providence rules all people, and we should not see other religions simply as 'Nothing', there is a differentiated level of participation for the Christian in comparison to that for the rest of humanity:

> His sovereignty is so great that it embraces both the possibility, and, as it is exercised, the actuality, that the creature can actively be present and co-operate in His overruling. There is no creaturely freedom which can limit or compete with the sole sovereignty and efficacy of God. But permitted by God, and indeed willed and created by Him, there is the freedom of the friends of God concerning whom He has determined that without abandoning the helm for one moment He will still allow Himself to be determined by them.[42]

The active participation of the believer in Christ in providence is such that, while God's sovereignty cannot be limited, the Christian is able to participate actively while the others participate only passively. What one can see here, therefore, is not a distinction based on limits of God's providential guidance, but instead a distinction based upon the response to providence. God's providential hand reaches all people; but by the power of the Holy Spirit, the Christian is able to respond to this providence by actively participating in it.

What does this mean for exclusion? Some extensions of Barth for other religions

This all too brief tour of Barth has attempted to suggest various ways in which his doctrine of providence might be related to questions of other religions. The purpose of this section of the chapter is to seek to draw some analytical comments from the foregoing discussion, and then to seek to think with Barth and, perhaps, point beyond him. In doing this, it is hoped that the theological themes tackled might be useful ones for the preacher to take back to scripture in order to aid him/her in preaching in today's age and generation in which conflict between the religions is such a dominant discourse.

Firstly, the strength and weight of Barth's doctrine of providence determine that we must all recognize the very breadth and distance of God's reach. It is all too easy for Christian systematic theology to engage in various dualisms or binaries, seeking to identify where God is or is not present. Due attention to providence

---

41. Ibid., 279.
42. Ibid., 285.

determines that one cannot think simply of God as present in some places and not in others. The God of the Christian faith is the God of all the world: there is no other god but the omnipresent Lord. Despite human, sinful rebellion, all of history is guided by Him, and the Christian is called to recognize the presence of God's will in all things – even when that will seems profoundly confusing and mysterious. To recognize the need to look outwards to the work of God in all the world from within the perspective of Christian faith is a healthy remedy to idolatrous propensities of identifying spaces in which God may be considered to be present and providentially guiding, and places in which God may be understood to be absent. Understanding the tremendous detailed engagement of God with all creation forces the Christian to be more positive in her assessment of the world, seeing it as a place in which she is called to see God's action not simply within her community but beyond the community as well. In an age of strife between the religions, rather than locating the idolatry of the religious other, the Christian is called away from the localizing of God (innate to idolatry) and towards true monotheism, which affirms that there is only one God.

This monotheism is, secondly, deeply Trinitarian for the Christian theologian. This Trinitarian dynamism leads to the need to articulate the differentiated exclusivisms and differentiated participation pointed to above. Through knowledge of Christ, the Christian is in the exclusive place from which to know the presence of God in all the world. Moreover, she is able to participate in this differently from all other peoples – actively participating in providence. Her faith, obedience and prayer in the power of the Spirit become an active participation in the providential workings of God. This does not determine that God is not present among non-Christians or that His providential power is somehow rendered impotent; simply that the Christian engages differently in God's providence than the non-Christian. There is a reason still to be Christian rather than a member of any other faith: particularity is retained.

Barth also, thirdly, points to a manner in which there might be deeper levels of differentiation between faiths. Barth is clear that providence is based on faith in Christ, and in that way the other Abrahamic faiths cannot know it in the same way as Christians, and he is clear that the Holy Spirit is the operation of God who allows for active participation in providence. However, Barth does point to Rabbinic Judaism and Islam in their articulations of providence. While he does caricature (unhelpfully) the versions of providence that these faiths articulate, he still recognizes the distinction between their expressions of providence, and between their expressions of providence and those of pantheism, panentheism and polytheism. There are clear levels of exclusivity in operation here, and the other monotheistic faiths, since they affirm there is only one God, will inevitably share some of the Christians' concerns with regard to providence. They will not share these, nor the Christian's fuller knowledge and active participation, in the same way as the Christian, nor will they share these in the same way as the pantheist and polytheist.

Thus, the Christian doctrine of providence is multiply differentiated: ontologically, God is Lord of all of the earth, but the reality of this is known only and exclusively in Christ, and this is known therefore by Christians most fully, who may – exclusively – by the power of the Spirit participate actively in this providence. However, this participation in providence presses beyond the closed confines of the church and back into the world of which God is Lord. Certainly, Barth's doctrine of providence enables the Christian to seek to live faithfully as a Christian in a world which is marked by pluralism and competing exclusivisms, without retreating to a sense of the exclusive operation of God as simply within the Christian community. For Barth, this is all held together in ultimate eschatological hope:

> God created the conditions and pre-conditions and pre-pre-conditions of all creaturely working. God gave them to the creature. All the preliminaries of creaturely activity were the effect of God's activity, of His friendly activity in the sense and to the end revealed and active in Jesus Christ, and in the history of the covenant of grace, of His activity as it was determined and controlled by His saving will. From the very first the purpose of God was to save and glorify the creature.[43]

From first to last, for Barth, God's plan for all creatures is their glorification; this is a plan not only for those who share in the special history of God with his church but also a plan for all creation, over which Christ is *Pantokrator*.

Conclusion

There are, however, places in which one may wish to press beyond Barth. The differentiated exclusivisms which underlie his work could helpfully be discussed in terms of the differentiated covenants of God with creation. While for the Christian these might all be a varied participation in God's covenant with humanity in the person of Jesus Christ, scripture is filled with varied covenants, and with God's differing relationships to creation. The Noahide covenant, for example, belongs specifically to the general sphere of God's covenant with all creation, and the promise of his preservation.[44] Furthermore, God's special history of salvation does not seem to be singularly focused on the people of Israel. Promises (or covenants) are made between God and Ishmael. In Gen. 16 and 21, one can see the promise of God to the descendants of Abraham through Hagar: there is a special purpose (more particular than the general purpose) present with these people. Differentiated exclusivism and participation require developing further beyond the simple binary of God's special and general operations in providence. There is a special relationship of God with the children of Ishmael, just as there is with the

---

43. Ibid., 119.
44. See Gerald O'Collins, SJ, *Salvation for All: God's Other Peoples* (Oxford: Oxford University Press, 2008), 7–12.

children of Isaac who do not enter the new covenant. Barth hints at this theme, but for those living today, there is perhaps the desire to develop his assertion:

> That world history in its totality is the history in which God executes His will of grace must thus be taken to mean that in its totality it belongs to this special history; that its lines can have no other starting-point or goal than the one divine will of grace; that they must converge on this one thin line and finally run in its direction. This is the theme of the doctrine of providence. It has to do with the history of the covenant, with the one thin line as such. Or rather, it has to do with it only to the extent that it for its part is undoubtedly one among the many other lines of general world-occurrence, and that these many other lines of general world-occurrence have their ontic and noetic basis in the fact that the God from whom they come and to whom they return pursues on this one line the special work which the creature must serve on these other lines.[45]

Recognizing God's ways with His other people is part of recognizing the covenant of grace uniquely revealed to the Christian. It recognizes that God is not only the God who is 'the Father of Jesus Christ, the God of Abraham, Isaac and Jacob, the God of the prophets and apostles'[46] but also the God of Ishmael, of Melchizedek, of Rahab, of Jethro and even of the pagan centurions. Systematic theology must take seriously the reality that the church's Lord is the Lord of all and should recognize that in breaking down boundaries, we are likely to find God on the other side, there already. It is this message which systematic theology must make clear to a generation of preachers facing the complexities of a pluralist world.

---

45. CD III/3, 36–7.
46. Ibid., 37.

Part III

ENGAGEMENTS WITH BONHOEFFER

Chapter 8

RELIGIONLESS CHRISTIANITY IN A COMPLEXLY RELIGIOUS AND SECULAR WORLD

Having discussed the relationship between Barth and Bonhoeffer, and the theology of Karl Barth, this book now turns to the work of Dietrich Bonhoeffer on related and associated themes.

This chapter in particular seeks to appropriate the inner logics of Bonhoeffer's discussion of religionlessness in order to help to reflect on the complex contemporary religious and secular situation in which religion is increasingly recognized as a geopolitical concern. Rather than seek to offer a further explanation of what Bonhoeffer meant by 'religionless Christianity',[1] the chapter aims to think through and beyond Bonhoeffer in order to allow his work to bear fruit for a world situation so different to the one he himself faced.[2] In this way, the chapter seeks to form Bonhoeffer's theology in a manner which is true to his own thinking and which allows that thinking a living voice.

A first section of the chapter will consider Bonhoeffer's historical reading of the 'coming of age' of the world. This will then, in a second section, be contrasted with contemporary sociological readings of religion, which present a situation in which Bonhoeffer's prophetic voice has not been realized. A third section will further consider the rise of religious people from various faiths (we might call them *fundamentalists*) who have felt very strongly that God should be at the centre of society and life, but in a manner very different from Bonhoeffer. A final section will consider the special significance there may be in Bonhoeffer's thought for Abrahamic religions, as they struggle with such fundamentalist resurgences of what might loosely be called *religion* and the false conceptions of God associated

---

1. For an excellent presentation of what Bonhoeffer meant by 'religionless Christianity', see Ralf K. Wüstenberg, *A Theology of Life: Dietrich Bonhoeffer's Religionless Christianity*, trans. Doug Stott (Grand Rapids, MI: Eerdmans, 1998). A briefer discussion can be found in Peter Selby, 'Christianity in a World Come of Age', in *The Cambridge Companion to Dietrich Bonhoeffer*, ed. John W. de Gruchy (Cambridge: Cambridge University Press, 1999), 226-45. Also of significance is Stephen Plant, *Bonhoeffer* (London: Continuum, 2004), chap. 8, especially in its ethical reflections, 136-8.

2. For a comparable methodological movement with regard to Barth's theology, see Chapter 7 in this volume.

with that. This chapter lays the foundations for the more constructive dialogue which is found in the following chapter.

Bonhoeffer on human autonomy

On 30 April 1944 Bonhoeffer wrote: 'We are approaching a completely religionless time; people as they are now simply cannot be religious anymore.'[3] These are stark words for a bleak time, but it is clear that they are underscored by a particular reading of history regarding the autonomy of humanity. This reading of human history is one in which the secularization of humanity is understood as an ongoing march leading to the obliteration of religion. Evidence that this conception of history underlies Bonhoeffer's concerns can be seen in the questions that he writes following the above quotation: 'How do we talk about God – without religion …? How do we speak (or perhaps we can no longer even "speak" the way we used to) in a "worldly" way about "God"?'[4] For Bonhoeffer, the progress of society towards complete secularization and religionlessness is taken as a given.[5]

This point is seen more clearly in Bonhoeffer's direct reflections on the history of human autonomy. He writes:

> The movement toward human autonomy (by which I mean discovery of the laws by which the world lives and manages its affairs in science, in society and government, in art, ethics, and religion), which began around the thirteenth century … has reached a certain completeness in our age. Human beings have learned to manage all important issues by themselves, without recourse to 'Working hypothesis: God'. In questions of science or art, as well as in ethical questions, this has become a matter of course, so that hardly anyone dares rock the boat anymore. But in the last hundred years or so, this has also become increasingly true of religious questions; it's becoming evident that everything gets along without 'God' and does so just as well as before. As in the scientific domain, so in human affairs generally, 'God' is being pushed further and further out of our life, losing ground.[6]

Regardless of the details of the dates with which he associates the beginnings of the movement towards human autonomy,[7] Bonhoeffer clearly pictures a world in which the 'space' God occupies is ever shrinking. This is not simply a space

---

3. DBWE 8, 30 April 1944, 362.
4. Ibid., 364.
5. For more nuanced considerations of the meaning of the secular and secularization, see below.
6. DBWE 8, 8 June 1944, 425–6.
7. For more on this, see David Martin, *The Religious and the Secular: Studies in Secularization* (London: Routledge & Kegan Paul, 1969), 3–4.

which is lost through the separation of the state from the church or an increased concentration on this age (*saeculum*) rather than the next.⁸ His presentation of the autonomy of humanity is one which he pictures in terms of an aggressive displacement of religion and God by the secular. Bonhoeffer's view of secularism might accord, therefore, with Quash and Jenkins's description of one particular form of secularization which 'claims to be the horizon of civilization, a final truth about humanity that will replace all local traditions, whether cultural, social, political, ethnic or religious in expression'.⁹ The importance of this reading of the world's history to Bonhoeffer's conceptual thinking is demonstrated further in his 'Outline for a Book'. The foundations for the opening chapters he pictures are 'The coming of age of the human being' followed by 'The religionlessness of the human being come of age. "God" as working hypothesis … has become superfluous' and 'worldliness and God'.¹⁰ It seems clear that the starting point for Bonhoeffer's reflections can be found in his reading of the history of the growth of human autonomy and a unified and aggressive progression towards secularization.¹¹ It is onto the backdrop of this view of the history of the world that Bonhoeffer paints his own thinking on 'religionless Christianity'.

No final triumph of secularity

Such readings of the history of humanity and the movement towards radical secularity, however, have been somewhat discredited since the time of Bonhoeffer's writing. Sociological studies have demonstrated that, while there may be a decline in the powers of ecclesial institutions and even in participation in religious rituals and practices, this has not led necessarily to the arrival of a totally religionless epoch. Statistics abound to that end; in 2017, 22 per cent of Western Europeans said they attended church at least once a month, with a further 22 per cent reporting they attended a few times a year. It is notable that 58 per cent of Western Europeans professed belief in God, with only Sweden, Belgium, the Netherlands

---

8. This is seen in the secularism that arose following the religious wars throughout Europe.

9. Ben Quash and Timothy Jenkins, 'Cambridge Inter-Faith Programme Academic Profile', accessed 7 November 2019, https://www.interfaith.cam.ac.uk/resources/journalarticlesandbookchapters/cipacademicprofile. This is contrasted with secularism as a set of 'minimal rules' that allow different religious communities to work together in a political unit.

10. DBWE 8, 'Outline for a Book', 500–1.

11. Here it is worth noting, with Selby, that for a contemporary audience, especially in the English-speaking world, 'a protest for adulthood and against tutelage might mean something very different in the context of Nazi imprisonment'. Selby, 'Christianity in a World Come of Age', 237. For more on Bonhoeffer's historical context, see the excellent presentation in Plant, *Bonhoeffer*, chap. 2.

and Norway with a figure at less than 50 per cent of their populations.¹² Nor is this belief professed without any suggested relation to institutional structures: in six Western European countries with church taxes in 2017, between 68 and 80 per cent paid the church tax, while only 8 to 20 per cent paid in the past but had stopped paying.¹³ Turning to church membership figures in the UK, while there was a general decline in membership between 2012 and 2017 affecting Anglican, Baptist, Roman Catholic, Methodist and Presbyterian communions, independent, Pentecostal and Orthodox churches grew in membership in the same period.¹⁴ Even an overall decline in church attendance in the UK has not been reflected in people's sense of religious self-identity. In 2017, 73 per cent of British people self-identified as Christian while only 23 per cent identified as religiously unaffiliated.¹⁵

Furthermore, improvements in communications have enabled Christians in Europe to see themselves as just one small part within worldwide Christianity. Considering patterns from all around the world, Davie observes that the assumption that as the world modernizes it secularizes has been proved quite simply untrue. In large parts of the world there is 'scant evidence for secularization, despite in many cases (if not all) convincing indicators of modernization – most noticeably in the United States (the most developed society in the world)'.¹⁶ Indeed, 45 per cent of Americans stated in 2018–19 that they attend church at least monthly,¹⁷ and in 2017, 80 per cent declared a belief in God.¹⁸ The path to secularity is not a global phenomenon.

This brief statistical survey demonstrates that the history of the world cannot be read in terms of a systematic and unidirectional movement towards secularity. What one may observe is numerous and discrete elements of secularism that have

---

12. 'Being Christian in Western Europe' (Washington, DC: Pew Research Center, 29 May 2018), 96, 99, https://www.pewforum.org/2018/05/29/being-christian-in-western-europe/. See also Grace Davie, *Europe: The Exceptional Case: Parameters of Faith and the Modern World* (London: Darton, Longman & Todd, 2002), 6–7.

13. 'In Western European Countries with Church Taxes, Support for the Tradition Remains Strong' (Washington, DC: Pew Research Center, 30 April 2019), https://www.pewforum.org/2019/04/30/in-western-european-countries-with-church-taxes-support-for-the-tradition-remains-strong/. See also David Martin, *Reflections on Sociology and Theology* (Oxford: Clarendon Press, 1997), 248.

14. Peter Brierley, *UK Church Statistics*, 3rd edn (Tonbridge: ADBC, 2018), 4. See also Grace Davie, *Religion in Britain since 1945* (Oxford: Blackwell, 1994), 46–7.

15. 'Being Christian in Western Europe', 81–2.

16. Davie, *Europe*, x.

17. 'In U.S., Decline of Christianity Continues at Rapid Pace' (Washington, DC: Pew Research Center, 17 October 2019), 12, https://www.pewforum.org/2019/10/17/in-u-s-decline-of-christianity-continues-at-rapid-pace/.

18. 'When Americans Say They Believe in God, What Do They Mean?' (Washington, DC: Pew Research Center, 25 April 2018), 4, https://www.pewforum.org/2018/04/25/when-americans-say-they-believe-in-god-what-do-they-mean/. See Davie, *Europe*, 28.

been lumped together in certain presentations of history as if they were part of one unified and singular movement.[19] Moreover, when one analyses these singular movements in detail, it becomes clear that a decline in certain institutional expressions of Christianity (especially in terms of historic churches) has not led to an overall and universal religionlessness. As Martin puts it:

> In spite of everything that may properly be said about how far disintegration has gone, there is a core moral understanding present in common language, and clustering around the Decalogue and injunctions not to steal, or injure, or kill, or covet, or lie. This is a very large fragment of the moral sense traditionally taught and recommended by the Church.[20]

Even if we live in an age in which a higher proportion of people do not attend churches (and even then there has been considerable growth even in Western Europe in Pentecostal communities),[21] we certainly do not live in a time when people are not religious anymore. They may simply be religious in a different way.

This is compounded by the contemporary reality of migration and increased mobility. The movement of Muslim communities into Europe has seen the numbers of Muslims in this continent increase from nine million in 1900[22] to nearly twenty-six million in 2016, or 4.9 per cent of the population of the European Union plus Norway and Switzerland. That figure is due to rise to 7.4 per cent by 2050 with zero migration of Muslims to Europe, 11.2 per cent with medium migration or 14.0 per cent with high migration.[23] While Europe may seem (at least) *less Christian*, one could argue it is *more religious* in terms of the increased number of religious minorities present throughout the twentieth century.

Even without reference to sociological studies, events such as 11 September in the United States or 7 July in the UK present people of our age and generation with religion as a geopolitical issue. If the Cold War defined the politics of the generation that succeeded Bonhoeffer, religion and issues surrounding religion define this generation. Religion is back on the agenda in a way it has not been for a long time.[24]

---

19. Martin, *The Religious and the Secular*, 2.
20. Martin, *Reflections on Sociology and Theology*, 248.
21. Ibid., 231–2.
22. David B. Barrett, George T. Kurian and Todd M. Johnson, *World Christian Encyclopaedia*, 2nd edn (Oxford: Oxford University Press, 2001), 14.
23. 'Europe's Growing Muslim Population' (Washington, DC: Pew Research Center, 29 November 2017), 4–5, https://www.pewforum.org/2017/11/29/europes-growing-muslim-population/.
24. At the 'Islam and Muslims in the World Today' consultation hosted by the British Government and facilitated by Cambridge Inter-Faith Project in 2007, David F. Ford commented on the change of focus between this century and the last: if the last were a very secular century defined by faiths' relationships to secularity, this century is presenting

Nevertheless, it must be acknowledged that this is combined with something of a *mentalité* of secularism. This *mentalité* is present particularly in public professional spheres that were once focused on the church, such as bodies of teachers, social workers, lecturers, counsellors, psychiatrists and so on.[25] Even if secularity does not in the end correspond to religionlessness, it is nevertheless present in many assumptions of and about contemporary society. As Talal Asad puts it: 'Because the secular is so much part of our modern life, it is not easy to grasp it directly.'[26] One must note, therefore, that even if the situation of contemporary society is significantly different to that of Bonhoeffer, secularity has established itself as a *perceived* reality even within an age in which religion is at the forefront of international concerns. The interrelation between the secular and the religious is a constant concern. Thus, rather than speaking of a completely religionless time, it is necessary to observe that the world is complexly secular and religious in all kinds of shifting coordinations.[27]

Fundamentalism as another response to secularity

This complex interdependent interrelation of the secular and the religious leads to anxiety among religious peoples as they perceive that their individual faiths are being pushed out of the centre of the world to the periphery, either as a result of a sense of secularism or the reality of pluralism. This is reflected in Bonhoeffer, though his solution is clearly somewhat different than most. The lack of the religious a priori of humanity means, in Bonhoeffer's words, that 'the foundations are being pulled out from under all that "Christianity" has previously been for us, and the only people among whom we might end up in terms of "religion" are "the last of the knights" or a few intellectually dishonest people. Are these supposed to be the chosen few?'[28] As Bonhoeffer observes, this sense about the world leads to an anxiety: 'It always seems to me that we leave room for God only out of anxiety. I'd like to speak of God not at the boundaries but in the centre, not in weakness but in strength, thus not in death and guilt but in human life and human goodness.'[29] The anxiety is that the space in the world for God is perceived as being ever-reduced – that God is being pushed to the boundaries and not allowed to be present at the centre.

---

itself as a very religious century, with concerns for the relationship of faith to secularism alongside relationships between faith communities.

25. Martin, *Reflections on Sociology and Theology*, 237–8.

26. Talal Asad, *Formations of the Secular: Christianity, Islam, Modernity* (Stanford, CA: Stanford University Press 2003), 16.

27. Cf. David F. Ford, 'Gospel in Context: Among Many Faiths', presented at the Fulcrum Conference, Islington, 2006.

28. DBWE 8, 30 April 1944, 363.

29. DBWE 8, 30 April 1944, 366–7.

This is not, however, a concern expressed only by Bonhoeffer. Fundamentalisms of all varieties have also laid claim to this anxiety: the desire to place God at the centre is an innate concern for them. The fundamentalist seeks to restore 'God' to a central position, a restoration which she believes is necessary for society to survive and morality to be retained. This leads to fundamentalism making its voice heard in governmental, educational, social and ethical issues.[30] Furthermore, power dynamics underlie this, as Martyn Percy rightly observes. Discussing one fundamentalist figure prominent in Britain, he states: '"The power of God" ... means that human, economic, geological, social and organizational powers – in fact power of any kind – can be subject at any moment to the superior power of God. Thus, the mission of Christ ... becomes an historic event in which power is lost and won.'[31] The basis of this power struggle arises as a reaction to the modern situation that is considered to undermine the centrality of religion: it is a response to the 'reductive possibility'.[32]

Even this, however, is complex. In many ways, fundamentalism is at home in the secular world, at least in terms of economics, market forces and profit.[33] Utilizing the market and improved communications, fundamentalism has, nevertheless, fed off the anxieties that the *mentalité* of secularism has brought about for religious peoples. It has required the sense of an ever-shrinking space for God in society in order to establish its own apocalyptic vision and to gain support from those who also wish to place God back at the centre and not at the fringes.

This is seen perhaps most visibly of all in the rise of Islamic fundamentalism.[34] While Christian fundamentalism grew as a movement to counteract liberalism's surrendering of space in the Christian world, Islamic fundamentalism arose in parallel to this but with the added dimension that most Muslim countries were under the direct or indirect control of colonial Western powers.[35] This added a further political edge to Islamic fundamentalism which was more sharp than the one already present in Christian fundamentalism. Secularism and democracy represented 'a usurpation of God's sovereignty'.[36] Secularization and the placing

---

30. See Martyn Percy, *Words, Wonders and Power: Understanding Contemporary Fundamentalism and Revivalism* (London: SPCK, 1996).

31. Ibid., 29.

32. Ibid., 43.

33. James Barr, *Fundamentalism* (London: SCM Press, 1977), 99–100. Barr observes that fundamentalism 'appears to be reasonably well established in our secularized society and prospering well within it' (100).

34. It is perhaps best to speak of 'fundamentalisms' since fundamentalism manifests itself in a variety of forms. However, for the sake of style, the singular has been preserved.

35. Ataullah Siddiqui, *Christian-Muslim Dialogue in the Twentieth Century* (London: Macmillan, 1997), 3–5.

36. Youssef M. Choueiri, *Islamic Fundamentalism*, rev. edn (London: Pinter, 1997), 106.

of control into the hands of humanity was perceived as God being pushed to the fringe, which in turn led to a fundamentalist desire to place God at the centre once again so God could exercise His sovereign rule.[37]

Thus, it is clear that not only has a completely religionless world failed to develop, but responses to the same concerns about God being pushed out of the centre to the boundaries from people who still seek to understand themselves as people of faith have been varied. This concern can clearly be seen in fundamentalism in both its Christian and Muslim manifestations.

Thinking through Bonhoeffer

So, what can Bonhoeffer's religionless Christianity offer to an age in which his prophetic vision of a world without religion has not been realized? Here, I think we need to be sensitive to the discipline Bonhoeffer believed himself to be pursuing. Bonhoeffer is at his best when he pursues not a sociological reading of human religiosity and secularity but when he gives theological reflection on religionlessness.[38] His primary concern is not to describe a religionless state but to advocate that religionlessness *theologically understood* through the Bible and the incarnation of the Word of God presents the Christian with the *necessity* of religionlessness. It is not that sociologically speaking the world has come of age by its own secularity; it is rather that theologically speaking one must speak of 'a world that has come of age *by Jesus Christ*'.[39] In this way, instead of seeing Bonhoeffer's vision as a prophetic understanding of the future of society, one is able to see him as a prophet in the other sense: Bonhoeffer tells forth to the church, instructing it to focus more on scripture and Christ in order to realize its true and religionless nature. This desire to reform the faith is ultimately a more helpful purpose that

---

37. Ibid., 110–11. Cf. Youssef Choueiri, 'The Political Discourse of Contemporary Islamicist Movements', in *Islamic Fundamentalism*, ed. Abdel Salam Sidahmed and Anoushiravan Ehteshami (Boulder, CO: Westview, 1996), 22–4.

38. Peter Selby notes along with Peter L. Berger that despite Bonhoeffer's professed interest in sociology, his sociological reflection is somewhat limited. Selby, 'Christianity in a World Come of Age', 237–8.

39. Dietrich Bonhoeffer, *Letters and Papers from Prison*, ed. Eberhard Bethge (London: SCM Press, 1999), 30 June 1944, 342, emphasis added. This translation is preferred over the DBWE 8 translation: 'the claim of Jesus Christ on the world that has come of age' (DBWE 8, 30 June 1944, 451). The translation in the main body of the text follows the German more closely: 'Lass mich nur schnell nochmal das Thema, um das es mir geht, formulieren: die Inanspruchnahme der mündig gewordenen Welt durch Jesus Christus' (DBW 8, 30.VI.44, 504). The new translation interprets 'durch Jesus Christ' as attached to *Inanspruchnahme*, while the earlier translation sticks more closely to the German word order.

Bonhoeffer's religionless Christianity can fulfil than a speculation on the future of society.[40]

Let us again return to the quotation with which I opened these reflections, but change the emphasis slightly: 'We are approaching a completely religionless age; *people as they are now* simply cannot be religious anymore.'[41] When we seek to emphasize the state of people in the contemporary world, the power of Bonhoeffer's words hits the reader even in an age in which religion has become a geopolitical issue. When we see acts of terror carried out supposedly in the name of God and hear rhetorical responses which conjure apocalyptic imagery,[42] for the Christian who believes that 'what is beyond this world is meant, in the gospel, to be there *for* this world ... in the biblical sense of the creation and the incarnation, crucifixion, and resurrection of Jesus Christ',[43] there is an imperative to assert that people simply cannot be religious *as they are now* any longer.

Here, there exists the necessity of careful formulation of theological statement for the sake of its implications on political action. As we have seen, one response to a perceived growth of secularity has been the rise of fundamentalism, which is itself underpinned with theological understandings of power related to the sovereignty of God and the re-establishment of that sovereignty at the centre of the world. In this, Bonhoeffer's words hold true: 'Human religiosity directs people in need to the power of God in the world, God as deus ex machina.'[44] In the fundamentalist approach, human religiosity even goes so far as to seek the establishment of the power and sovereignty of God in the world in the here and now. That means fundamentalism is by definition political in nature.[45] However,

---

40. Indeed, Wüstenberg's wise assertion that Bonhoeffer is ahead of his times in not formulating any one concept of religion is helpful here. See Wüstenberg, *A Theology of Life*, 159. Bonhoeffer's 'loose' understanding of religion forces one back to theological interpretations of religion rather than settling on one single sociological definition of the word. As Martin observes: 'The religions and the secular are in one sense opposites but in another way intertwined. There is almost nothing regarded as religious which cannot also be secular, and almost no characteristic appearing in secular contexts which do not also appear in religious ones.' Martin, *The Religious and the Secular*, 3; cf. chap. 4.

41. DBWE 8, 30 April 1944, 362, emphasis added.

42. For example, see these lines from former US President George W. Bush: 'So we are determined to fight this evil, and fight until we are rid of it. ... We act now, because we must lift this dark threat from our age.' 'Remarks by the President to the Warsaw Conference on Combatting Terrorism' (6 November 2001), https://avalon.law.yale.edu/sept11/president_086.asp.

43. DBWE 8, 5 May 1944, 373.

44. DBWE 8, 16 July 1944, 479.

45. The view that fundamentalism rests singularly upon literal interpretation of scripture cannot be held. In the example of the Christian fundamentalist, the Bible is often interpreted with great sophistry in order to justify certain perspectives. So, for example, to justify substitutionary atonement, a complex understanding of the relations between the covenants is required along with a Trinitarian logic that allows for such a view of

its unpinning cannot come from the political sphere (which would be seen only as part of the usurping of God's sovereignty) but must come from within the theological sphere. Furthermore, within the theological sphere, any discussion with fundamentalism must come on its own terms with reference to scripture. To this situation, Bonhoeffer's words present Christian fundamentalists with a prophetic admonition:

> Thus our coming of age leads us to a truer recognition of our situation before God. God would have us know that we must live as those who manage their lives without God. The same God who is with us is the God who forsakes us (Mark 15:34!). The same God who makes us to live in the world without the working hypothesis of God is the God before whom we stand continually. Before God, and with God, we live without God. God consents to be pushed out of the world and onto the cross; God is weak and powerless in the world and in precisely this way, and only so, is at our side and helps us. Matt. 8:17 makes it quite clear that Christ helps us not by virtue of his omnipotence but rather by virtue of his weakness and suffering![46]

Such words have great power in the present climate of unhelpful theo-politics. They are words which present a counter-interpretation of God's sovereignty and its relationship with human religion.[47] Moreover, such an interpretation seeks to be genuinely biblical in a manner necessary if one is to be able to communicate with those who have aggregated to themselves the false title of 'biblical Christians'. In an age which has not fully come of age and done away with false conceptions of God, but in which such false conceptions have burgeoned like weeds in a garden, words such as these genuinely help to do away with those types of idols and open up a way 'to see the God of the Bible, who gains ground and power in the world by being powerless'.[48] It is the true God and His genuine sovereignty who must be told

---

God. Similarly, on the political level, ancient oracles are read as commentary on present-day society, which also involves some level of hermeneutical sophistication. Christian fundamentalism is grounded in certain readings of scripture, granted, but those readings often arise out of other concerns, such as doctrinal standpoints and certain readings of the political situation.

46. DBWE 8, 16 July 1944, 478–9.

47. Plant notes helpfully that Bonhoeffer does not

> make the mistake, typical of many theologies of the suffering of God, of equating the weakness of Christ and the powerlessness of God with a divine inability to make any difference. Bonhoeffer's deep conviction is that it is *through* weakness, suffering and power *that* God is with us and helps us. Being 'pushed out' onto the cross, God is not reduced to absenteeism, but helps us by virtue of his weakness. (Plant, *Bonhoeffer*, 136)

48. DBWE 8, 16 July 1944, 479–80.

forth prophetically against the many and varied advocates of false conceptions of Him for the sake of this complexly religious and secular world which the true God has created and providentially guided. Bonhoeffer's use to this age is not his sociological description of human autonomy and the victory of secularization but his message of the 'gospel impetus towards autonomy'.[49] His work is not descriptive; it is imperative.

But what of other fundamentalisms? As has been asserted, secularity has not conquered religion but has in certain cases led to a fundamentalist backlash against the perceived secularity of the world. This has not simply been a Christian phenomenon but a phenomenon which has been witnessed in a number of religions.[50] Bonhoeffer's reflections on the Old Testament in December 1943,[51] prior to his move to religionlessness (albeit these reflections continue after that move),[52] may offer a positive contribution to the problem of fundamentalism not only for Christianity but for the Abrahamic traditions more generally. Bonhoeffer points briefly to the unutterability of the name of God.[53] The unutterability of God's name is an element that each of the Abrahamic faiths retains to a greater or lesser degree. Most clearly, in Judaism, the name is considered so holy that it cannot be spoken, and is instead replaced most often with *Ha-shem* or 'the Name'. Furthermore, in Christianity, there remains an unutterable, or better unknown, name even for those who know Christ. Rev. 19.12-13 reads: 'His eyes are like a flame of fire, and on his head are many diadems; and he has a name inscribed that no one knows but himself. He is clothed in a robe dipped in blood, and his name is called The Word of God.' The Word of God has a name which is known only to Him. Similarly, of the many names of Allah, only ninety-nine have been revealed. Allah also has at least one unknown name, and in most traditions many, many more. Clearly, there is a distinction between a name being known but unutterable and a name not being known at all. However, in the latter case, the name remains unutterable as it is unknown. In both cases, the reality for people of faith is the same. This reality is, in the words of R. Kendall Soulen, thus:

> To say that God cannot be circumscribed is to say that human beings can never bring God under their control. God is inexhaustible. … God cannot be caught

---

49. This phrase is borrowed from Selby, 'Christianity in a World Come of Age', 235.

50. This chapter has pointed to Islamic and Christian fundamentalism as a pressing issue that the West must consider. However, in different social or geographical settings, issues such as Kali worship in Sri Lanka might be those perceived as most important.

51. DBWE 8, Second Sunday in Advent [5 December 1943], 213-14.

52. This is prior to the 1944 shift to Bonhoeffer's mature thinking on religionlessness. See, for example, Wüstenberg, *A Theology of Life*, 59.

53. DBWE 8, Second Sunday in Advent [5 December 1943], 213.

by our definitions, nor domesticated by human thought or feeling. ... Although humans are name-giving animals, they cannot give a name to God.[54]

This is not to say that God lacks His uniqueness or His particularity.[55] It is to say, however, that God's very particularity is one in which our perception and speech about Him fall woefully short of His reality. That He cannot be fully named (either because there are names we do not know or because His name is unutterable) reminds us of this. In this way, God is allowed genuinely to be sovereign and is not reduced to a false sovereignty manufactured by human creating.

Although not fully developed, this issue of the unutterability of God's name by the Israelites is connected to Bonhoeffer's concerns about religion: 'I will definitely not come out of here as a *homo religiosus*! Quite the opposite: my suspicion and fear of "religiosity" have become greater here than ever. That the Israelites *never* say the name of God aloud is something I often ponder, and I understand it increasingly better.'[56] Reclaiming the unutterability of God's name, the mystery of God's being, a mystery which is no ignorance but an ever-fuller glory as indicated in the unknown names of Allah and Christ in Islam and Christianity, respectively, allows God to be God and not to be reduced to human's religion. It prevents people of faith from second guessing God. It saves people of faith from idolatry, an idolatry with enormous political implications.

Conclusion

Let us here make three summative comments before proceeding to some formative closing remarks. Firstly, if it cannot be said that we live in a religionless world, other (and dangerous) reactions to perceived secularity may mean it is possible to say that we live in a world with Godless varieties of religion. Secondly, if it cannot be said that Bonhoeffer prophetically predicted the end of religion, it must be said that Bonhoeffer prophetically speaks out against our continued religion. Thirdly, if it cannot be said that Bonhoeffer has a unified concept of religion, it should be said that his 'loose' understanding of religion has much to offer to the multiple

---

54. R. Kendall Soulen, '"Go Tell Pharaoh", or, Why Empires Prefer a Nameless God', in *The Economy of Salvation: Essays in Honour of M. Douglas Meeks*, ed. Jürgen Moltmann, Timothy R. Eberhart and Matthew W. Charlton (Eugene, OR: Cascade Books, 2015), 65–6.

55. As is the case in theologies which look to a shared essence or core to religions. The unutterability of God's name is not synonymous with God being entirely unknown. It is in the history and narrative of the life of the Hebrew people, recorded in the Old Testament, that God makes Himself known as the God whose name is unutterable: the tension between the cataphatic and the apophatic must be maintained. Put otherwise, it is the God whose name is unutterable who is the Word that speaks and becomes flesh (Jn 1.1-14): God *reveals* Himself as the God whose name is unutterable.

56. DBWE 8, 21 November 1943, 189.

particularities of the religions in a complexly religious and secular age in which these issues have geopolitical magnitude.

What Bonhoeffer has to offer for such an age as ours is a recognition that we must purge ourselves of religion in order to take seriously the incarnation in our contemporary lives.[57] It is this which perhaps Christianity has to offer to the present age: a message that in order to be genuinely children of God (however uniquely and exclusively 'God' is understood by each faith), we must not confuse our God with our human and religious representations of Him. Bonhoeffer leaves us with a need and desire to purge ourselves of our religion. To an age in which terror is enacted in the name of religion, there can be fewer more important imperatives.

---

57. It is, in the words of Wüstenberg, a 'life-christological interpretation'. Wüstenberg, *A Theology of Life*, 157.

Chapter 9

RELIGIONLESS CHRISTIANITY AND THE POLITICAL IMPLICATIONS OF THEOLOGICAL SPEECH

To appropriate Bonhoeffer's religionless Christianity for contemporary theological speech might not seem an obvious or apparent thing to do. Whereas the last century (to which Bonhoeffer belonged)[1] proved to be a century in which secularism sounded the loudest note,[2] with religions seeking to understand themselves in relation to what was perceived to be a great triumph for the antagonizers of religion, this century has begun in a remarkably religious vain. One needs only to look to headlines to see this: from the terrors of 11 September 2001 to the 2007 outcry in Sudan over a British primary schoolteacher naming a class teddy bear 'Mohammad', religion is a huge factor and concern in community relations both in terms internal to nations and in terms of foreign policy. If geopolitics in the twentieth century revolved around the Cold War, geopolitics in the present century revolves around the so-called 'clash of civilizations' between Muslim and Christian nations.[3] To look, therefore, as a resource, to one who sought a 'secular interpretation' of the Bible, and who advocated that 'as a working hypothesis for morality, politics, and the natural sciences, God has been overcome and done away with'[4] may not seem wise for the twenty-first-century theologian and ethicist.

As I have argued in the previous chapter, however, Bonhoeffer's articulation of 'religionless Christianity' should be understood as offering not primarily

---

1. For an excellent presentation of Bonhoeffer's context, see Stephen Plant, *Bonhoeffer* (London: Continuum, 2004), chap. 2. For a more detailed biography of Bonhoeffer, see Eberhard Bethge, *Dietrich Bonhoeffer: Theologian, Christian, Contemporary* (London: Collins, 1970).

2. At least in the case of Europe and communist countries. See Grace Davie, *Europe: The Exceptional Case: Parameters of Faith and the Modern World* (London: Darton, Longman & Todd, 2002); Peter L. Berger, 'The Desecularization of the World: A Global Overview', in *The Desecularization of the World*, ed. Peter L. Berger (Washington, DC: Ethics and Public Policy Center, 1999), 9–11.

3. Samuel P. Huntington, 'The Clash of Civilizations?', *Foreign Affairs* 72, no. 3 (1993): 22–49. Cf. Samuel P. Huntington, *The Clash of Civilizations and the Remaking of World Order* (London: Touchstone, 1998).

4. DBWE 8, 16 July 1944, 478; cf. 8 July 1944, 455–7.

a sociological but a *theological* interpretation of religion.⁵ Bonhoeffer was incorrect in his prophetic sociological expectation of an imminent end to the 'age of religion';⁶ and contemporary sociologists of religion may well question Bonhoeffer's presentation of a unitary and unidirectional secularization thesis,⁷ especially from a globalized perspective.⁸ As Berger puts it: 'The assumption that we live in a secularized world is false. The world today … is as furiously religious as it ever was.'⁹ Religion has clearly not been brought to an end, as Bonhoeffer anticipated. In fact, far from it, religion has gained a heightened role in social and political discourse at the start of the new millennium. However, even if Bonhoeffer is not a prophet simply in his (failed) role as a seer of future trends and events, he is a prophet in another sense of the word – one who speaks out against the church's wrong religion, admonishing and challenging us to change our theology and our behaviour. Thus, for Bonhoeffer, it is not that sociologically speaking the world has come of age by its own secularity; it is rather that *theologically* speaking one must speak of 'a world that has come of age *by Jesus Christ*'.¹⁰ Bonhoeffer tells forth to the church, instructing it to focus more on scripture and Christ in order to realize its true and religionless nature. This is the key to reading Bonhoeffer now: religionless Christianity is for Bonhoeffer a theological category and imperative, as opposed to any sociological description.¹¹ Though concerning a differing field, the words of

5. This chapter marks a sequel to Chapter 8 in this volume.

6. 'We are approaching a completely religionless time' (DBWE 8, 30 April 1944, 362). This theme reoccurs in DBWE 8, 30 April 1944, 8 June 1944, 30 June 1944, 16 July 1944 and 'Outline for a Book'.

7. See, for example, DBWE 8, 8 June 1944 and 16 July 1944. Such a view should be compared to the more recent depictions given in the likes of Grace Davie, *Religion in Britain since 1945* (Oxford: Blackwell, 1994); David Martin, *The Religious and the Secular: Studies in Secularization* (London: Routledge & Kegan Paul, 1969); David Martin, *Reflections on Sociology and Theology* (Oxford: Clarendon Press, 1997); and Timothy Jenkins, *Religion in English Everyday Life: An Ethnographic Approach* (New York: Berghahn Books, 1999). This theme is also explored with regard to 'post-secularism' and Bonhoeffer in Christoph Schwöbel, ' "Religion" and "Religionlessness" in *Letters and Papers from Prison*: A Perspective for Religious Pluralism?', in *Mysteries in the Theology of Dietrich Bonhoeffer: A Copenhagen Bonhoeffer Symposium*, ed. Kirsten Busch Nielsen, Ulrich Nissen and Christiane Tietz (Göttingen: Vandenhoeck & Ruprecht, 2007), esp. 275–83.

8. To understand secularization from a globalized perspective, see Davie, *Europe*; and Berger, 'The Desecularization of the World'.

9. Berger, 'The Desecularization of the World', 2.

10. Dietrich Bonhoeffer, *Letters and Papers from Prison*, ed. Eberhard Bethge (London: SCM Press, 1999), 30 June 1944, 342, emphasis added. As in the previous chapter, the earlier translation is preferred to DBWE 8, since it more closely follows the German.

11. Religion as a theological category should, therefore, be thought of as the attempt of humanity to locate God in a sacred space, and the related attempt of humanity at reaching God separate from revelation through the incarnation of the second person of the trinity. In short, religion as a theological category is innately related to idolatry. Religion is,

Walter Moberly seem apposite: 'Theology classically is concerned with constructive questions of what belief and practice *can* and *ought* to be as a living reality in the present rather than simply descriptive, albeit suggestive, accounts of what it has been in the past.'[12] This desire to reform the faith, and to seek what theology ought to be saying and what the path of Christian discipleship ought to be like is ultimately a more helpful purpose that Bonhoeffer's religionless Christianity can fulfil than a failed speculation on the future of society. Schwöbel puts this well in reference to Bonhoeffer's religionless Christianity:

> A theology that follows Bonhoeffer's inspirations in reading the 'signs of the times' and in seeing the theological diagnosis of the religious situation as a central element of the theological task cannot simply repeat Bonhoeffer's diagnosis of *his* time and apply it to *our* time as if nothing had changed. Rather it seems much more in keeping with the spirit of Bonhoeffer's theology to attempt careful description of the phenomena and to try to assess them theologically.[13]

It is this theological interpretation of religionlessness that provides the basis for a useful appropriation of Bonhoeffer's ideas at a very different stage of world history.

This chapter seeks to use Bonhoeffer's theology in a formative and constructive way in order to offer a reading of the theology of the religions in the twenty-first century that takes the political implications of theological discourse seriously. Rather than simply thinking *towards* Bonhoeffer, it seeks to think *through* and *with* his work on religionless Christianity in order best to fulfil its promise.[14] It will begin by seeking to highlight unhelpful trends in contemporary theo-politics,[15]

furthermore, to understand and confuse this human localizing of God to a sacred space and the penultimacy of human speech about God with God in Godself and God in God's own Self-revelation in the world. It is hoped that this chapter further teases out this theological understanding of religion in contrast to standard sociological definitions.

 12. R. W. L. Moberly, *The Old Testament of the Old Testament: Patriarchal Narratives and Mosaic Yahwism* (Minneapolis, MN: Fortress Press, 1992), 152.
 13. Schwöbel, '"Religion" and "Religionlessness"', 176.
 14. Excellent presentations of Bonhoeffer's religionless Christianity already exist, and it is not my purpose to repeat the work carried out so successfully by others. The reader is directed to Ralf K. Wüstenberg, *A Theology of Life: Dietrich Bonhoeffer's Religionless Christianity* (Grand Rapids, MI: Eerdmans, 1998); and Peter Selby, 'Christianity in a World Come of Age', in *The Cambridge Companion to Dietrich Bonhoeffer*, ed. John W. de Gruchy (Cambridge: Cambridge University Press, 1999), 226–45.
 15. Clearly, this chapter is not suggesting that all theo-politics are unhelpful: it is itself an exercise in theo-political thought. For positive and helpful exercises in theo-politics, see for example, Oliver O'Donovan, *The Ways of Judgment* (Grand Rapids, MI: Eerdmans, 2005); and William T. Cavanaugh, *Theopolitical Imagination: Discovering the Liturgy as a Political Act in an Age of Global Consumerism* (Edinburgh: T&T Clark, 2002). The focus of the chapter is, instead, the *unhelpful* theo-politics that can arise from fundamentalist approaches to religion. The chapter does not wish to replace these with what might broadly

and locate these in the interconnection of secular and religious forms of fundamentalism. From there, it will consider how a theological interpretation of Bonhoeffer's religionless Christianity might assist in undermining such fundamentalisms. A further section will seek to apply this theological thinking to theo-politics, in order to see what Bonhoeffer's thought on religionlessness might yield to the contemporary situation.

Diagnosing the problem: Fundamentalisms and unhelpful theo-politics

Although I argued in the previous chapter that Bonhoeffer's presentation of the history of secularization does not correspond to either a global or a contemporary perspective on the theme,[16] it does, nevertheless, correspond to the *mentalité* many religious people possess about secularization. Many religious people are fearful that secularization is taking place – and perhaps even has taken place – in a unified and aggressive manner.[17] Although sociological studies of religion suggest that the world remains deeply religious (albeit perhaps in Europe in a different way to the way in which it was before),[18] there still exists in many religious people an anxiety that the space and room for religion has been reduced. Even if the reality is one in which religion continues to thrive in most parts of the world and that Christianity (and indeed Islam) continues to grow, and even if it is the case that many people are not irreligious but simply religious in a different way, this does not determine that religious people will *perceive* reality to be thus. Many religious people work from a basis of the fear that their faith is fizzling out rather than moving towards a great eschatological *crescendo*:[19] one can see this simply in concerns over the numbers in congregations. Moreover, one can perhaps, strangely, also find this

---

be called a secular liberal or pluralist approach. Rather, it seeks a genuinely faith-centred approach to these themes, beginning exclusively from *within* the faith community and justified on the grounds of faith.

16. See chap. 9, 'Religionless Christianity in a Complexly Religious and Secular World'.

17. See Ben Quash and Timothy Jenkins, 'Cambridge Inter-Faith Programme Academic Profile', accessed 7 November 2019, https://www.interfaith.cam.ac.uk/resources/journalarticlesandbookchapters/cipacademicprofile, 2–4, which differentiates between 'the secular settlement' and secularism as the 'horizon of civilization'.

18. Davie, *Europe*, chap. 1; Davie, *Religion in Britain Since 1945*, chaps. 5 and 6; Jenkins, *Religion in English Everyday Life*; 'Being Christian in Western Europe' (Washington, DC: Pew Research Center, 29 May 2018), https://www.pewforum.org/2018/05/29/being-christian-in-western-europe/; 'Europe's Growing Muslim Population' (Washington, DC: Pew Research Center, 29 November 2017), https://www.pewforum.org/2017/11/29/europes-growing-muslim-population/.

19. The preoccupation of American Christian fundamentalism with pre- and post-millennialism may well be symptomatic of this concern, attempting to make sense of the *seeming* decline of Christianity from an eschatological perspective.

concern present underneath the surface of Bonhoeffer's discussions of religionless Christianity, although he clearly offers a rather different and radical resolution to this fear. The lack of the religious a priori of humanity means, in Bonhoeffer's words, 'the foundations are being pulled out from under all that "Christianity" has previously been for us'.[20] And this *mentalité* of secularization leads to an anxiety: 'It always seems to me that we leave room for God only out of anxiety.'[21] Elsewhere Bonhoeffer puts it thus: 'Human religiosity directs people in need to the power of God in the world'.[22] The anxiety of religious people is that the room in the world for God is perceived as being ever-reduced – that God is being pushed to the boundaries and not allowed to be present at the centre.

The anxiety Bonhoeffer observes does not only lead to a reaction in terms of the way in which his own theology develops. Fundamentalisms of all varieties also respond to the same perceived problem.[23] Fearful that their 'God' is losing space in a dualistic battle of good and evil, fundamentalists seek to restore 'God' to a central position, a restoration which they believe is necessary for society to survive and morality to be retained. Anxious that 'God' may be losing power, a power struggle ensues between what is perceived as the secular and what is thought to be the power of God.[24] This serves to demonstrate the complex interdependence of fundamentalism and so-called secularization. As David Ford puts it: 'The pathologies of the religions are of course made worse by their mirror opposites in the secular sphere, as the extremes reinforce each other. Unwise, fundamentalist religious dogmatisms feed off unwise, fundamentalist secular ideologies, and vice versa.'[25] Put otherwise, perceived aggressive secularization which leads to a reduction in the perceived power of God in the world leads to the aggressive assertion of religion in a fundamentalist form, which in turn leads to the assertion of an even more fundamentalist and aggressive form of secularization, which in turn leads to a fiercer form of fundamentalism from

---

20. DBWE 8, 30 April 1944, 363.
21. Ibid., 30 April 1944, 366–7.
22. Ibid., 16 July 1944, 479.

23. For the relationship between fundamentalism and secularity, see Berger, 'The Desecularization of the World', who speaks of fundamentalism as '*counter*-secularization' and as 'counter-secularizing forces' (6–7).

24. To understand the relationship between fundamentalism (in its Christian form) and power, see Martyn Percy, *Words, Wonders and Power: Understanding Contemporary Fundamentalism and Revivalism* (London: SPCK, 1996).

25. David F. Ford, 'God and Our Public Life: A Scriptural Wisdom', *International Journal of Public Theology* 1, no. 1 (2007): 78. This point is put similarly by Martin: 'The religions and the secular are in one sense opposites but in another way intertwined. There is almost nothing regarded as religious which cannot also be secular, and almost no characteristic appearing in secular contexts which do not also appear in religious ones.' Martin, *The Religious and the Secular*, 3; cf. chap. 4.

the religious side, and so on. Secularization and religious fundamentalisms are therefore intertwined.

In an age of globalization, the anxiety that leads to an aggressive and reactionist reassertion of the power of God in the world by fundamentalists (and which in turn leads to reactionism by extremist forms of secularization) is exacerbated by a shift in power dynamics between religions. Whereas once those of another religion tended to be distant and exotic figures detached from normal day-to-day existence, a hundred years of vast improvements in transport and revolutions in communications determine that, even if the other religionist does not live next door, one is more than aware of her in the vast array of news carried to us from around the world through newspapers, television and the internet.[26] Far from a distant (and perhaps unimportant) figure, the religious other has become in recent times a real person who affects the communities and the world to which each of us belongs. Christians may not only feel they are losing ground to secularism but also that the space for their one particular religion in society is also shrinking in terms of the increased role other religionists are playing on both a national and international stage. This has led some groups to feel the need to reassert a definitive identity, usually underscored in teleological religions by definitive apocalyptic determinations which are all too readily associated with contemporary and existent communities. Thus, fundamentalism has grown as it has fed off and reacted to those who replace its eschatological world view with another – whether that be a future religionless society or an eschatology based on another religionist's perspective.[27]

Fundamentalism, therefore, I would argue, is not simply about literal approaches to texts.[28] In fact, given that a literal reading of any scripture as one single text leads to an ever-greater complexity in the hermeneutical process, fundamentalism (at least in its Christian variety, the form I know best) often involves a deeply complex approach to individual scriptural texts to bring about a unity of meaning within

---

26. The exception to this is Judaism as a diaspora religion, which has nevertheless in a different way contributed to the growing recognition of the pluralist society of which we are a part: the horrors of the Shoah determine that one cannot but recognize the importance of inter-faith commitments for a wise and civilized society.

27. This is not only the case for Christianity in Europe. One can also see this in the rise of Islamic fundamentalism (or fundamentalisms given its manifestation in a variety of forms), which arose in parallel to Christian fundamentalism but with the added dimension that most Muslim countries were under the direct or indirect control of colonial Western powers. See Ataullah Siddiqui, *Christian-Muslim Dialogue in the Twentieth Century* (London: Macmillan, 1997), 3–5; Youssef M. Choueiri, *Islamic Fundamentalism*, rev. edn (London: Cassell, 1997); and Youssef Choueiri, 'The Political Discourse of Contemporary Islamicist Movements', in *Islamic Fundamentalism*, ed. Abdel Salam Sidahmed and Anoushiravan Ehteshami (Boulder, CO: Westview, 1996), 22–4.

28. Nevertheless, literalism clearly is also an important factor as James Barr has pointed out. See James Barr, *Fundamentalism* (London: SCM, 1977), esp. chap. 3.

the multivocality of scripture. Within the Christian tradition, this often involves long discussions on such themes as dispensationalism, covenants, soteriology and millennialism (pre and post) in order to allow the literal reading to stand by virtue of a complex hermeneutical process.[29] The essence of fundamentalism is thus not merely a literal approach to texts but also a common belief that the deep mysteries of God are plainly and visibly obvious and given, and that one can draw a clear and definitive boundary around them: one can determine, for example, the eschatological determination of individuals and groups of people based on whether they are an insider or an outsider to one's own perspective; and the work, will and kingdom of God is patently clear for all who – being on the inside – have eyes to see.

Literal readings do not alone constitute fundamentalism, but a more general hermeneutic of identity formation vis-à-vis the world and others is constitutive of its nature. Rather than allowing God to speak to it through scripture, fundamentalism seeks, therefore, to speak on behalf of God and claims to know the mind of God. Fundamentalists do not understand themselves as speaking as religionists or as those speaking on behalf of their own or their religion's interpretation of God; they instead believe their view of God to be equivalent to God. Their historically relative interpretation assumes ultimate meaning and thus becomes 'radical' in Bonhoeffer's negative sense of the word. This determines that ironically, their religion (and not God) becomes their God. Drawing boundaries of identity around their religion so sharply, and thinking in binary terms of insiders and outsiders, fundamentalists begin to draw very clear boundaries around God. In that way, fundamentalism is a form of idolatry – an idolatry of imagining if not of imaging: to presume the position of God by imagining that one's own religious or theological community can deliver the judgement of God is in some way a sin of idolatry. It enforces a definition and limitation onto God and seeks to shackle God to that pre-decided and normative definition and space which God is allowed to occupy.

This is not to say that any speech about God is idolatrous, nor is it to say that any attempt at speaking on behalf of a religious community is an act of idolatry. It is to say that one cannot equate a community's interpretation of God's speech or of the nature of God with God's speech or with the exhaustive entirety of the nature of God. Our speech, our religious communities, our interpretations, our theology, our religion are always ours and therefore penultimate to the ultimacy of God.[30] The very Godness of God relativizes all speech about God to the realm

---

29. It is also worth noting that most Christian fundamentalists (excluding those who belong to what might be termed 'extra ecclesial' sects such as Latter Day Saints and Jehovah's Witnesses) hold orthodox beliefs in terms of Christology and the doctrine of the trinity, both of which are theological articulations on the church that arise from scripture but are not explicitly there.

30. The language of 'ultimate' and 'penultimate' here arises from reflection on Bonhoeffer's categories of the 'ultimate' and the 'penultimate' (albeit applied to different

of at best the penultimate. This is not to say that theologians must understand their existence as simply within the confines of relativism; nor is it to say that there is, therefore, no sense in speaking at all if all claims are only penultimate.[31] The penultimate is still the penultimate – in a unique relation to that which is ultimate. But this is only so *qua* penultimate. The penultimate is not the ultimate because in the end is God. Fundamentalism confuses this issue, making that which is penultimate ultimate by confusing theological speech with God in God's ultimacy. Put otherwise, as a response to what is perceived to be the reduced space for God, God is actually allocated space by fundamentalists – space in which they perceive God is.[32] The localizing of God to space is in essence the nature of idolatry – a confusing of God with the spatio-temporal limitations of the world (to which religion belongs).

Bonhoeffer's religionless Christianity

Where, then, does Bonhoeffer's religionless Christianity fit into all of this? Since, as I have stated, Bonhoeffer responds to the same anxiety to which fundamentalists also respond but in an entirely different and creative way, Bonhoeffer's response marks a helpful counterbalance to the excesses of Christian fundamentalism. Bonhoeffer's religionless Christianity offers tremendous promise in terms of the theo-political speech in an age in which the complex dynamics of secular-faith and inter-faith relations are all too evident: Bonhoeffer undermines the bad politics that arises from bad theology by cutting out the root of that bad theology. Moreover, Bonhoeffer's sketched response to these anxieties arises from scriptural reflection, which is the only ground on which fundamentalists (ostensibly at least) will allow debate. Bonhoeffer not only responds in helpful and creative ways to the same anxiety from which fundamentalists suffer, but he also responds on the same and the only basis that fundamentalists will allow – scripture. Let me present what I see as the promise of Bonhoeffer's work to today's age in three movements: a distinction between God and religion, a genuine understanding of God's sovereignty, and an inability to separate secular–religious concerns from inter-faith concerns.

---

areas of theological reflection) in DBWE 6, 146–70. Space does not allow a thorough going and detailed discussion of these terms.

31. One can also see this in Karl Barth. See Chapter 6 in this volume.

32. Or else, in other words, one might say that ironically by confusing the penultimacy of theological speech with the ultimacy of God, the fundamentalist is in terms of Bonhoeffer's ultimate–penultimate distinction, the 'radical' with disdain for creation and for the *Inneren Wesensgesetze* which pertain in the penultimate world. This is not only hermeneutically problematic but also for Bonhoeffer contrary to the very nature of the incarnation. See DBWE 6, 146–70.

Distinction between God and religion

In response to the sort of definitions of fundamentalism I have offered above, religionless Christianity provides a great resource in its simultaneous consideration of God and religion.[33] Bonhoeffer is useful in countering aggressive fundamentalist assertions of so-called 'God' over and against secularism or other religions because of his refusal to allow the religionist to confuse her religion (which can only ever be penultimate) with God (who is ultimate). The 'God of the Bible' is only allowed genuine space when the world has 'eliminat[ed] a false notion of God'.[34] God in Godself is not rejected; that which is rejected is the *deus ex machina*, or 'God' as a working hypothesis.[35] What Bonhoeffer disallows is any confusion of God with so-called 'God' – any confusion of religious articulations of God with God in Godself. Bonhoeffer, I would argue, rejects any notion that theological questions about God are synonymous with historical questions about the development of religion or religious speech: the death of the 'God' of religion in the 'world come of age' allows the theologian to engage in articulating the God of the Bible, the God of the whole person. Even if those attempted religionless articulations of God fall prey to the same failings as religious articulations of God (as perhaps they inevitably will), they will at least do so with the recognition and suspicion of that failing, and thereby guard against any confusion of God with so-called 'God': their great achievement will not be articulating a religionless doctrine of God but recognizing the dangers and failings of confusing their viewpoints about God and God's action in the world with God in God's ultimacy.

Bonhoeffer's reflections on the Old Testament in December 1943 may help to unpack this.[36] In his discussions of the Old Testament, Bonhoeffer points briefly to the unutterability of the name of God: 'Only when one knows that the name of God may not be uttered may one sometimes speak the name of Jesus Christ.'[37] Although not historically perhaps true, the unutterability of God's name by the Israelites is connected to Bonhoeffer's concerns about religion and the inability to limit the conception of god to even linguistic conceptualizations: 'I will definitely not come out of here as a *homo religiosus*! Quite the opposite: my suspicion and fear of "religiosity" have become greater here than ever. That the Israelites *never* say the name of God aloud is something I often ponder, and I understand it increasingly better.'[38] The revelation of this name to Moses is a revelation which

---

33. Albeit the definition of religion is one which is not formed sociologically but theologically.

34. DBWE 8, 16 July 1944, 479.

35. Ibid.

36. DBWE 8, Second Sunday in Advent [5 December 1943], 213–14. This is prior to the 1944 shift to Bonhoeffer's mature thinking on religionlessness. See, for example, Wüstenberg, *A Theology of Life*, 59.

37. DBWE 8, Second Sunday in Advent [5 December 1943], 213.

38. DBWE 8, 21 November 1943, 189.

simultaneously reveals and shrouds God.[39] This is evident in the very enigmatic nature of the name in response to Moses' request that God name Himself.[40] This point is not to deny the particularity of the God of the Bible – a particularity which is more than evident in God's identifying Godself as 'the God of Abraham, Isaac and Jacob' and in God's promise that God will be with this people, and in the narrative that follows this event.[41] This is no generalized notion of deity; this is the LORD, the God who is made known in the history of a particular people, and this new revelation to Moses indicates a 'subtle and complex blend of both continuity and discontinuity' with the stories that have preceded it.[42] This is a particular God, on whom the penultimacy of our theological speech can reflect in a way which is uniquely penultimate; but this is simultaneously the God who cannot be grasped and idolized in our human imaginings as if those imaginings were ultimate as God is. The particularity and exclusivity of religious speech about God by religionists is upheld, and not reduced to the silence of mysticism or atheism, nor displaced by a bland lowest common denominator approach to religion as found in secular liberalism. But that very exclusivity is relativized not by an external pluralist mandate that requires all members of one religious tradition to recognize the validity of any other religious traditions but by the very nature and ultimacy of God.

But, still, what has this to do with fundamentalisms and unhelpful theo-politics? The unutterability of God's name as a concern for Bonhoeffer in his rejection of religion may provide some theological way of interpreting his belief that the coming of age of the world removes false notions of God and makes way for the God of the Bible.[43] The God of the Bible, the name of whom the Israelites never uttered, is a God who is not to be confused with the world of religion. This is not to say that God lacks His uniqueness or His particularity.[44] It is not to say that as a result of this, all paths to God are of equal validity. Rather, it is to say that religion (however highly it is viewed by religionists) is only ever penultimate to the ultimacy of God. There are no fundamentals, therefore, but only one fundamental – God. All that is

---

39. My thinking here owes much to Barth's dialectic of veiling and unveiling. See CD I/1, 162–86, 315–33.

40. Exod. 3.13-15. Similarly, the bush that is ablaze but does not burn up is an indicator of the event itself being enigmatic.

41. Exod. 3.12; 15-22; 6.3-8.

42. Moberly, *The Old Testament of the Old Testament*, 163.

43. DBWE 8, 16 July 1944, 479-80.

44. This is the case in theologies which look to a shared essence or core to religions. The unutterability of God's name is not synonymous with God being entirely unknown. It is in the history and narrative of the life of the Hebrew people, recorded in the Old Testament, that God makes Himself known as the God whose name is unutterable: the tension between the *kataphatic* and the *apophatic* must be maintained. Put otherwise, it is the God whose name is unutterable who is the Word that speaks and becomes flesh (Jn 1.1-14): God *reveals* Himself as the God whose name is unutterable.

seen to be fundamental other than God is at best only penultimate to His ultimacy. It may, as the penultimate, stand in a unique relation to God's ultimacy, but it is still only penultimate to God. However important our religion may seem, it is not ultimate, and to see it otherwise (to presume it is God) is to engage in idolatry, for in the end is not religion but God. God's very particularity and uniqueness is one in which our perception and speech about Him falls woefully short of His reality. That He cannot be fully named (either because there are names we do not know or because His name is unutterable) reminds us of this. In this way, theology is able to recognize God's genuine sovereignty, rather than this sovereignty being reduced to a false kingship manufactured by human creating. God is not delineated or imprisoned by our religion but allowed to be God, and allowed to reign.

Reclaiming the unutterability of God's name and the mystery of God's being, a mystery which is no ignorance but an ever-fuller shining glory, allows – in a suitably Lutheran turn of phrase – God to be God and not to be reduced to an element of humanity's religion. It prevents people of faith and theologians from second-guessing God and saves them from the sin of idolatry, an idolatry with enormous political implications. For in understanding the Godness of God, one is not allowed to confuse God with a space out of which He is being pushed. This means that religionists cannot define the places in which God is found in the world and aggressively push at the boundaries of the religious or secular other. Instead, the religionist is forced with Bonhoeffer to recognize the transcendence of God (however particularly conceived at least for each of the Abrahamic faiths) who is 'the beyond in the midst of our lives'.[45] For the monotheist, this is all the more acute, as there *is* only one God who cannot lose space to the world but is the creator, sustainer and providential guide of the world. This is surely what it means for the theologian of religionless Christianity to read the New Testament in light of the Old. When we do this, we are enabled to see ourselves for who we are before God: we are freed from our sovereignty over God, aware of our own idolatry and less anxious to locate the idolatry of the other. And in this, we are careful of fighting (in whatever way) for our space, as we are aware that to locate and assign to God a space is to make of God an idol.[46]

Genuine understanding of God's sovereignty

Secondly but relatedly, I wish to address the potential Bonhoeffer's reinterpretation of God's sovereignty has to aid unhelpful theological discourse, and the political implications that arise from it. While fundamentalisms seek to find God's power

---

45. DBWE 8, 30 April 1944, 367.
46. I am struck by Bonhoeffer's spatial language of identifying and locating boundaries for God and of reserving space for God in comparison to God's being at the centre (DBWE 8, 30 April 1944, 366–7). It is this thinking that underlies much of my thought in this paragraph.

in the world in visible forms which echo or mirror human power,[47] Bonhoeffer writes:

> God consents to be pushed out of the world and onto the cross; God is weak and powerless in the world and in precisely this way, and only so, is at our side and helps us. Matt. 8:17 makes it quite clear that Christ helps us not by virtue of his omnipotence but rather by virtue of his weakness and suffering![48]

Rather than battling against secularity, and – indeed in certain quarters – enacting violence in order to seek victory in this battle,[49] Bonhoeffer directs Christians to 'stand by God in God's own pain'; and it is this act which 'distinguishes Christians from heathens'.[50] He writes further that this is

> the opposite of everything a religious person expects from God. The human being is called upon to share in God's suffering at the hands of a godless world. ... Being a Christian does not mean being religious in a certain way. ... It is not a religious act that makes someone a Christian, but rather sharing in God's suffering in the worldly life.[51]

These ideas remove unhelpful theo-politics at root by undermining false presentations of the *theos*. They remove the instinct, so well articulated by the great anti-theologian Feuerbach, to see God as 'man writ large'.[52] God's power and sovereignty is not a grander version of human power and sovereignty, but a sovereignty which is evident and most sovereign in God's willingness to be weak.[53]

---

47. The reader is again referred to Percy, *Words, Wonders and Power*.
48. DBWE 8, 16 July 1944, 479. This idea is also echoed in the second and third stanzas of Bonhoeffer's poem 'Christians and Heathens', DBWE 8, 460–1.
49. This is not only considered in terms of terrorist acts but also in terms of such events as anti-abortion campaigns in the United States.
50. DBWE 8, 18 July 1944, 480; cf. DBWE 8, 461.
51. DBWE 8, 18 July 1944, 480.
52. See Ludwig Feuerbach, *The Essence of Christianity* (New York: Harper and Row, 1957). In his introductory essay in this volume, Karl Barth speaks of Feuerbach's benefit in highlighting the danger of theology becoming anthropology (xxi). This danger is perhaps all the more significant when the anthropology confused with theology is even confused with God (as can be the case in fundamentalisms).
53. As Barth puts it in CD IV/2, 86:

> The sovereignty of God dwells in His creaturely dependence as the Son of Man, the eternity of God in His temporal uniqueness, the omnipresence of God in His spatial limitation, the omnipotence of God in His weakness, the glory of God in His possibility and mortality, the holiness and righteousness of God in His adamic bondage and fleshliness – in short, the unity and totality of the divine which is His own original essence in His humanity.

Against the idols of our own imagining, Bonhoeffer seeks theologically to open up a way 'to see the God of the Bible, who gains *ground and power* in the world by being powerless'.[54] Thus, our reading of scripture should be a reading of scripture before God in His ultimacy, and not a reading of scripture to justify our religious existence, power or standpoint. Over and against fundamentalisms, Bonhoeffer offers a different reading which forces us to be critical of the religious presuppositions brought to the text, and to engage the hermeneutic of suspicion back towards ourselves. The point is not that we should not bring presuppositions to the text (how could we do other?), but that we should recognize these presuppositions and allow the text to contradict them. This is no neutral, context-free reading of scripture; this is reading scripture before the LORD whose ultimacy is pointed towards in the text, and whose ultimacy undoes our claimed knowing as God does.[55] Rather than an external liberalism or pluralism devaluing the text's uniqueness and call to the religionist (a pluralism which in itself leads to more aggressive forms of fundamentalism), it is the very God pointed to in the text who cannot be confused with our religious speech about God. Scripture relativizes the confidence with which the theologian can speak of God because scripture is not the LORD but points to the LORD who is not only within but also beyond the text itself. Put otherwise, the Bible will not allow fundamentalism as the Bible relativizes the Bible before God. It may still be the closest we can come to exceeding penultimate statements about God (I am not lessening its unique status), but it nevertheless belongs to that penultimacy and should not be confused with God. There must be no idolatry, not even biblio-idolatry. This reading of scripture takes on fundamentalism on its own terms with a more fundamentalist approach to the Word of God: it seeks the true God, the LORD, who is the God not confined within the Bible but is the God *of* the Bible, and it is suspicious of its own temptation to desire sinfully, as did Adam and Eve, to know as God knows. This message is the still, small voice of calm within an age that includes the earthquakes of acts of terror supposedly carried out on behalf of God, but at best only ever on behalf and at the behest of an idol.

Inability to separate secular-religious concerns from inter-faith concerns

Bonhoeffer's consideration of religionless Christianity paradoxically directs us at once to the inseparability of God and religion, and to the distinction of God from religion. His theological imperative and prophetic telling forth of religionless Christianity directs Christians to recognize the religious garments we wear and to seek to purge ourselves of them. It recognizes that our expression of God is and has been clothed in religion. But it simultaneously recognizes that God and His Word cannot be confused with a particular stage in human religious evolution: 'The Word of God does not ally itself with this rebellion of mistrust,

---

54. DBWE 8, 16 July 1944, 479–80, emphasis added.
55. This is the temptation involved in the original sin in Gen. 3.5.

this rebellion from below.'[56] Bonhoeffer advocates that Christian 'lives must be "worldly"'.[57] However, he does so because it is by this that the Christian can come to share in God's sufferings in the world.[58] Bonhoeffer's concern is to seek the right and fitting articulation of Jesus Christ today in light of religion, secularity and God. He realizes that any speech as a Christian about any one of these three themes involves consideration of the other themes. Moreover, Bonhoeffer refuses to accept any one definition of 'religion' (no doubt as part of his rejection of 'this rebellion from below'). As Wüstenberg helpfully advocates, Bonhoeffer's 'loose' understanding of religion forces one back to theological interpretations of religion rather than settling on one single sociological definition of the word.[59] Bonhoeffer determines that one must think theologically, that is, about God, when one seeks to interpret religion: his religionless Christianity is a Christianized version of the secular critiques of religion, and his concern is not for a sociological or anthropological exercise in defining terms but for a theological engagement in formative interpretation. Furthermore, while in seeking to speak of religionlessness Bonhoeffer determines that one should simultaneously think about God, about religion and about the secular, his drive towards religionlessness nevertheless also determines a recognition of the distinct nature of each of these three. There is a symbiotic intellectual relationship between each of these ideas: religious speech presupposes God; the secular presupposes religion and so on. Clearly, there is both unity and distinction here, and I wish to advocate that this unity and distinction has three beneficial implications for inter-faith approaches, especially at a time of unhelpful political implications to theological speech.

Firstly, the recognition that one must not make an idol out of religion, and that God is not equivalent to religious speech about God (with all of the above provisos we have stated in terms of ultimates and penultimates) determines that the religionist at the inter-faith table, or any one religionist approaching any other, cannot presume to take the place of God (however uniquely or even exclusively one may conceive of one's God within one's own religion) in relation to any other.[60] Theological speech requires all the necessary humility that a recognition of the Godness of God should bring. In comparison to

---

56. DBWE 8, 8 July 1944, 457.

57. Ibid., 18 July 1944, 480.

58. Ibid., 18 July 1944, 480–2.

59. Wüstenberg, *A Theology of Life*, 159. For an example of this 'loose' definition of religion in Bonhoeffer, see DBWE 8, 30 April 1944, 362.

60. See Chapter 6 in this volume. Also of note is David Clough, 'Karl Barth on the Idolatry of Religion', in *Idolatry: False Worship in the Bible, Early Judaism and Christianity*, ed. Stephen C. Barton (London: T&T Clark, 2007). Clough seeks to recognize the tension between Christian speech about God and idolatry by simultaneously emphasizing humility and faithfulness: Christian speech cannot give way to saying nothing or understanding itself as of equal validity to any other speech about God; nor can it proceed without recognizing the dangers of idolatry.

any other religionist, it may understand itself to be unique in its penultimate relationship to the ultimate, but – as a penultimate compared to an ultimate – it shares infinitely more in common with the speech of other religionists than it does with God.[61] Secondly, the symbiotic relationship between the secular and the religious determines that, in inter-faith relations, one is directed back to a recognition of the complexity of gathering as religionists in the twenty-first century, aware of the dynamics of secular-faith issues alongside inter-faith issues: religious people in our globalized world are confronted by both. Furthermore, as Christians we are confronted by other religions and secularity before God, and we must seek wisely how to live before God who is LORD of all the world and all history. Thirdly, Bonhoeffer's unwillingness to define religion by any one definition allows the possibilities of recognizing the need for multiple theological particularities in inter-faith relations.[62] This is not to state that the Christian involved in inter-faith dialogue should be a two-faced Janus. Rather, it is meant that any one-size-fits-all universal inter-faith approach is never sufficient.[63] Different religions have to deal differently with each other, and resourcing wise dialogue between religions will require rethinking for each community, situation, generation and religion.[64] These three helpful pointers to resourcing inter-faith dialogue (however telegrammatically they have been stated) are crucial to working against unhelpful theo-political articulations of God in the globalized political sphere.

61. I would wish to relate this idea of the notion of *creatio ex nihilo*. From a Christian perspective, there is infinitely more in common between religions as things belonging to creation (even if any one of those is understood uniquely in relation to each of the others) than there is between God and any one religion.

62. I owe much in my thinking here to friends in Scriptural Reasoning in the University (née Scriptural Reasoning Theory) and to the attentive care given by all involved to the particularities of each.

63. Here, I am rejecting each one of the generally accepted threefold typologies for theologies of the religions (exclusivism, inclusivism and pluralism). For a summary of these positions, see Gavin D'Costa, 'Theology of Religions', in *The Modern Theologians: An Introduction to Christian Theology in the Twentieth Century*, ed. David F. Ford, 2nd edn (Oxford: Blackwell, 1997).

64. For example, a Christian relating to a Jew is in a very different situation concerning issues such as supersession than a Christian relating to a Muslim; or else relationships between Abrahamic faiths might be resourced in a very different way to relationships between Abrahamic and non-Abrahamic faiths. For further philosophical reflection on the issues surrounding the particularities and difficulties in this type of dialogue, see Alasdair MacIntyre, *Whose Justice? Which Rationality?* (London: Duckworth, 1988). MacIntyre writes: 'There are no preconceptual or even pretheoretical data, and this entails that no set of examples of action, no matter how comprehensive, can provide a neutral court of appeal for decision between rival theories' (333).

Conclusion

In conclusion, Bonhoeffer's speech about secular interpretations of the Bible and religionless Christianity benefits a world of fundamentalisms precisely because in speaking of the 'secular' or the 'worldly' it leads us back to this world and to this age.[65] This is a world and an age which faces conflict between different unhelpful theo-political understandings of civilizations and religions. Bonhoeffer helps us to recognize the reciprocity of the 'inner' and 'outer' life for the '*whole*' person: our spiritual life and our life in the world are at once reciprocal and one, and we should live as Christians 'as much from … "outer" to … "inner" selves as from … "inner" to … "outer" selves'.[66] Not only should our faith affect the world, but the world must affect our faith. In an age in which there is unhelpful political rhetoric, incitements to hatred of the religious other and acts of mindless terrorism carried out supposedly in the name of God, the Christian cannot simply smuggle God into 'the very last, secret place'[67] but must speak of their faith in today's age with all of its globalized and theo-political problems in order to break the idols of our own creating. We must speak out because life is so central to the concerns of the Bible, just as it is to Bonhoeffer. We must speak out because, against the death and destruction that ultimately results from religious fundamentalism, in the words of Bonhoeffer, 'Jesus calls … not to a new religion, but to life.'[68]

---

65. This is a use of the word 'secular' in the literal sense of *saeculum* meaning this age or world.
66. DBWE 8, 8 July 1944, 457.
67. Ibid.
68. DBWE 8, 18 July 1944, 482.

Chapter 10

BEARING SIN IN THE CHURCH

Having discussed how Bonhoeffer's critique of religion and discussion of religionless Christianity guards the church against falling prey to religious and political fundamentalisms, the discussion can now turn positively to the action of God in putting humanity right with itself. How does God operate in a world of fallen ecclesio-political realities? To consider these issues in relation to Bonhoeffer's theology, it is necessary first to consider the nature of systematic theology itself. Systematic theology is a theological discipline which involves not only the rational explication of the Christian gospel through description, reflection and critique of the church's teaching but also the selective placement, arrangement and locating of doctrinal loci within the theological description offered. The arrangement of doctrines in the description is significant in the enterprise not only in terms of the presentational form of the doctrine offered but also in terms of the material dogmatic content. Within systematic theology it is possible always to have ultimate and immediate foundational *res* for different loci. Beginning with, let us say, the inner life of God as a foundation will determine that all other loci exist underneath or stem from this doctrine: one could imagine a doctrine of God's immanent life, leading to an account of God's economy and from there to an account of creation, Christology, reconciliation and so forth – each locus stemming from a previous intermediate *res* or directly from the ultimate foundational *res*.[1] Key here is this ordering and differentiation – the point that there are immediate foundational *res* and there is an ultimate foundational *res*. Here, in this example, the ultimate foundational *res* is the inner divine life, and we might consider that the other dogmatic loci have their foundation in this doctrine; but other doctrines which have their foundation in the ultimate foundational *res* might also become immediate foundational *res* for successive dogmatic loci. For example, the inner divine life is the ultimate foundational *res* for the external works of God, of which we might list creation, but creation itself might become the immediate foundational *res* for, let us say, theological anthropology, which in turn might become the immediate

---

1. We might think of Thomas Aquinas's *Summa Theologiae* in this way. Karl Barth's *Church Dogmatics* might be thought to take a foundation of Christology. Friedrich Schleiermacher's *Christian Faith* might be considered to have its foundation in a theology of human experience.

foundational *res* for accounts of sin and so forth: all of these doctrines have their ultimate foundational *res* in this scheme in the account of the inner life of God but may have successive immediate foundational *res* in other dependent loci.[2] The derivative doctrines will take a particular form materially by virtue of the structural dogmatic foundation on which they rest: having a particular dogmatic foundation will give a particular shape to the doctrine which exists underneath it. For example, a theological anthropology which has Christology as its immediate foundational *res* will produce a distinctive account of what it means to be human in comparison to an account of theological anthropology which has its immediate foundational *res* in the doctrine of creation. Similarly, an account of the person and work of Jesus Christ as a human will take a particular form and shape dependent on whether its immediate foundational *res* is theological anthropology, or the external operations of the divine life, or the doctrine of reconciliation and so forth; or dependent on whether it is itself the ultimate foundational *res* for the given system. All of this is to say that dogmatic topography matters: where a particular doctrine becomes the focus or foundation of theological thinking, it may well become a foundational *res* for other areas of dogmatic enquiry. By doing so, it will invariably shape the material form of the locus which has its foundational *res* in the more primordial doctrine. This account of the systematic task in theology clearly concerns primarily the order of derivation rather than the order of presentation, though we might think that in a mature account of theology, these two become one or can be seen as one (even if certain material derivations of doctrines receive only more explicit presentational statements in later work).

What has this abstracted engagement with the scientific task of theology to do with Dietrich Bonhoeffer? Within Dietrich Bonhoeffer's account of the Christian gospel and the Christian life, one might identify the ultimate foundational *res* of his theology as ecclesiology;[3] this may be a contentious claim, but I think it can be

---

2. Anna Williams sees this aspect of the task of theology as being related to the desire for coherence. On the interconnection of doctrines in relation to the issue of rational coherence, see A. N. Williams, *The Architecture of Theology: Structure, System, and Ratio* (Oxford: Oxford University Press, 2011), 4–6.

3. See Bonhoeffer DWBE 1, 141: one should 'start with the doctrine of the church'. Others have suggested different hermeneutical keys. For example, sociality has been offered in Clifford J. Green, *Bonhoeffer: A Theology of Sociality*, rev. edn (Grand Rapids, MI: Eerdmans, 1999); a theology of life has been offered by Ralf K. Wüstenberg, *A Theology of Life: Dietrich Bonhoeffer's Religionless Christianity* (Grand Rapids, MI: Eerdmans, 1998); reality as a key by André Dumas, *Dietrich Bonhoeffer: Theologian of Reality* (London: DBWE 1M, 1971) and Heinrich Ott, *Reality and Faith: The Theological Legacy of Dietrich Bonhoeffer* (London: Lutterworth, 1971); or freedom in Ann Nickson, *Bonhoeffer on Freedom: Courageously Grasping Reality* (Aldershot: Ashgate, 2002). Even those such as Nielsen who claim that Christology forms the centre of Bonhoeffer's theology nevertheless see Christology as existing surrounded by an 'ellipse' of anthropology and ecclesiology; see Kirsten Busch Nielsen, 'Community Turned Inside Out: Dietrich Bonhoeffer's Concept of the Church and of Humanity Reconsidered', in *Being Human, Becoming Human: Dietrich*

made. While Bonhoeffer's theology does not form a regular dogmatics offering a systematic account of the whole breadth and schema of Christian doctrine, as an irregular dogmatics it nevertheless follows from a foundational basis,[4] or else is at least a theology which is centred upon the theological account of the church. From a first doctoral dissertation on the theological study of the sociology of the church to final searching questions on the meaning of the church in a post-Christian era, Bonhoeffer's theology is resolutely and continuously ecclesiologically orientated, or better still ecclesiologically founded. Such an orientation and foundation determines that the loci which flow from and derive from Bonhoeffer's account of the church will take a particular form and have particular dogmatic content by virtue of the ecclesiological centeredness of the theological account offered. This shapes in interesting ways the doctrines which have their immediate derivative *res* in this ecclesiological account. This has material as well as presentation effects (effects on content as well as form) and determines that creative and new ways of thinking about derivative loci occur: thinking loci from the doctrine of the church has a material effect on dependent loci which are formed in different ways because of the dogmatic ultimate *res* and the subsequent intermediate immediate *res*.

In this chapter, I wish to examine the effect of this ultimate foundational *res* of ecclesiology on one (under-studied) area of Bonhoeffer's thought in which Bonhoeffer offers distinctive and creative accounts of Christian doctrine – his hamartiology. Given Bonhoeffer's ecclesio-centrism, the account offered of the doctrine of sin has a significantly corporate dimension, compared to accounts of sin which find their *res* (immediately or ultimately) in the doctrine of creation or human freedom, and so forth. Exploring this ecclesial effect on the materially derived doctrine of sin, the first section of this chapter will explore the individual and corporate nature of sin for Bonhoeffer, and Bonhoeffer's account of the way in which these interrelate. The nature of the fall as being separated from the community and choosing the life of an individual will be explored in the second section of this chapter; here, I consider what it means to speak of sin as 'horizontal' as well as 'vertical'. The third section seeks to understand the act of God, for Bonhoeffer, in putting right this horizontal disorder both internal to the church and in relation to the church's role in the world. A brief conclusion will seek to discuss what contemporary theology might take from Bonhoeffer on this topic and how the theme might further be explored.

Bonhoeffer and Social Thought, ed. Jens Zimmerman and Brian Gregor (Eugene, OR: Wipf and Stock, 2010), 91–2.

4. On regular and irregular dogmatics, see Barth, CD I/1, 275–87. Williams helpfully differentiates between two approaches to systematicity: one a 'reasonably comprehensive account of Christian doctrine, ordered locus by locus'; the other 'theological writing in which the treatment of any one locus indicates, at least in some measure, how it is informed by other loci or how it will itself determine the shape of others'. See Williams, *The Architecture of Theology*, 1–2.

The individual and corporate nature of sin

Bonhoeffer's account of original sin is one which recognizes both the individual and the corporate nature of sin. Rather than focusing primarily on the nature of the original sin and its effects, Bonhoeffer recognizes the relationship between the culpability of the individual and the culpability of the entire race. In the classical Augustinian account, through Adam's turning away from God in the fall, the soul of the human is made chaotic and subject to perturbation. It is, for Augustine, the pride of the first human which is wholly the basis for his fall.[5] It is the character of the first sin which is the reason for its heinousness: it is worse than any other sin because Adam was nobler than any other subsequent (fallen) human. Indeed, such was the gravity of the first sin that it resulted in the ruin of the entire race (the *massa damnata*): sinful itself, the first sin propagates sinners. Through this first sin, humans have no freedom over their sinfulness. Augustine uses the analogy of the inherited disease to illustrate this: the disease has weakened humanity and cannot be cured by human agency. In Adam's fall, humans lost the power to do good because a permanent twist had occurred; and Adam lost the freedom of choice for the good because he could choose only one thing (for ill) and this had a universal effect which required God to put it right. Sinning, in a sense, becomes a natural thing for humankind, as Augustine sees in Adam a sin which flaws the very nature of the human; humans can no longer turn God-wards unaided by God and require God to enable them to do good, as a permanent change in human nature has occurred through corruption in sin. Thus, in Augustine it is possible to see a system of *inherited* sin as a result of Adam's fall.

For Bonhoeffer, the incapacity of humans to escape sinfulness (the universal quality of sin) is affirmed in classical Augustinian manner (as one would expect from a Lutheran).[6] But Bonhoeffer focuses particularly on individual humans' *cooperation* with and *participation* in the first sin (rather than primarily the inheritance of its effects): original sin is, for Bonhoeffer, corporate and something for which we are co-responsible. He writes:

> The culpability of the individual and the universality of sin should be understood together; that is the individual culpable act and the culpability of the human race must be connected conceptually. ... Everything obviously depends upon *finding the act of the whole in the sinful act*, without making the one the reason for the other.[7]

---

5. Augustine, *De Civitate Dei*, PL 41, 13–14; and *De Libero Arbitrio*, PL 32, 2–3.

6. On the relation of Luther to Augustine (and for very helpful accounts of the hamartiology of both Luther and Augustine), see Matt Jenson, *The Gravity of Sin: Augustine, Luther and Barth on* homo incurvatus in se (London: T&T Clark, 2006), chapters 1 and 2. On the relation of Bonhoeffer to Lutheran accounts of sin, see Michael P. DeJonge, *Bonhoeffer's Theological Formation: Berlin, Barth, and Protestant Theology* (Oxford: Oxford University Press, 2012), 121–8.

7. DBWE 1, 110–11, 115, emphasis original.

For Bonhoeffer the individual human participates fully in the act of Adam. This is a drawing out of a particular emphasis of Augustine's account of original sin, which points to the co-responsibility of every human being for human fallenness: we too are culpable in the sharing of our wills in Adam's willing. Augustine writes: 'All sinned in Adam on that occasion, for all were already identical with him in that nature of his which was endowed with the capacity to generate them.'[8] Although Augustine has a system of inherited sin passing like a disease from Adam through to all his descendants in humanity,[9] Augustine nevertheless also points to the reality that all human beings are identical with Adam,[10] though he leaves space for this to be further developed or explored. Bonhoeffer expands on and develops this tradition away from straightforward notions of inheritance. He writes, 'In *my* fall from God, humanity fell. … Before the cross, the debt of the I grows to monstrous size; it is itself Adam, itself the first to have done, and to do again and again, that incomprehensible deed – sin as act.'[11] One's own individual sin is the first sin, is original sin, for Bonhoeffer. The reason for this is that for Bonhoeffer each individual is connected to humanity as a whole.[12] There is not simply inheritance on display in this concept; instead, there is a *reciprocity* here. He continues:

> In this act, for which I hold myself utterly responsible on every occasion, I find myself already in the humanity of Adam. I see humanity in me necessarily committing this, my own free deed. As human being, the I is banished into this old humanity, which fell on my account. The I 'is' not as an individual, but always in humanity. And just because the deed of the individual is at the same time that of humanity, human beings must hold themselves individually responsible for the whole guilt of humankind. … I myself am Adam – am I am humanity in one. In me humanity falls. As I am Adam, so is every individual; but in all individuals the one person of humanity, Adam, is active.[13]

Bonhoeffer's account of original sin is a *corporate* account in Adam – an account of human co-responsibility which develops the Augustinian account and moves away from notions of sin as inherited towards the participation in and culpability of all individual humans in the first sin, and the first sin's participation and responsibility in any individual sin. The hamartiology here is concerned with the corporate and the individual in relation to the corporate: there is no capacity to separate Adam from other individuals or other individuals from Adam; the

---

8. Augustine, *De Peccatorum Meritis et Remissione et de Baptismo Parvulorum*, PL 44, 3.14.
9. See Karl Barth's critique of inheritance, CD IV/2, 501–12.
10. Bonhoeffer relates this to Luther (see DBWE 2, 147–8), but Luther himself, a former Augustinian monk, draws upon the tradition of Augustine for it.
11. DBWE 2, 146.
12. See Nielsen, 'Community Turned Inside Out', 96–7.
13. DBWE 2, 146.

human being is understood in her fallenness in Adam as identical with Adam and fully responsible not only for her own sin but also for the sin of all human beings. This corporate effect is a result of the immediate theological *res* of Bonhoeffer's account of the doctrine of sin finding its locus within an account of the church. The topography of the doctrine shapes its form and determines its content.

Let me explain what I mean. The metaphysical underpinning for this manoeuvre lies in Bonhoeffer's theological ontology of 'being in'. For Bonhoeffer, the essence of humanity is found not in an independent metaphysics of humanity but in a genuine *theological* account of human ontology.[14] For him:

> There is no ontological specification of that which is created that is independent of God being reconciler and redeemer, and human beings being sinners and forgiven. In the Christian doctrine of being, all metaphysical ideas of eternity and time, being and becoming, living and dying, essence and appearance must be measured against the concepts of the being of sin and the being of grace or else must be developed anew in light of them.[15]

The prior knowledge that there is no humanity independent of being in Adam or being in Christ establishes the theological anthropological ontology necessary for the individual and corporate understandings of sin that Bonhoeffer gives. For Bonhoeffer, this point about ontology is a fundamental distinctive of Protestant theology compared to Roman Catholic theology. Any account of metaphysics based upon an account of being in creation, rather than being in Adam and sin, leads, according to Bonhoeffer, directly to the *analogia entis* and a pure metaphysics of 'being'. Instead, for Bonhoeffer, the human is either in Adam (in sin) or in Christ (in the church): 'The human being only "is" in Adam or in Christ, in unfaith or in faith, in Adamic humanity and in Christ's community.'[16] There is no humanity apart from these two communities – the community of Adam (of sin) and the community of Christ (which is concretely the church).[17] Clearly, the church continues to sin and fall (and exists within the *communio peccatorum*),[18] but humans do not exist independent of the community of which they are a part; and the ontology of both individual humans and all humanity must be thought of in relation to the *community* of Adam or of Christ. Adam and Christ are both in one sense corporate persons [*Gesamptperson*].[19] Again, this account flows from the ecclesial (community) *res* of the account of humanity and sin offered.

There is, furthermore, an epistemic consequence of this claimed ontology: the order of being (as being in) affects the order of knowing, as this knowledge of

---

14. Ibid., 109.
15. Ibid., 151.
16. Ibid., 153.
17. Bonhoeffer: 'Being in Christ means being in the church'. Ibid., 199.
18. DBWE 1, 213.
19. DBWE 2, 111.

human ontology as 'being in' is known only in the context of being in Christ, that is, being in the 'corporate person of the Christian community of faith'.[20] It is only within the corporate context of the church that humanity can know itself as sinful and the individual know herself as a sinner. Since for Bonhoeffer, there is no independent metaphysics beyond the ontology of 'being in', and that reality is one that is only known theologically, true knowledge of who one is is only possible in relation to one's being in the life of the church. There is no knowledge of who one is outside of Christ, and outside of the church there is no knowledge of Christ: 'For only through the person of Christ can the existence of human beings be encountered, placed truth, and transposed into a new manner of existence. But as the person of Christ has been revealed in the community of faith, the existence of human beings can be encountered only through the community of faith.'[21] Or, as Luther puts it: 'sola fide credendum est non esse peccatores'.[22] The possibility of knowing one's own sin outside of the community of faith is itself (we might say) semi-Pelagian: it would mean that outside of the Gospel and faith one could know the truth of oneself by oneself. This consequence is not simply intellectual: the epistemic component of sin is as a result of the ontology of 'being in Adam'. For humans in Adam, knowledge begins and ends in themselves: pulling themselves away from God and the community of faith, they stand alone. That standing alone is in itself an untruth about human existence: it is a making of oneself lord and creator, a standing alone in a false belief in one's own individual identity.[23] Standing alone is the desire to be creator and creature all at once: 'Only in Christ,' writes Bonhoeffer, 'do human beings know themselves as God's creatures; in Adam they were creator and creature all at once.'[24] This theme is developed in *Discipleship* where Bonhoeffer is able to state arrestingly:

> Only those who are bound to Jesus in discipleship stand in complete truthfulness. They have nothing to conceal from their Lord. They live unveiled before him. Jesus knows them and places them into the truth. They are revealed as sinners before Jesus. They did not reveal themselves to Jesus, but as soon as Jesus revealed himself to them in his call, they knew themselves revealed in their sinfulness. Complete truthfulness emerges only from sin that is unveiled and forgiven by Jesus.[25]

---

20. Ibid.
21. DBWE 2, 114.
22. Luther, *Lectures on Romans*, in LW 25, 215.
23. DBWE 2, 137. There is a consequence here for homiletics. Clearly, the preaching of repentance is meaningful only within the community of the church, as a second manoeuvre, after the sinner has been met by Christ in the community.
24. DBWE 2, 151.
25. DBWE 4, 131.

Yet, this relationship to Jesus is not possible without living in community with other people: the two cannot be prized apart. It is an untruth that one tells oneself outside of Christ not to recognize and confess oneself a sinner. This untruth is itself an aspect of the heart turned towards itself, and only turned outside of itself (in salvation, we may say) can it live in the community of Christ with other people: 'There is no truth toward Jesus without truth toward other people.'[26] In denying one's sinfulness and standing outside of community with Christ (known only in the community of the church), the human does not know herself and corrupts her own being from one of relationality towards others to one of self-preservation over and against others. This standing alone aside from the community is in itself a horizontal component (and not merely consequence) of the fall. It is to this we now turn.

Horizontal sin: The individual separated from the community

For Bonhoeffer, the sinful act is not simply a disruption of the divine–human relationship but a fundamental altering of the human in Adam such that the person ceases to be a person in relation and instead believes that personhood is an individual standing alone. Thus, the vertical fallenness (humanity in relation to God) and the horizontal fallenness (humans in relation to one another) are both two sides of the same coin: in the fall humans cease to be persons in relation and become those whose hearts are turned in on themselves. Bonhoeffer is able to write, therefore,

> Community with God by definition establishes social community as well. It is not that community with God subsequently leads to social community; rather, neither exists without the other. ... With their act of disobedience against God ... [a] rupture has come into the unbroken community. Losing direct community with God, they also lose – by definition – unmediated human community. A third power, sin, has stepped between human beings and God, as between human beings themselves.[27]

Given Bonhoeffer's ecclesially orientated theological foundation as the ultimate *res* of his theological thought, the connection between divine–human and human–human relationality cannot be prized apart, as both belong within an account of theology which stems from an account of the life of the church. Sin is not about a single individual's relationship with God which has consequences for her relationship with other humans: sin is about the alteration of human beings such that we cease to be orientated eccentrically and relationally and become orientated interiorly and individually.

26. DBWE 4.
27. DBWE 1, 63.

For Bonhoeffer, the *cor curvum in se* determines that humans are pulled away from community – both from God and other humans – and 'stand alone' in solitude.[28] Humans have rent themselves away from God and each other and continue to defend themselves and decide for themselves. This is a theme which Bonhoeffer develops in *Creation and Fall*. In seeking to remove his limits by disobeying God and seeking to be like God, Adam finds himself alone in his desire to be his own god, his own creator: in this Adam seeks to lose his creaturely identity.[29] But this rejection of creatureliness is not only a rejection of God but also a rejection of the relationality which comes from God: it is a bounding of oneself to oneself and one's own limits, having rejected the limits placed upon one by God; it is a stepping out of relationship and a stepping into individualism. The fall, therefore, is horizontal as much as it is vertical since Adam and Eve exist not only in relation to God but also in relation to one another. Having been created from the rib of Adam, the violation that takes place towards God at the tree and the subsequent discussion of blame is at the same time a violation of the other person.[30] What was a gift of God in the alterity and unity of the other becomes a perceived curse of God in division and seeking to place responsibility for the fall at the feet of the other. As the human is turned in on herself, the other exists not as gift but as a burdensome limit. Bonhoeffer writes:

> [Adam] no longer sees the limit that the other person constitutes as grace but as God's wrath, God's hatred, God's begrudging. This means that the human being no longer regards the other person with love. Instead one person sees the other in terms of their being over against each other; each sees the other as divided from himself or herself. The limit is no longer grace that holds the human being in the unity of creaturely, free love; instead the limit is now the mark of dividedness.[31]

This dividedness is symbolized in the act of the human in covering herself up: in the perceived shame of nakedness, the human recognizes her limited nature over and against the other.[32] The heart turned in on itself is not only a standing apart

---

28. DBWE 2, 137. See Jüngel:

> The Christian faith understands this ontic tendency towards self-grounding as *sin*. For faith, identity as self-identification is the mark of one who is losing him or herself. For according to faith's understanding of the matter, we never find ourselves in ourselves. In ourselves we cannot come to ourselves. We come to ourselves when we come to someone other than ourselves. (Eberhard Jüngel, *Theological Essays I*, trans. John Webster [Edinburgh: T&T Clark, 1989], 134)

29. DBWE 3, 115.
30. DBWE 3, 117–18.
31. Ibid., 122.
32. Ibid., 124.

as an individual in relation to God; it is also a standing alone in relation to other human beings. This is an idea which Bonhoeffer rehearses in *Sanctorum Communio*: 'With their act of disobedience against God, human beings realize their sexual difference and are ashamed before one another. A rupture has come into the unbroken community,'[33] writes Bonhoeffer. It is by losing their direct relationship with God that they lose their direct relationship with each other and the community is broken.

If sin is a life turned in on itself, then sin arises from altered human relationality, a relationality which now fails to be orientated not only towards God but also towards one another. We see this in Bonhoeffer's unpacking of the effect of the fall. Humans find themselves in solitude, and in this solitude, they cling to themselves and their own self-knowledge. This self-knowledge is untruthful and self-justifying or despairing in its form; Bonhoeffer names this 'conscience'.[34] This postlapsarian situation is a desperate one in which in their solitude humans find themselves hopeless in light of their limits and guilty in light of their conscience.[35] The turning in on the self produces an existence in which one cannot know one's reality in light of God and of others and in which we hide in our solitude from one another.

The intermediate dogmatic *res* for Bonhoeffer between his ecclesial-centric doctrinal foundations and his hamartiology is his concept of the person.[36] Altered personhood determines that humans no longer share in the divine form of personhood as that which exists in relation. Bonhoeffer is clear that 'Community with God by definition establishes social community as well.'[37] It is clear in his thought that the '*concepts of person, community, and God* are inseparably and essentially interrelated'.[38] For him, it is not that one is the subsequent creation

33. DBWE 1, 63.
34. DBWE 2, 139–41. For a further account of Bonhoeffer on conscience, see DeJonge, *Bonhoeffer's Theological Formation*, 118–27.
35. DBWE 2, 145–7.
36. My claim in dogmatic locatedness is the reverse of Nielsen, who states that Bonhoeffer's understanding of the church is influenced by his anthropology (including his hamartiology under this): I am wanting to argue that the distinctive flavour of his hamartiology stems from his ecclesial approach, which is the reason why there is a preoccupation with communal sin. The logical consequence of the influence of anthropology on the church does not necessitate either a relationality or a propensity to focus on the community; whereas the logical consequence of an ecclesial ultimate *res* (as I am arguing) would necessitate an anthropological account involving relationality and sociality, and an hamartiological account which focuses on the corporate as well as the individual. Nielsen herself, however, seems to reverse the doctrinal direction in her account of the movement from Bonhoeffer's ecclesiology to his anthropology, and then recapitulates it in the other direction once more. I am wishing to clarify the dogmatic topography in relation to these themes. See Nielsen, 'Community Turned Inside Out', 92–5.
37. DBWE 1, 63.
38. Ibid., 34, emphasis in original.

of the other (presumably, we would wish to add doctrinally, within the created order). He asserts: 'It is not that community with God *subsequently* leads to social community; rather, neither exists without the other.'[39] The basis for this claim is the personhood and relationality of God. For Bonhoeffer, 'God only "is" as the creator, reconciler, and redeemer, and that being as such is personal being.'[40] There is no independent divine metaphysics for Bonhoeffer out with the relationship of God to humanity: or else, we might say, there is (at least for humanity) no immanent trinity independent of God's divine economy.[41] As Bonhoeffer famously states in the second doctoral dissertation: 'There is no God who "is there" [*Einen Gott, den 'es gibt', gibt es nicht*]; God "is" in the relation of persons, and the being of God is God's being person [*das Sein ist sein Personsein*].'[42] This is something which accompanies Bonhoeffer throughout his theological career,[43] and to which he points later in his life in his suggestive *Letters and Papers from Prison* in his questioning and critique of metaphysical approaches to speaking of God.[44] For Bonhoeffer, personhood and sociality are concepts which are bound together. Human personhood arises from the gracious external operations of divine personhood; and each is known only in relationship to the other. Since the only God there is is God for creation only known in relation to creation, creation is also creation only in relation to the creator, reconciler and redeemer God.

To unpack what this means, it is useful to turn to Bonhoeffer's account of the likeness of God in humanity in relation to his account of the *analogia relationalis*.[45] Bonhoeffer yet again firmly rejects the *analogia entis* and affirms that the image of God in humanity is one based on an analogy of relationship. Although Bonhoeffer affirms divine aseity in the order of being (and by virtue of this differentiates God's being from human being), Bonhoeffer nevertheless points to God's relationship which he freely establishes with that which is not God in creation. Divine aseity

39. Ibid., 63, emphasis added.
40. DBWE 2, 153.
41. See Bruce L. McCormack on this. McCormack, *Orthodox and Modern: Studies in the Theology of Karl Barth* (Grand Rapids, MI: Baker Academic, 2008), 133.
42. DBWE 2, 115.
43. For more on this concept, see Green, *Bonhoeffer*, esp. 29–45.
44. Being for others is contrasted to 'conceptual forms of the absolute, the metaphysical', with the word metaphysical added later in the manuscript as a definitive addition, DBWE 8, 501. The metaphysical also comprises components of Bonhoeffer's critique of religion, ibid., 372. Indeed, Bonhoeffer asks the question: 'How do we talk about God – without religion, that is, without the temporally conditioned presuppositions of metaphysics, the inner life, and so on?', ibid., 364.
45. It is notable here that Bonhoeffer uses the idea of the likeness or analogy (*analogia*) and not directly the image of God. Classical theology has tended to suggest that humans lose the likeness but not the image of God; see for example, the *locus classicus* of Irenaeus, *Adversus haereses*, PG 7, 5.6.1 and 5.16.2 (though at other points Irenaeus is not quite so consistent).

protects the graciousness of God's relationality, but there can be no concept of God independent of God's free self-offering to humanity. Bonhoeffer writes:

> God – who alone has self-sufficient being in aseity, yet at the same time is there for God's creature, binding God's freedom to humankind and so giving God's self to humankind – must be thought of as one who is not alone, inasmuch as God is the one who in Christ attests to God's 'being for humankind'. The likeness, the analogia, of humankind to God is not analogia entis but *analogia relationalis*. What this means, however, is, firstly, that the *relatio* too is not a human potential or possibility or structure of human existence; instead it is a given relation, a relation in which human beings are set, a *justitia passiva*![46]

For Bonhoeffer, moreover, this likeness is not something which humans have in possession in and of themselves, but which they have only strictly in likeness from the prototype and which always points back to the prototype: '*Analogia relationalis* is therefore the relation which God has established, and it is *analogia* only in this relation which God has established. The relation of creature with creature is a relation established by God.'[47] This establishment finds its analogy in God's own freedom to be for another in creation based in the form of personhood the divine life has: a form of personhood which lives in relationality not only internally in the eternal trinity but also externally in the economy of grace – in creation, reconciliation and redemption. What we can see here is that the intermediate *res* of Bonhoeffer's doctrine of sin, based upon the foundational *res* of ecclesiology, is an account of divine personhood in external relationality which forms itself as an immediate foundational *res* of Bonhoeffer's theological anthropology through the *analogia relationalis* in his description of the divine likeness in humanity. The fall, therefore, relates to human relationality which is both vertical (centred upon God) and horizontal (centred upon other humans): one is not a consequence of the other, but both are a consequence of the altered fallen human ontology of being 'in Adam'. Being in Adam, and seeking to be one's own creator and god, the human is tempted to a life *in se* – a sinful replication of the divine aseity which fails to understand that the freedom of the divine life *a se* is not something which God has grasped and claimed for Godself, but something which only establishes the full graciousness of the God who, although He is free from creation, chooses in creation to be free for creation in the divine economy of salvation. It is only in relearning what it means to be a creature in light of Christ that the human can once again become human in the community of Christ, and be saved from the individualistic solitude that seeking to be *sicut deus* produces in its perverted attempt at the false replication of divine aseity. As Bonhoeffer puts it: 'To be in the centre and to be alone means to be *sicut deus*. Humankind is now *sicut deus*. It now lives out of its own resources, creates its own life, is its own creator; it no longer

---

46. DBWE 3, 65.
47. Ibid., 65–6.

needs the Creator.'[48] It is only an act of God which can rescue humanity from this desire to be as it considers wrongly and falsely God to be.

Horizontal salvation: Turning out towards the other

Existence in Christ is the only way in which the human is able to know herself as creature, and the only way in which she can be saved from the desire to be her own creator and a creature all at once. Existence in Christ is a salvific act of God's economy as the human moves from being 'in Adam' to, in the life of the church, being 'in Christ': 'The person *in se conversus* is delivered from the attempt to remain alone – to understand itself out of itself – and is turned outwards towards Christ.'[49] This turning out towards Christ involves gaining a new humanity found in Christ as the one 'for others'. Humanity being 'in Christ' regains its original created human form, regains the likeness of God in the *analogia relationalis*, through the work of Christ. For Bonhoeffer, the being and work of Christ is such that in Christ's human form, humanity finds its restored and renewed human form. Reversing the classical account of divine salvation which acclaims that God became human in order that humans might become like God,[50] for Bonhoeffer Christ takes human form in order that humans can become like Jesus in His humanity: God became human, we might say, so that humans might become genuine human creatures. For Bonhoeffer, salvation is by *anthroposis* not *theosis*. Bonhoeffer writes: 'In Christ's incarnation all of humanity regains the dignity of bearing the image of God. … In community with the incarnate one, we are once again given our true humanity.'[51] Through community with the incarnate one, humanity is saved from the individualized isolation of its uncreaturely inhumanity. This *anthroposis*, therefore, is one which allows the fulfilment of the *analogia relationalis* in mirroring the personhood of God as a personhood which exists in relationship and sociality – not in isolation, even though God's divine aseity determines that God is the only One who can live in and of Godself. Bonhoeffer continues in relation to human solitude: 'With [our true humanity given by Christ], we are delivered from the isolation caused by sin, and at the same time restored to the whole of humanity.'[52] Salvation is, for Bonhoeffer, in part a sharing in the corporate life of the whole of humanity. For him, 'the destruction of humanness is sin'.[53] In the reception of salvation, the Christian takes on the form of Christ, and the form of Christ takes form in human beings.[54] Christians live

---

48. Ibid., 115.
49. DBWE 2, 150.
50. See Athanasius, *De Incarnatione Verbi*, PG 25, para 54.
51. DBWE 4, 285.
52. Ibid..
53. DBWE 6, 157.
54. Ibid., 95–6.

in the world like anyone else and differ seemingly only little from those others who are 'in Adam'. The difference is that they are not individualized and isolated from others, concerned to promote themselves and their own individual ego; instead, writes Bonhoeffer, they are 'not concerned to promote themselves, but to lift up Christ for the sake of their brothers and sisters'.[55] Their life is not ordered to themselves but is ordered to Christ and through Him to others. As Bonhoeffer writes in *Act and Being*:

> Only through the person of Christ can the existence of human beings be encountered, placed into truth, and transposed into a new manner of existence. But as the person of Christ has been revealed in the community of faith, the existence of other human beings can be encountered only through the community of faith. It is from the person of Christ that every other person first acquires for other human beings the character of personhood.[56]

Christ, known in the community of faith, enables humans to be open in relationality to the personhood of other humans, and by this creates a new existence for the believer who now has an ontology 'in Christ'.[57]

This life in Christ is experienced and known concretely in the church, and it is in the church that the forgiveness of God is found. The mechanism for forgiveness is confession, but even confession, for Bonhoeffer, has an immediate *res* in ecclesiology. Confession is not an individual's engagement with God apart from the community, since sin is itself corporate. Confession involves the community and is a breakthrough of community. As Bonhoeffer writes in *Life Together*, 'In confession there takes place a *breakthrough to community*. Sin wants to be alone with people. It takes them away from the community. The more lonely people become, the more destructive the power of sin over them.'[58] Sin in its individualism wants to hide, to be alone to be in darkness. It, therefore, needs to be exposed and to have light shone on it. This exposure is by necessity ecclesial: it involves there being others in front of whom this exposure can take place, individuals who can be present as a gift to overcome the solitude and hiddenness of sin. In public confessing, sin is taken away from the individual and is exposed to the community; as such its individualizing power, which tears the individual away from community, is undermined. In Bonhoeffer's words:

> Sin that has been spoken and confessed has lost all of its power. ... It can no longer tear apart the community. Now the community bears the sin of the individual believer, who is no longer alone with this evil but has 'cast off' this

---

55. Ibid., 95.
56. DBWE 2, 114.
57. 'Christ is the *Kollektivperson* of the new humanity, superseding Adam as the *Kollektivperson* of the old humanity.' Green, *Bonhoeffer*, 53.
58. DBWE 5, 110.

sin by confessing it and handing it over to God. The sinner has been relieved of sin's burden. Now the sinner stands in the community of sinners who live by the grace of God in the cross of Jesus Christ. Now one is allowed to be a sinner and still enjoy the grace of God. We can admit our sins and in this very act find community for the first time. The hidden sins separated the sinner from the community and made the sinner's apparent community all a sham. The sins that were acknowledged helped the sinner to find true community with other believers in Jesus Christ.[59]

To confess sin means that the individual joins a community of confession, in which individuals confess sins *to one another*. It is in this community that one finds forgiveness because by acknowledging and confessing our sin before one another, the human is enabled to participate in a community and by that is freed from her individualized solitude in which by her conscience she attempts to adjudicate her sinful standing herself and yet in that finds her guilt. In the act of confessing publicly, Christians are joined in solidarity to one another in the church.

There is a subjective and objective component to this act of confession and the forgiveness which flows from it. Firstly, subjectively, so long as Christians confess their sins to each other, there is no way in which the Christian can feel alone anywhere.[60] Bonhoeffer unpacks this idea from *Life Together* in his Finkenwalde material, which formed the basis of his later book. In this, confession before others means that for us subjectively God is not a phantom who makes us *feel* as though we are forgiving our own sins by ourselves. Public confession means that our sins are brought into the open and that the pride which is the root of sin is in public confession before others uncovered such that we are made to feel small. From this smallness we are enabled to surrender entirely to the mercy of God, and in this surrender and joint confession, there emerges the creation of fellowship. For Bonhoeffer, we are not alone in our confession.[61] It is not that the church qua church releases people from their personal confession of guilt: the church does not give absolution; only Christ judges and restores humanity. But in confessing guilt together, the church draws people into a community of confession.[62] This, in itself, overcomes the fall – taking away the human's covering over of sin, sense of blame, individual conscience and solitude.

Secondly, objectively from this, forgiveness is not only given existentially to the believer through the words 'I am forgiven' but also objectively in the life of the community. The believer may know forgiveness only in the life of the community through the practices of the community in word and sacrament:

---

59. Ibid.
60. DBWE 5, 111.
61. DBWE 14, 593–4.
62. DBWE 6, 142.

The community of faith really does have the word of forgiveness at its disposal. In the community faith the words 'I am forgiven' can be spoken not merely existentially; as the Christian church, the congregation may declare in sermon and sacrament that 'you are forgiven'. Through such proclamation of the gospel, every member of the church may and should 'become a Christ' to the others.[63]

Furthermore, it is not simply that *my* hearing and reception of forgiveness is grounded in the individual self even in the context of the community. It is the church *qua* church which hears and receives forgiveness *and* the individual within the life of the church, that is, the individual whose being is 'in Christ'. This is what preserves the *being* of forgiveness vis-à-vis the *act* of forgiveness in time and space. The words of forgiveness are proclaimed and heard *in the community of faith*, that is, in the community of Christ. Continuity of human reception of forgiveness does not stem, therefore, from any individual state of faith or existential individualism or subjective identity but from the word of the gospel addressed to, heard in and proclaimed by the church. In Bonhoeffer's words, 'The continuity does not lie in human beings, but rather it is guaranteed suprapersonally [*überpersönlich*] through a community of persons.'[64] The reception of forgiveness by the community in Christ, one could say, is in part an overcoming of the solitariness of the guilt and conscience of the human in Adam.

This corporate sin and confession is itself expanded to a confession and acceptance of guilt by the church on behalf of the whole world. The internal ordering of individuals towards the other in the church is replicated in its community orientation corporately in an external ordering towards the world. Just as the individual confesses sin in the context of the church, and through the church is ordered towards another (becomes, we might say, a true person), so the church as the individual corporate community of Christ is ordered towards the world and its sin. This outwards, relational orientation is not simply something which the individual has in relation to the corporate identity of the church, but something which the church has corporately in relation to the whole world. The church has a vicarious role in accepting the sin of those outside of the church. This idea clearly relates to the sharing of the individual's sin in original sin: we are all co-responsible for the sin in the world and in the church's confession of its members' own sins, it must also confess the sin of the world to which it has contributed. In his provocative *Ethics*, Bonhoeffer writes:

> With this confession [*mea culpa, mea culpa, mea maxima culpa*] the whole guilt of the world falls on the church, on Christians, and because here it is confessed and not denied, the possibility of forgiveness is opened … for there are people here who take all – really all – guilt upon themselves, not in some heroic self-sacrificing decision, but simply overwhelmed by their very own guilt toward

---

63. DBWE 2, 112–13.
64. Ibid., 114.

Christ. In that moment they can no longer think about retributive justice for the 'chief sinners' but only about the forgiveness of their own great guilt.[65]

Even in the church there is a contribution to the sin of the world in the church's continued sinfulness as the sins of those who previously had been in Adam and now find themselves in Christ. In recognition that to calculate or weigh sin is in and of itself fallen, part of the individual's activity of conscience and self-justification (a result of eating from the tree of the knowledge of good and evil), genuine admission of guilt 'no longer calculates and argues, but which acknowledges my sin as the origin of all sin, as, in the words of the Bible, the sin of Adam'.[66] We require the other to be forgiven, indeed, as we have the power to excuse every other sin but our own, and concomitantly we too require the other to be excused. Furthermore, the church as Christ existing as community shares in the work and power of Christ in accepting vicariously the sins of those outside of the community which exists in Christ.[67] Brought together in Christ's forgiveness in the collective I [*Gesamtich*] of the church, the church confesses and acknowledges its guilt in and through the rest of the world. The nexus of sin 'in Adam', in the individual, community and world determines that there is an ecclesial and relational component to forgiveness as well. Sin and forgiveness are not simply about the individual in relation to God but also simultaneously and resultantly about the individual in relation to others in the church, and the church in relation to the rest of the world.

Conclusion

For Bonhoeffer, theological thought finds its ultimate foundational *res* in the doctrine of the church. His thought in other areas of theology has its locatedness in relation to this ultimate *res* of ecclesiology. This approach to the system of systematic theology shapes subsequent and dependent loci which emerge from this ultimate and the intermediate immediate dogmatic *res*. Bonhoeffer's hamartiology takes a distinctly corporate and ecclesial focus as a result. The doctrine of sin that Bonhoeffer produces is one which explores more fully than most the horizontal nature of sin, but distinctively from social gospel accounts of corporate sin, Bonhoeffer offers a determinedly biblical and classical account of original sin:[68] the key distinctive for Bonhoeffer is the nature of the church and the effect of thinking about the church on the dogmatic locus of hamartiology.

But what does this mean for theology today? On a meta-level in terms of the nature of doctrinal thought, Bonhoeffer offers us an important lesson. Clearly,

---

65. DBWE 6, 136.
66. Ibid., 137.
67. Ibid., 135.
68. On Bonhoeffer's criticism of social gospel accounts of sinfulness, see DBWE 12, 241–2.

there are different ways of accounting for each locus depending on the differing foundational and immediate *res* that one offers for dogmatics. Or else, we might suggest different irreducible narratives of the Christian faith and life,[69] and the theologian is wise to explore how dogmatic locatedness and topography in relation to immediate and foundational *res* affect individual loci. Bonhoeffer may help us to learn that thinking of doctrines from different loci as immediate or foundational *res* may create a plurality of accounts of doctrines and may help us both recognize the descriptive and critical task of systematic theology as well as the possibility for new and creative ways of thinking rationally about the gospel, which can never be reducible to a single system.

On a micro (or locus-specific) level, thinking with Bonhoeffer on the corporate nature of sin, we might be prepared to say that what Bonhoeffer makes plain for Magisterial Protestant believers is what it means in a deeply Protestant setting to speak of the church as salvific: or, in more classical theological terms, to claim that *extra muros ecclesiam nulla salus est*.[70] To be in the church is to be in Christ and to have a distinctive ontology. Realizing the horizontal as well as the vertical nature of sin makes the church a genuine act of the salvation of God as in the church we are given forgiveness and restored to true humanity as a humanity not ordered to the self but to others.

Should we, then, simply repeat Bonhoeffer's findings uncritically? Here, I am not so sure as a theologian, and especially as one interested in ecclesiology. Bonhoeffer opens interesting and exciting avenues, but mere repetition does not do justice to his thought: to be a true student of Bonhoeffer is surely to learn from him and respond to him, to take his promise and think along with and beyond it.[71] Thinking beyond Bonhoeffer, there are questions to be asked about the role of the Spirit in his account. Recognizing that (despite caricatures to the contrary) Bonhoeffer does talk about the Spirit (especially in terms of actualization), does locating the church so closely with the person of Christ risk the danger of reducing the particularity of the historical person, Jesus, and the once-for-allness of the cross and resurrection? Might contemporary theology, drawing from Bonhoeffer, wish to deepen an account of the Spirit to unpack the way in which the church is Christ existing as community – a church which is such as the Spirit enables it to participate in, encounter and be transformed by the Living Lord Jesus? Perhaps for Bonhoeffer, the foundational *res* of ecclesiology requires being founded upon the divine person who creates and sustains the church, and either a more foundational *res* of pneumatology is needed or an intermediate *res* of pneumatology should be

---

69. The notion of irreducible narratives is borrowed from David Kelsey, *Eccentric Existence: A Theological Anthropology* (Louisville, KY: Westminster John Knox, 2009).

70. Cf. Brendan Leahy, '"Christ Existing as Community": Dietrich Bonhoeffer's Notion of Church', *Irish Theological Quarterly*, 73, nos. 1–2 (2008): 41.

71. This parallels Barth's account of the way in which students of Calvin should learn from Calvin; see Karl Barth, *The Theology of John Calvin* (Grand Rapids, MI: Eerdmans, 1992), 1–10.

offered in relation to how the church is 'in Christ'. Either way, there is much to be learned and developed from Bonhoeffer's understanding of the corporate and ecclesial nature of the way in which we should think of sin and the way in which God in His grace offers humans salvation, especially within the Protestant and more particularly Pietistic communities. How Bonhoeffer understands God to do this work of reconciliation in Christ is explored in the next chapter in relation to Bonhoeffer's understanding of the priestly community of the church.

Chapter 11

PRIESTLY MEDIATION IN THE CHURCH

Dietrich Bonhoeffer is not a theologian who immediately springs to mind if one were to ask about a theology of priestly mediation. Standing in the Lutheran tradition (though with significant ecumenical commitments), Bonhoeffer could be excused for a lack of concern on priesthood. Luther attacked the idea that the priesthood of Christ is transferred to the apostle Peter, and then on to the succession of popes.[1] In his 'The Freedom of the Christian', Luther discusses the priesthood of Christ and relates this to believers in the church, and it is here that we begin to find the classical Protestant doctrine of the priesthood of all believers.[2] For Luther, the priesthood of Christ is related both to his status as first born and the discussion in Hebrews about Melchizedek. The meaning of this is unpacked in two ways – in relation first to prayer and intercession, and second to instructing in the word. It is participation in these acts which then determines the priesthood of each member of the church. Priestliness is not a quality that belongs only to a particular *clerus* and, indeed, other possible forms of priestly action beyond teaching and prayer are not discussed.

Bonhoeffer, however, took this Lutheran approach to priesthood further. In one sense, he was entirely uninterested in priesthood as an operative theological category of significance. Not only do his Christology lectures have little concern for Christ as priest, but he even displays a lack of formal interest in the priesthood of all believers. This is a doctrinal commitment which hardly appears within Bonhoeffer's corpus, though he assented to it. His main discussion of the doctrine comes in *Sanctorum Communio*. In one sense, Bonhoeffer's use here is classical, in that he used the doctrine polemically to differentiate Lutheran forms of polity from other forms:

> In the Protestant church there is no theurgy, and no magical authority invested in the office or its bearers. The concept of the *priesthood of all believers* is merely another way of expressing this. The reality off the church-community, which has only one head, namely Christ, protects us from the idea of a spiritual-earthly

---

1. Martin Luther, 'Proceedings at Augsburg' (1518), in LW 31, 279–81; cf. LW 31, 388–9.
2. On the priesthood of Christ in Luther, see LW 31, 353–4.

head, which, as Luther aptly states, cannot exist because he (that is, the pope) obviously would not know those whom he was governing.[3]

In contrast to this, Bonhoeffer affirmed the more Lutheran account of office in relation to the ordering of the assembly around word and sacrament. He also offered some discussion of the priesthood of all believers in relation to the rule of the Word of God over the church: because of the priesthood of all believers, 'No empirical body "in itself" can claim to have authority over the church-community. Every claim derives from the word.'[4] Other than these uses in terms of polity, more theologically, Bonhoeffer does see the doctrine as a means to affirm the 'invisible' equality of Christians and the 'concrete dissimilarity of individuals'.[5]

Despite this seeming lack of interest in priestliness, Bonhoeffer was the head of an illegal seminary to train ministers for the Confessing Church and gave lectures on Christology. Is it simply the case, therefore, that Bonhoeffer ignored the issues relating to the priestliness of Christ and of all believers, and the representative function of the minister in relation to this? How did Bonhoeffer, and how should those who follow after him, deal with the material in the Bible that addresses the priestly tradition – in relation to Israel, the temple, Christ and the church? Certainly, elements of Christ's work as priest are picked up in Bonhoeffer's Christology lectures in relation to Christ's work as mediator. However, I will argue that the primary way in which Bonhoeffer construes priestliness is in relation to certain motifs associated with mediation focused on his theological approach to the church. There is a symbiotic twofold relationship in this. Firstly, the priestliness of the church is felt internally: Christ establishes a mode of sociality in the church which arises from mediation not only between God and humanity but also between human beings and other human beings; this is part of Christ's salvific work. Secondly, there is an external relationality which is established between the church and the world, whereby in Christ, the church shares in the task of vicarious representative responsibility for the world. This bears the hallmarks of priestliness. Priesthood is an identity held collectively in the church as the person of Christ in the world today, rather than being a quality possessed by individuals, whether for all Christians or merely some.

Christ as the human-to-human priestly mediator of community

Mediation is a central concern of priesthood throughout scripture. The priest in scripture mediates between God and humanity, placing himself in the space where the two meet in sacrifice (Exod. 28–29; Lev. 8–11). This mediation on behalf of God to humanity and on behalf of humanity to God is one which is fulfilled and (in a

---

3. DBWE 1, 236.
4. Ibid., 266.
5. Ibid., 206–7.

way which is difficult for a post-Shoah setting) superseded in Christ's priesthood, which itself is grounded in a more ancient form of priesthood, in relation to the order of Melchizedek (Heb. 7.17). Christ is both high priest and perfect sacrifice:

> But when Christ came as a high priest of the good things that have come, then through the greater and perfect tent (not made with hands, that is, not of this creation), he entered once for all into the Holy Place, not with the blood of goats and calves, but with his own blood, thus obtaining eternal redemption. For if the blood of goats and bulls, with the sprinkling of the ashes of a heifer, sanctifies those who have been defiled so that their flesh is purified, how much more will the blood of Christ, who through the eternal Spirit offered himself without blemish to God, purify our conscience from dead works to worship the living God! (Heb. 9.11-14)

As such, Christ is the 'mediator of a new covenant' (Heb. 9.15). This is a theme which Bonhoeffer picked up in relation to his Christology. For him, Christ mediates between the old existence and the new existence, standing at the centre.[6] And he stands as mediator between nature and God, standing for all creatures before God.[7] In this way, Bonhoeffer offers something of a classical understanding of Christ's mediating role.

Bonhoeffer, however, did not only pick up on the soteriological implications of this mediation in relation to the relationship between God and the world. For Bonhoeffer, this soteriological aspect of Christ's mediating role is conjoined with an anthropological/ecclesiological function. As Leahy puts it:

> Bonhoeffer brings together two important categories that flow from Christ who is present and are essential for all members of the church – the soteriological motif of vicarious representative action (*Stellvertretung*) and the motif of reciprocity of being *with* one another (*miteinander*) and *for* one another (*füreinander*). All the communitarian life of the church is rooted in Christ's vicarious action on our behalf.[8]

The representative work of Christ on the cross is such that it mediates not only between humanity and God but also between human beings and other human beings. In one sense, Bonhoeffer recognizes that the discussion of Christ's priestly mediation in scripture has implications for both community formation and ethics. The writer of Hebrews identifies this in his seeing that the effect of the high priestliness of Christ is to create not only a new and restored relation with God but also a new and restored relation with one another:

---

6. DBWE 12, 324–5.
7. Ibid., 327.
8. Brendan Leahy, '"Christ Existing as Community": Dietrich Bonhoeffer's Notion of Church', *Irish Theological Quarterly* 73, nos. 1–2 (2008): 41.

> Therefore, my friends, since we have confidence to enter the sanctuary by the blood of Jesus, by the new and living way that he opened for us through the curtain (that is, through his flesh), and since we have a great priest over the house of God ... let us consider how to provoke one another to love and good deeds, not neglecting to meet together, as is the habit of some, but encouraging one another, and all the more as you see the Day approaching. (Heb. 10:19-25)

So, too, for Bonhoeffer – Christ's work as priest is one that sees him mediate not only between God and humanity but also between human beings to form community. Such community cannot be created simply by nature or human will but requires the active mediation of Christ. According to Bonhoeffer, part of Christ's work in salvation involves the formation of the community of the church. He identifies three basic sociological relationships in and through Christ which are known to humanity:

> [Christ's] death isolates the *individuals* – all of them bear their own culpability and have their own conscience; in the light of the resurrection the community of the cross is justified and sanctified in Christ as *one*. The new humanity is seen synoptically in *one* point, in Christ. And since the love of God, in Christ's vicarious representative action, restores the community between God and human beings, so the *community of human beings with each other has also become a reality in love once again*.[9]

Thus, the vicarious representative action of Christ creates not only the (previously impossible) possibility of genuine community of human beings, it also makes this a reality in the church. Notably, the relationship of Christ to the church is not merely representational: the church *is* present in Christ and is seen as such 'in God's eyes'.[10] This reality is actualized in the working of the Holy Spirit in the creation of the church in time. Thus, the church is not a creation of the human exercise of will but comes into being as the result of the work of Christ and the Spirit: 'The church does not come into being by people coming together (genetic sociology), rather its *existence is sustained* by the Spirit who is a reality within the church community; therefore, it cannot be derived from individual wills.'[11] For Bonhoeffer, Christ's mediating work as priest does not terminate singularly in putting right the relationship between humanity and God; it also mediates between humans to form community.

As Bonhoeffer saw it, this is equally a work of salvation as that which puts right relations between God and humanity. Bonhoeffer's concept of person is relational:[12] a person exists always in relation to another human being. As Clifford

---

9. DBWE 1, 157.
10. Ibid.
11. Ibid., 160.
12. See ibid., chap. 2.

Green has identified, it is not the case for Bonhoeffer that to be a human being involves being able to say, 'I think, therefore, I am', but being able to say, 'I relate ethically, therefore I am'. The human being is essentially 'relational and social'.[13] As Green puts it, 'God is the one who establishes the other as You in relation the self, thus constituting the self as a person.'[14] Bonhoeffer drew on the Lutheran *cor incurvatum in se* as that situation from which the human needs to be rescued by God. His soteriology is one which the ego is able to move beyond its own self-imprisonment to be centred instead in Christ; and in Christ one is able to find a freedom for the other. Christ mediates in judgement and grace between the old self in Adam and the new self.[15] As Bonhoeffer puts it in *Act and Being*: 'Christ, the crucified and risen one, gives Christ's own self to be known by human beings, who live to themselves. It is in being known by God that human beings know God. But to be known by God means to become a new person. … It affects the existence of human beings.'[16] The way in which this existence is affected is in terms of the capacity to live not only genuinely as a creature before God but also in relation with human beings. Bonhoeffer wrote: 'Human beings have torn themselves loose from community with God and, therefore, also from that with other human beings, and now they stand alone.'[17] As well as being set aright with God in Christ, humans are able to encounter one another – to become relational, or fully human. This comes from Christ's work: 'It is from the person of Christ that every other person first acquires for other human beings the character of personhood.'[18] In Christ's work of mediating our relationships to other human beings, he sets humanity aright and makes human beings the creatures they are called to be, that is, makes human beings into persons.

The mediation of relationships through Christ is a theme addressed in *Life Together*. Establishing that Christ opens the way both to God and to other people,[19] Bonhoeffer implicitly asserted a classical Lutheran understanding of priesthood (in relation to the priesthood of all believers). He claimed that we need one another to speak God's word to each other, to be 'bearers and proclaimers of the divine word of salvation'.[20] But this was developed beyond the classical Lutheran perspective. As well as affirming that the discord between God and humanity is ended in Christ, Bonhoeffer said that enmity between humans is also ended. Thus, he stated:

---

13. Clifford J. Green, *Bonhoeffer: A Theology of Sociality*, rev. edn (Grand Rapids, MI: Eerdmans, 1999), 30–1.
14. Ibid., 35.
15. Clifford J. Green, 'Trinity and Christology in Bonhoeffer and Barth', *Union Seminary Quarterly Review* 60, nos. 1–2 (2006): 137.
16. DBWE 2, 134.
17. Ibid., 137.
18. Ibid., 114.
19. DBWE 5, 33.
20. Ibid., 32.

Christ has become the mediator who has made peace with God and peace with human beings. Without Christ we would not know God; we could neither call on God nor come to God. Moreover, without Christ we would not know other Christians around us; nor could we approach them, the way to them is blocked by one's own ego [*das eigene ich*]. Now Christians can live with each other in peace; they can love and serve one another; they can become one. But they can continue to do so only through Jesus Christ. Only in Jesus Christ are we one; only though him are we bound together. He remains the one and only mediator throughout eternity.[21]

Thus, Christ's priestly work as mediator is enacted in person-to-person mediation; and in the community of the church, this is the only form of relationship that there should be.[22] Through the priestly work of Christ, those in Christ (in the community of the church) are put right with one another and are made into a priesthood. Just as there can be no priest without other people, so human personhood demands other people in relationship, and this is provided in the life of the church. Within the church, the mediating work of Christ as priest is fulfilled in the mediated encounter of human beings with one another: mediation is found in restored humanity and is thereby an anthropological and ecclesial reality.

Priestliness of the church for the world

The priestly mediating work of Christ in the church is not only an internal mediation but determines the relationship of the church to the world. The priestly mediation of Christ determines the relationships of persons within the world: the 'structural being-with-each-other [*Miteinander*] of church-community and its members, and the members acting-for-each-other [*Füreinander*] as vicarious representatives'.[23] It also determines the relationship of the church to the world. Just as with human persons, the ontology of the church is fully relational: the church is in this relationship with the world. The church exists provisionally for the world: it is determined not for itself but in order to mediate God's word of salvation to the world. Christ is the *Kollektivperson*,[24] and as such the church has the 'collective personality' [*Gesamtpersönlichkeit*] of Christ (though a complete identification is impossible since Christ remains in heaven and we await his return):[25] 'The church is the presence of Christ in the same way that Christ is the presence of the God,' claimed Bonhoeffer.[26] Where Bonhoeffer sees the difference between Adam

21. Ibid., 32–3.
22. Ibid., 41.
23. DBWE 1, 191.
24. Ibid., 79.
25. Ibid., 140.
26. Ibid., 140–1. However, a complete identification of church and Christ is impossible since Christ remains in heaven and we await his return.

11. Priestly Mediation in the Church

(and the community of Adam) and Christ (and the community of Christ) is in terms of *Stellvertretung* (vicarious representation). Christ represents the whole of humanity in his life.[27] In this, we find the beginnings of an understanding of priestly mediation structured not only towards sociality within the church but equally and also towards the church's corporate priestly mediation to the world. The concept of mediation expanded in the more mature Bonhoeffer from a primary preoccupation with the internal operations, structure and organization of the church, to include the relationship between the church and the world: the structural ordering of the internal workings of the church becomes the structural ordering of the life of the church in relation to the world. In this, a priestly relation of the church to the world can be identified: Christ's priesthood extends not to individuals – not even to the sum of all individuals as in Luther – but to the church as a body; the church is the priest of the world.

This is a theme which one can find powerfully articulated in Bonhoeffer's *Ethics*. Here, Bonhoeffer's concern was explicitly the relation of the church to the world. The Christocentric focus on the unity of God and the world through the mediation of Jesus Christ becomes the basis for the action of the Christian. The unity of God and the world must be understood singularly in Jesus Christ and his action which produces a corresponding action for the church. Thus,

> this unity exists solely in the person of Jesus Christ, in whom God became human, acting in vicarious representative responsibility [*stellvertretende Verantwortung*] and entering out of love for the real human being into the guilt of the world. Originating from Christ alone, there is now human action … [which] springs … from the already accomplished reconciliation of the world with God. … It is an action of vicarious representative responsibility, of love for the real human being, of taking on oneself the guilt that burdens the world. What is 'Christian' and what is 'worldly' are now no longer defined from the outset. Instead, both are understood in their unity only within the concrete responsibility of action that is based on the unity accomplished in Jesus Christ.[28]

The church joins in Christ's priestly work of various representation to God on behalf of the world. Like the priests of the Old Testament, the church (and Christians) now stands before God on behalf of the world: united in Christ's own person, the church joins Christ in loving vicarious representative responsibility for the world, its guilt and its burdens. This became, for Bonhoeffer, in one sense the defining feature of the church's external relations. Modelling the internal relationality of the unity 'with one another' and 'for one another' that Christ produces, the church's external relationality (indeed, its purpose) is defined in this corporate priestly

---

27. DBWE 1, 146–7, and more generally, 146–65.
28. DBWE 6, 238–9. This is a theme which is picked up in Bonhoeffer's poem 'Jonah'; see DBWE 8, 547–8.

function in Christ. The church fulfils its purpose by focusing not on itself but the world and realizing its instrumentality.

Just as God and the world are the essential coordinates of priesthood so too are they the essential coordinates of the church: the church does not exist for itself but for the world on whose behalf it acts; that is its purpose and determination. Thus, Bonhoeffer stated: 'The concept of vicarious representative action [*Stellvertretung*] defines this ... relationship most clearly. The Christian community stands in the place in which the whole world should stand. In this respect it serves the world as its vicarious representative; it is there for the world's sake.'[29] Standing in the place of the people (indeed, the world as such) and mediating on the world's behalf is precisely the position of the priest with his people. For Bonhoeffer, this priesthood is one held by the church in Christ in relation to all the world. Furthermore, the church witnesses, proclaims and testifies back to the world. This activity of witness and proclamation is one central to the Aaronic priesthood. Indeed, the word for priest (*kōhēn*) stems from a Semitic root form meaning 'truthsayer'.[30] In this stem is found the idea that the priest testifies to the activity of God. Priests are in this way witness to God's covenant with His people: they point beyond themselves and their activity to the mercy and forgiveness of God. As a priest for the world, the church exists to proclaim God's work of salvation to the world. Thus, Bonhoeffer asserts:

> Th[e] space of the church does not, therefore, exist just for itself, but its existence is already always something that reaches far beyond it. This is because it is not the space of a cult that would have to fight for its own existence in the world. Rather, the space of the church is the place where witness is given to the foundation of all reality in Jesus Christ. ... The space of the church is not there in order to fight with the world for a piece of territory, but precisely to testify to the world that it is still the world, namely the world that is loved and reconciled by God.[31]

This act of testimony could be thought in many ways as being closely aligned to Luther's concept of the priesthood of all believers, where priesthood is defined in a twofold way: speaking of Jesus Christ to one another (teaching) and interceding for one another. In speaking to the world of its reality in Jesus Christ, Bonhoeffer's theology might suggest that the church acts as a priest for the world in precisely this sense of Luther's. This is a theme which is also brought out in Bonhoeffer's *Letters and Papers from Prison*, which contains an outline for a planned book. In this outline, Bonhoeffer pointed to Jesus as fundamentally the one who has 'being-for-others'. In faith, Christians are able to participate in this being of Christ, and in doing so become human (*Menschwerdung*). Bonhoeffer redescribed human

---

29. DBWE 6, 404.
30. T. F. Torrance, *Royal Priesthood: A Theology of Ordained Ministry*, 2nd edn (Edinburgh: T&T Clark, 1993), 1.
31. DBWE 6, 63.

11. Priestly Mediation in the Church

relationship to God as 'a new life in "being there for others", through participation in the being of Jesus'.³² Perhaps in this one might find the beginning and direction of an answer to Bonhoeffer's pressing and prophetic question: 'What does a church, a congregation, a sermon, a liturgy, a Christian life, mean in a religionless world?'³³ Their meaning, for Bonhoeffer, is their existence for the world, as a church which is a vicarious representative: in one sense, to be the church means to be the world's priest.

Moreover, for Bonhoeffer, this sense of how one is to be for the world is deeply priestly. Priests in the Old Testament bore the sin of the people: they stood in their place to such an extent that they held the sins of the people on their forehead. For example, in the sacrifice offered on the day of atonement, the priest stands in a precarious position before God in two ways. First, he risks his own life for the sake of the people in the coming into the very presence of God; and second, he bears the iniquity of the people on his own head (Exod. 28.38; Lev. 10.17; Num. 18.1, 23). According to Philo, we also see this in the mediatory activity of Moses, whom Philo saw as the 'high-priestly Logos': Moses communed with God and pleaded for Israel's forgiveness even if this were to involve his own damnation (Exod. 25.22; Num. 7.89).³⁴ Bonhoeffer's account of ecclesial mediation for the world included this priestly activity. However, rather than it being focused internally on the forgiveness of the sins of the community, it came to focus externally beyond the bounds of the church upon the world. The church genuinely and supremely exists not for itself but for the world in its preparedness to take upon itself the sins of the world: there is real vicarious representative responsibility enacted here. The task of the church in a religionless age is to bear the sin of the world before God. This point is made powerfully by Bonhoeffer:

> The church is today the community of people who, grasped by the power of Christ's grace, acknowledge, confess, and take upon themselves not only their personal sins, but also the Western world's falling away from Jesus Christ as toward Jesus Christ. … With this confession the whole guilt of the world falls on the church, on Christians, and because here it is confessed and not denied, the possibility of forgiveness is opened.³⁵

Like Moses and like the Aaronic priesthood (indeed, ultimately like Christ), the church should be prepared to be a community which stands before God with the sins of others upon it: confessing these sins and opening the possibility of forgiveness. There is no heroism in this act, but – like the priest who represents the people and shares in their sin – there is a sense of joining in the sinfulness of the

---

32. DBWE 8, 501.
33. Ibid., 364.
34. Torrance, *Royal Priesthood*, 3. Cf. G. Schrenk, 'ἱερός, etc.', in *Theologisches Wörterbuch zum Neuen Testament*, vol. 3, ed. Gerhard Kittel (Stuttgart: Kohlhammer, 1957), 259.
35. DBWE 6, 135–6.

world and being genuinely responsible for it in a representative way. The church confesses as the 'collective I' aware of being guilty towards the whole.[36] Thus, as a participant in sin, the church mediates confession and the forgiveness of God to the world. It does this because 'there are people here [in the church] who take all – really all – guilt upon themselves, not in some heroic self-sacrificing decision, but simply overwhelmed by their very own guilt toward Christ'.[37] The effect of this is that those confessing do not think of those other sinners (who might be considered greater) but only about the forgiveness of their own great guilt. The priestliness of the church is related to its standing with the world as well as for it: – *miteinander* and *füreinander*.

Conclusion

While Bonhoeffer may not seem to have been particularly concerned with the theological category of priestliness as regards individual priesthood, the priesthood of all believers or the priesthood of Christ, it is clear that Bonhoeffer is concerned with certain theological themes often associated with priestliness. There is a twofold relationship in this: firstly, Christ's mediating work mediates between God and humanity, but also (innovatively) mediates humans and other humans, in a way which makes Christ's priestly work the grounds of the community and expands the sense in which Christ's mediation is salvific. Secondly, in Christ, the church now engages as a corporate priest for the world, existing for it, witnessing to it and confessing its guilt, even to the point of taking that guilt to itself. Bonhoeffer's understanding of priestliness is, therefore, more corporate and strictly ecclesial than his Lutheran forebears who taught the individual priesthood of each person. This is not to say that Bonhoeffer was uninterested in ministerial formation: he headed a seminary in which his practices were sometimes considered 'popish'.[38] But even his theological description of this time is one which is corporate: Bonhoeffer thought first of *Life Together* (*Gemeinsames Leben*) before he thought of the life and practices of the individual minister, and even the eucharist and confession are thought of as corporate acts.

---

36. Ibid., 137.
37. Ibid., 136.
38. Eberhard Bethge, *Dietrich Bonhoeffer: A Biography*, ed. Victoria J. Barnett, rev. edn (Minneapolis, MN: Fortress, 2000), 433.

Part IV

READING BARTH AND BONHOEFFER TOGETHER IN A FALLEN PLURALIST WORLD

Chapter 12

PESSIMISTIC UNIVERSALISM

This chapter seeks in many ways to bring together many of the themes discussed discretely in relation to Karl Barth and Dietrich Bonhoeffer in the preceding chapters – an awareness of the realities of a world outside of Christendom, a central place for Jesus Christ, a consciousness of our propensity to be sinners, the need to consider the place of religious and secular others in our theological reflection. And to attempt to focus on bringing these themes together, there is an intended irony to the title of this chapter. 'Pessimism' is not a word most often associated with universal salvation, except perhaps with regard to the way in which its opponents have viewed its orthodoxy: universal salvation has been variously condemned by churchmen and theologians alike. While it would be incorrect to suggest that it was anathematized in 553 CE, since the church could not condemn *apokatastasis* (a word meaning 'universal restoration' used by the Holy Spirit in scripture in Acts), all versions of universal salvation have been seen as heterodox by the majority mainstream tradition. Although there has been an almost universal rejection of universalism, it cannot be said, however, that the mode in which the rejection has taken place has been universal: universalism has many varied forms, and there are resultantly various different reasons why universalism has been denied. Some of these are connected to the strangeness of other doctrines with which it has been associated (such as a belief in pre-existing souls); some connected with the effect of universalism on other doctrines (such as the freedom of God); some connected with scripture (principally regarding whether the New Testament does allow for the possibility of a non-binary or non-separationist judgement); and some connected to philosophy (such as what this doctrine does to freedom, or to temporality and history).[1]

It is necessary, therefore, to be clear about the form of universalism that is the focus of this chapter and the reasons it has been rejected. This chapter concerns what might broadly be spoken of as 'Christian universalism'. This is a type of universalism which arises from within the Christian faith and tradition[2] and

---

1. For more on this, see Trevor Hart, 'Universalism: Two Distinct Types', in *Universalism and the Doctrine of Hell*, ed. Nigel M. de S. Cameron (Carlisle: Paternoster, 1992), 1–34.

2. For more on why this needs to be the case, see my *Barth, Origen, and Universal Salvation: Restoring Particularity* (Oxford: Oxford University Press, 2009).

utilizes those resources in order to suggest a wider hope that will encompass all of humanity. This version of universalism might be contrasted with pluralism which, while it need not necessarily be universalist, may suggest some version of 'salvation' (whatever can be meant broadly by this term in a pluralist setting) for all.[3] Most often, Christian universalism is seen to arise out of a theological and philosophical consideration of what has been termed 'the omnipotence of God's love'.[4] Critical responses to this kind of universalism are often some version of the argument from free will. Trevor Hart cites J. A. T. Robinson as a prime example of this version of universalism. Robinson's thesis spends the majority of its time attempting to answer this issue of free will by proving that ultimate salvation is compatible with people's freedom either to choose or to reject it.[5] In the end, Robinson arrives at the view that all will be saved because ultimately all will choose Christ.[6] Often, this version of universalism draws principally on the biblical imagery of Christ preaching to the dead,[7] which is indicative of a future opportunity to choose Christ. In many ways such arguments conform to the typology of Christian universalism as described by Trevor Hart: '[This form of] universalism does not deny that judgement and hell are real: but simply that the judgement will find any wanting, and that hell will be occupied.'[8] However, it must be noted that, as generally articulated, so-called Christian universalism, while it seeks as I do to be innately Christian, does arise ultimately to some degree from an optimism about humanity's capacity to choose God, or else an optimistic hope that it will be the case that God's love will be unconquerable. The root of this optimism can be focused on either perspective (God, as perhaps classically articulated by Schleiermacher,[9] or humanity, as expressed in other more liberal versions of Christian theology). These two versions of universalism (while often

---

3. An example of this can be found in the likes of John Hick, *God and the Universe of Faiths: Essays in the Philosophy of Religion* (London: Macmillan, 1973).

4. Hart, 'Universalism', 16–17.

5. Ibid., 17–19. Cf. George Hunsinger, *Disruptive Grace: Studies in the Theology of Karl Barth* (Grand Rapids, MI: Eerdmans, 2000), 234–9.

6. J. A. T. Robinson, *In the End God* (London: Collins Fontana, 1968), 118–19. One finds a very similar argument (from a different perspective) in the excellent book written by Robin Parry under the *nom de plume* of Gregory MacDonald, *The Evangelical Universalist: The Biblical Hope That God's Love Will Save Us All* (London: SPCK, 2008).

7. MacDonald, *The Evangelical Universalist*.

8. Hart, 'Universalism', 23.

9. Friedrich Schleiermacher considered the capriciousness of certain separationist presentations of God, and instead advocated that all humanity is elected to salvation in Jesus Christ and that, in this, divine omnipotence cannot fail. See Friedrich Schleiermacher, *The Christian Faith*, ed. H. R. Mackintosh and J. S. Stewart, trans. D. M. Baillie, W. R. Matthews, Edith Sandbach-Marshall, A. B. Macaulay, Alexander Grieve, J. Y. Campbell, R. W. Stewart and H. R. Mackintosh, English translation of the 2nd German edn (Edinburgh: T&T Clark, 1968), §§117–20, 163.

linked) clearly are not the same. However, the key concern that I wish to address is the (perhaps symbiotic) optimistic world view that underlines both expressions.

Such Christian universalism as outlined either holds an optimistic view of humanity or in its God-focused form prioritizes or aggrandizes the Christian and her place in salvation, not only making the believer stand in a superior position to the unbeliever but also making the believer – rather than God – central to salvation. Effectively, salvation belongs to Christians really, as those who have freely chosen God in this life, and others are allowed in because God has even more love and patience (enough to stretch to the furthest reaches of non-Christians), or because they become Christians and are thereby lovely to God. This taxonomy places the Christian in a superior or privileged position; sees salvation as hers properly; and, while nevertheless seeking to be charitable, degrades the other to a secondary place or forces an alternate identity upon her. To some degree, in both versions there is a positive reading of humanity which is focused on the Christian's having chosen God. This optimistic universalism is overly optimistic about the human capacity to choose correctly (and this idea of choice anyway seems so horribly Gnostic) and about the superior place of the Christian in the plans and purposes of God (which to my mind seems so contrary to grace and the reality of the empirical church).[10] While the position forwarded in this chapter hardly precludes but is rather underscored by God's inexhaustible love, in place of this optimism I propose a version of universalism which arises from a pessimistic view of humanity,[11] sketched in three movements. Through a dialogical engagement with Barth and Bonhoeffer, and drawing heavily from their writings, I wish also to demonstrate in passing that this form of universalism underlies each of their thought processes about salvation. As two theologians who wrestled with expressions of the Christian faith in a world marked by increased secularism, and who posited original and distinctive versions of universalism, they provide useful interlocutors for this enterprise.

The depravity of all humanity

Eberhard Bethge speaks in his biography of Bonhoeffer's lack of formal engagement in eschatology outside of his student years, despite the personal stimulation the topic brought to him.[12] To some degree this is undoubtedly true. If eschatology is understood simply to be a focus on other-worldly matters, an orientation away

---

10. The one who has forgiven more loves more; cf. Lk. 7.47.

11. In this way, there is perhaps a relation between my thinking and that of James Relly. For a brief summary of his thought, see Morwenna Ludlow, 'Universalism in the History of Christianity', in *Universal Salvation? The Current Debate*, ed. Robin A. Parry and Christopher H. Partridge (Carlisle: Paternoster, 2003), 205.

12. Eberhard Bethge, *Dietrich Bonhoeffer: Theologian, Christian, Contemporary*, ed. Edwin Robertson, trans. Eric Mosbacher, et al. (London: Collins, 1970), 61.

from the world or a speculative engagement in chronologically identifying the various points associated with the coming of the end, there could be little that is at a further distance from the thinking of Bonhoeffer. Indeed, as the mature Bonhoeffer would state:

> Unlike believers in the redemption myths, Christians do not have an ultimate escape route out of their earthly tasks and difficulties into eternity. ... This-worldliness must not be abolished ahead of its time; on this, [New Testament] and [Old Testament] are united. Redemption myths arise from the human experience of boundaries. But Christ takes hold of human beings in the midst of their lives.[13]

And within a fortnight, Bethge was replying: 'It makes great sense to me that it is unbiblical to regard eschatology as a means of evasion.'[14] However, there does exist (telegrammatically perhaps – though it may be wise to suggest that one can never find little more than this in Bonhoeffer) some discussion of the *apokatastasis* in Bonhoeffer's writings, as we shall see in the course of this chapter, at all periods of his life – from the first doctoral thesis, *Sanctorum Communio*, to the prophetic and enigmatic prison writings of his final years.[15]

That Bonhoeffer was supposedly uninterested in eschatology may not in the end, however, stand in contradiction to passing interests in universal salvation. Of all the ways to deal with eschatology, universalism is almost certainly the most 'worldly' in one sense: it arises out of a sense of God's ultimate purpose for all creation, and the firm weddedness of the Christian to the world and to all humanity.[16] It is not surprising, therefore, that one who considers the *sanctorum communio* as existing within the *peccatorum communio* and who seeks later to give secular interpretations of the Bible should, in expressing his eschatology, seek to do so in this way. While Bonhoeffer may be uninterested in themes traditionally associated with eschatology, perhaps that very lack of interest provides the possibility of a more open approach to universal salvation than might otherwise be considered normally the case for a theologian whose interest lies more in the beyond than in this world.

---

13. DBWE 8, 27 June 1944, 447–8.
14. Ibid., from Eberhard Bethge, 8 July 1944, 472.
15. In the prison writings, the reader is directed to DBWE 8, 18 December 1943, 228–9; and to the discussion of the restoration of all things in Advent IV, 18 December 1943, 170. For an identification of the various places in which Bonhoeffer discusses universal salvation, see Sabine Dramm, *Dietrich Bonhoeffer: An Introduction to His Thought*, trans. Thomas Rice (Peabody, MA: Hendrickson, 2007), 63–6.
16. Christians are not types of people, or superior to creation, but in the first instance, simply human beings and creatures of God, with infinitely more in common with all other arts of creation than with the God who creates *ex nihilo*.

For the purpose of this chapter, however, what is of particular note is that Bonhoeffer's articulation of universal salvation is not expressed in the usual positive and optimistic manner. In short, it is not simply expressed in terms of the overwhelming love of God (though, sure, this plays some part); nor is it expressed in terms of the capacity of humans ultimately to choose God. Rather it is expressed somewhat – for want of a better way to describe its logic – pessimistically and arises from a very realistic assessment of the Christian's condition before God. Certainly, for Bonhoeffer, 'this very talk of *apokatastasis* can never be more than a sigh of theology whenever it has to speak of faith and unfaith, election and rejection'.[17] But this very sigh itself arises from a groan about the depravity of all humanity – Christians being no exception.

The continued sinfulness of the Christian is a theme which preoccupies much of what Bonhoeffer has to say in the fourth chapter of *Sanctorum Communio* on 'Sin and Broken Community'. Bonhoeffer is concerned in much of his discussion of the doctrine of sin to recognize the simultaneous universality of and individual culpability for sin. He writes: 'The culpability of the individual and the universality of sin should be understood together; that is, the individual culpable act and the culpability of the human race must be connected conceptually.'[18] However, one is not to understand this symbiotic relationship in a singular direction: it is not simply as a result of the heinousness of the first and original sin that presently humanity sins. Instead, for Bonhoeffer, all humanity falls with each sin, and thus no human is different in principle to Adam. Effectively, this means every sin is original sin: 'Everyone is also the "first" sinner.'[19] As a result of this, there is no exoneration of the individual's sin by virtue of the common experience of sinfulness. Rather, the sinner 'associates his own guiltiness with the consciousness that the sin of the whole people has awakened in him – that his sin stands in closest connection with that of the whole people.'[20]

Moreover, for Bonhoeffer, this sin is not simply removed in the present following the experience of salvation and sanctification: the church, too, stands under this sinful judgement: 'The reality of sin and the communio peccatorum remain even in God's church-community: Adam has really been replaced by Christ *only eschatologically, ep elpidi (in spe)* [in hope].'[21] So long as sin remains, the whole sinful humanity remains also in each and every human being. What one can note, therefore, in Bonhoeffer is a strong sense of the depravity of all humanity, which continues in the church crucially because of the connection between each sin and all sins, and thus each sinner and all sinners. As stated, this relationship is not unidirectional (i.e. I sin because of original sin) but genuinely symbiotic (i.e. my sin is in original sin; original sin is in my sin): each individual shares in the

---

17. DBWE 2, 160–1.
18. DBWE 1, 110–11.
19. Ibid., 115.
20. Ibid., 116.
21. Ibid., 124, emphasis added; Greek transliterated and italicized.

sin of the world and thus in the sin of other sinners even for the Christian who has confessed her sin and sought God's forgiveness.[22] For Bonhoeffer, there can be no binary categorization of sinners and saints, no binary separation of church and world.

In turning to eschatology, a strong sense of the sinfulness of humanity is certainly at odds with much that is liberally hopeful and optimistic regarding humanity's capacity eventually to choose God freely. There is, instead, a strong sense of pessimism here, even in terms of the capacity of the Christian to be freed from sin: needless to say, this is a Lutheran approach in which – in this life at least – one must recognize the status of *simul iustus et peccator* for the Christian. As one might expect from Bonhoeffer's popular writings, *Discipleship* and *Life Together*, no simple jump can be made from here into a 'wishy-washy' or non-rigorous form of universalism which fails to recognize the important role of the church and of decision and a life of faithful obedience: a recognition of the seriousness of sin surely demands this; there can be no 'cheap grace'.[23] Bonhoeffer certainly does speak clearly and strongly of a dual outcome;[24] and as a result of this pessimistic understanding of the Christian's failure in terms of sin, the danger may well indeed seem to be whether there is any good news at all for the Christian so culpable for her own and the world's sin. However – and this is the key point – this speech is not without the 'sigh' spoken of earlier in terms of universal salvation. Bonhoeffer writes:

> We must not speak of a dual outcome ... without at the same time emphasizing the inner necessity of the idea of apocatastasis. ... On the one hand, the concept of the church, as Christ's presence in the world which calls for a decision, necessarily demands the dual outcome. The recognition that the gift of God's boundless love has been received without any merit would, on the other hand, make it seem just as impossible to exclude others from this gift and this love.[25]

Thus far, one might detect here a classical 'love of God' approach reminiscent of the aforementioned optimistic appraisals of God's ultimate loving purpose. However, Bonhoeffer's grounds for this are not simply to be found in the usual places – no recourse to God's patient allowing of a future choice, no suggestion of a love principle as binding on God's nature, no positive assessment of humanity as capable ultimately of making the correct decision and choosing for God. Rather, Bonhoeffer points to the argument I have already rehearsed about the co-sinfulness of all humanity. In the very next sentence, he continues: 'The strongest reason for accepting the idea of apocatastasis would seem to me that all Christians must

---

22. One might note here a connection to the idea in Bonhoeffer's *Ethics* of the Christian taking on the guilt of the world. See DBWE 6, 134–45.
23. On 'cheap' and 'costly' grace, see DBWE 4, 43–56.
24. DBWE 1, 286.
25. Ibid., 286–7.

be aware of having brought sin into the world, and thus aware of being bound together with the whole of humanity in sin, aware of having the sins of humanity on their conscience.'[26] Crucially, it is a pessimistic view of humanity that leads Bonhoeffer to this ultimate hope. Rather than his universalism detracting from the seriousness of sin, or impugning the righteousness of God, Bonhoeffer grounds his universalist 'sigh' in a full recognition of the seriousness of sin and the precariousness of humanity's situation before God. In this, Bonhoeffer recognizes that in offering God's grace to any (Christian or non-Christian) there is always involved the sin of all, and thus any assumptions about universalism impugning God's righteous require re-examination.

This theme of universal salvation grounded in the co-sinfulness of all humanity is one which is also brought out in Bonhoeffer's discussion of paedo-baptism in his discussion of the child in *Act and Being*. Bonhoeffer claims that there is a defining of the infant about to be baptized by the future, by the eschatological possibility.[27] He writes: 'In faith the future is present; but in as much as faith suspends itself before the future. ... The human being "is" in the future of Christ.'[28] Thus, the very hope which is expressed in infant baptism is one which has a broader implication for all people, since for Bonhoeffer the community of Christ recognizes itself always as the children of the future.[29] However, as Bonhoeffer reminds us in *Sanctorum Communio*, the church must 'refrain from premature attempts to transform this hope into a present reality'.[30] In this, the church cannot simply identify itself with this future hope. Again, the Christian and the non-Christian find themselves united, albeit the Christian may realize in faith and anticipation the presence of the future now. Bonhoeffer addresses these matters directly with regard to universalism: 'Our discussion of the *actus directus* – as something which can never be captured in reflection ... – and of infant baptism – as of faith that excludes itself – allows a perspective to open up in which not all roads appear blocked to the eschatology of apocatastasis.'[31] Clearly the co-sinfulness of humanity is far from optimistic in its approach to humanity and to the Christian life, but as expressed by Bonhoeffer it is nevertheless not one of doom, hellfire and damnation. Rather, it is a pessimism which determines a broader future hope which arises from a strong sense that one cannot place boundaries too firmly around the Christian church

---

26. Ibid., 287.
27. DBWE 2, 159.
28. Ibid. Cf. DBWE 8, 27 July 1944, 373, on Luther's distinction between *fides directa* and *fides reflexa*, as related to the faith of children at baptism. For a further discussion of this latter passage and its relation to the theme of reality, see Heinrich Ott, *Reality and Faith: The Theological Legacy of Dietrich Bonhoeffer*, trans. Alex A. Morrison (London: Lutterworth Press, 1971), 190–1.
29. DBWE 2, 161.
30. DBWE 1, 289.
31. DBWE 2, 160.

as those who alone are saved in any separationist account, as paedo-baptism emphasizes.[32]

While it might seem that Bonhoeffer's approach is little more than another version of universalism based on the absoluteness of the love of God, the subtle differences are important. A simultaneous emphasis on the co-sinfulness of the Christian with the non-Christian undermines inevitable comparative value judgements. When we emphasize universal salvation as a result of Christian sinfulness, salvation is no longer ours to offer in a slightly superior way to the others;[33] now the salvation of the other is the only hope of our own salvation: not 'us then them', but 'only us if them', or an 'if even us then surely them'. In this way, human particularity is not undermined, but salvation is enabled still to be fully dependent on grace (and not on the making of grace into a work). In this account, the righteousness of God is upheld to the height in realizing the impugned righteousness of God in the continued sinfulness of the Christian – perhaps a graver version of sin than that of those who know not what they do. Therefore, the charge against universalism that it does not treat sin or God's righteousness seriously enough cannot be maintained. This pessimistic universalism finds benefit on both sides – more fully universalist than more optimistic accounts, but without certain of the failings that some separationists identify in universalism.

Faith and unbelief

The second section of this chapter moves from the implications of the continued sin of the believer to the issue of doubt and unbelief. For the more traditionally minded may rush to say something along the lines of: 'This may well be true, but does this not emphasize all the more the importance of faith as the means of salvation?' More orthodox Protestants will no doubt rush to remind us that it is no good simply having *sola gratia* unless *sola fide* is also taken into account. Faith in Christ's salvation alone can overcome the perils of sin, and the faithful must be constant in their confession and in their seeking forgiveness and absolution. For the orthodox Protestant Christian, this is no doubt true. However, even here there is a problem: how do we account for those moments (fleeting or

---

32. There is a similar movement here with Barth in CD, IV/4. Although he does reject the position ultimately, he is able to write this of arguments for infant baptism: 'The strongest – I myself used it for some decades – is that infant baptism is so remarkably vivid a description of the free and omnipotent grace of God which is independent of all human thought and will, faith and unbelief' (189).

33. Even many accounts of universalism still work within this logic, prioritizing the Christian's salvation and seeing the other's salvation as some form of Christianization. One may see this sort of logic in Rahner's articulation of anonymous Christianity. See Karl Rahner, SJ, 'Anonymous Christians', in *Theological Investigations*, vol. 6, *Concerning Vatican Council II* (London: Darton, Longman & Todd, 1974), 390–8.

otherwise) of doubt, of unbelief, of faithlessness within the purported category of 'the Christian'? Indeed, is it not a rather arbitrary distinction to speak of sin as in some ways separate to faithlessness or unbelief from sin? When the fool says that there is no God, this is hardly an epistemological statement but rather one grounded in morality and sin.[34] Bonhoeffer deals very well with the inseparability of sin and faithlessness when he states, 'The concept of a situation in which faith is possible is only a description of the reality contained within the following two statements: *only the believers* obey, *and only the obedient* believe.'[35] However, the theologian that this section of the chapter will draw on principally is Karl Barth.[36] It is true to say that both Barth and Bonhoeffer deal with both of the aspects of the pessimism that this chapter addresses – sin and doubt – but the dominance of concern for the latter is perhaps to be found in the Basel professor.

The interrelated nature of these concerns regarding sin and unbelief (and Barth's focus on unbelief) is found in Barth's strong sense of sin *being* unbelief. He writes, for example, 'Man's sin *is* unbelief in the God who was "in Christ reconciling the world to himself", who in Him elected and loved man from all eternity, who in Him created him, whose word to man from and to all eternity was and will be Jesus Christ.'[37] The idea that doubt or unbelief is simply some form of questioning knowledge (whatever that might mean) is rejected by Barth who realizes that faith is not the simple assent to a *credo* which might wipe sins magically away: unbelief [*Unglaube*] *is* faithlessness, is sin. There can be no crude distinction between faith and works in this way: Christians cannot simply understand their continued sin as being cancelled out by their faith; rather their continued sin is indicative of their continued faithlessness and unbelief. For the question of salvation and impugning the righteousness of God by offering a broader hope, there can be no easy recourse to the *sola fide* that separates faithlessness from sinfulness.

---

34. One does well here to be reminded by Bonhoeffer that folly is a 'moral rather than an intellectual defect', DBWE 8, 8.

35. DBWE 4, 63. For further reflection on this phrase in Bonhoeffer, see Christiane Tietz, '"Nur der Glaubende ist gehorsam, und nur der Gehorsame glaubt." Beobachtungen zu einem existentiellen Zirkel in Dietrich Bonhoeffers "Nachfolge"', in *Dietrich Bonhoeffer Jahrbuch 2: 2005/2006*, ed. Christian Gremmels, Hans Pfeifer and Christiane Tietz (München: Gütersloher Verlagshaus, 2005), 170–81.

36. There has been much discussion about whether Barth can be spoken of as a universalist; it is not the purpose of this chapter to make that judgement, but simply to draw upon Barth's discussion of unbelief. For a sample of the issues at stake, the reader is directed to the following: G. C. Berkouwer, *The Triumph of Grace in the Theology of Karl Barth*, trans. Harry R. Boer (London: Paternoster, 1956); Joseph D. Bettis, 'Is Karl Barth a Universalist?', *Scottish Journal of Theology* 20, no. 4 (1967): 423–36; Thomas F. Torrance, 'Universalism or Election?', *Scottish Journal of Theology* 2, no. 3 (1949): 310–18; Oliver Crisp, 'On Barth's Denial of Universalism', *Themelios* 29, no. 1 (2003); and Chapter 5 in this volume.

37. CD IV/1, 415, emphasis added.

The recognition of the faithlessness even of the Christian determines that there can be no sharp binary distinction of the believing who continue in sin (as those who assent to Christianity) from the unbelieving who sin: such a distinction simply does not make sense. Thus, for Barth, there is a constant awareness – even personally – of the Christian's unbelief. This is perhaps most famously summarized in Barth's comments on the atheism of Max Bense: 'I know the rather sinister figure of the "atheist" very well, not only from books, but also because it lurks somewhere inside me too.'[38] Barth explores these themes variously in his writings, but continuous in all his work is the connectedness of the Christian to the non-Christian even in the life of faith; for in this faith there still exists 'ambivalence, impotence, confusion and peril'.[39] While Barth is able to state that Christians 'are the children of God by faith in Jesus Christ',[40] Barth goes on to define this faith as follows: 'Faith is a new act each day and hour, *at war each day and hour with newly insurgent unbelief*. Thus Christians, in Luther's words, have never become but are always *becoming*.'[41] No sharp divisive binary line can be drawn between Christians and non-Christians, but this is not simply because of the grace and love of God for all humanity: this lack of a binary arises from the faithless propensities of Christians. Barth realizes (as in the words of a verse he often quotes)[42] that the Christian faith is the enactment of the cry: 'Lord, I believe; help thou mine unbelief.'[43] No false or crude categorization of believing and unbelieving can be made.

Moreover, for Barth the real precariousness in gaining God's salvation lies with those who are thought to be in a situation 'of faith'. With an apocalyptic tone, Barth asserts:

> Christians who regard themselves as big and strong and rich and even dear and good children of God, Christians who refuse to sit with their Master at the table of publicans and sinners, are *not* Christians at all, have still to become so, and need not be surprised if heaven is gray above them and their calling upon God sounds hollow and finds no hearing.[44]

This seems apposite given the New Testament's warnings to the Scribes and Pharisees, whom clearly Barth associates with the contemporary Christian.[45] As in the story of the rich man and Lazarus in Lk. 16, Christians, too, may find

---

38. Karl Barth, *Fragments Grave and Gay*, ed. Martin Rumscheidt (London: Collins, 1971), 45–6.
39. CD IV/4, 150.
40. ChrL, 78.
41. Ibid., emphasis added.
42. E.g. CD I/1, 24; II/2, 337; IV/1, 616, 699, 748; and IV/2, 138.
43. Cf. Mk 9.24.
44. Barth, ChrL, 80.
45. Bonhoeffer also discusses the Pharisees. See DBWE 6, 309–17.

themselves in the fearful position of the rich man's five brothers: Christians know and have had the warnings of scripture, and if they have not heard them what hope may be expected? Those brothers were also, after all, people of faith in some sense – children of Abraham who have the words of Moses and the prophets. Barth continues:

> Only the eyes of the blind can be opened, only the ears of the deaf can be unstopped, only the lame can be told to take up their bed and walk. ... Only for prisoners is there liberation ..., only for the hungry and the thirsty is there the promise of being filled ..., only to those who take a low place can the call come: 'Friend, go up higher'. To Christians who will not call upon God as those who are blind, deaf, lame, prisoners, hungry and thirsty, *and who will not take the lowest place*, those acts of salvation cannot apply and will not happen.[46]

Again, one can detect here a subtlety with regard to usual expressions of the wider hope. The point is not simply that God's love can touch even the most unlovely (true as that may be) but rather more acutely that the Christian is likely to be that most unlovely of persons. Salvation will come only to the Christian who does 'take the lowest place'.[47] Thus, it is not that Christians have the first access to salvation, and God lets the others in as second-class citizens. Instead, the first step is to recognize that, in the words of Barth, 'All man's unbelief, error and superstition cannot alter this original relationship of God to him or its far-reaching implications.'[48] The second is to realize as a result of this that Christ's love and grace does not come firstly to the Christian and only subsequently to the non-Christian: realizing the unbelief even of the Christian, there is a need to appreciate that for the non-Christian Christ 'is not merely their hope as well, but their hope specifically'.[49] As with Bonhoeffer, only if there is hope for them can there be hope for us – ultimately because there is no simple us and them with regard to sin and unbelief.

---

46. Barth, ChrL, 80. Cf. Luther:

> God receives none but those who are forsaken, restores health to none but those who are sick, gives sight to none but the blind, and life to one but the dead. He does not give saintliness to any but sinners, nor wisdom to any but fools. In short: He has mercy on none but the wretched and gives grace to none but those who are in disgrace. Therefore no arrogant saint, or just or wise man can be material for God, neither can he do the work of God, but he remains confined within his own work and makes of himself a fictitious, ostensible, false, and deceitful saint, that is, a hypocrite. (LW 14, 163)

47. This is methodologically akin to the place of the Christian at the inter-faith table that I have suggested might arise from Barth's consideration of religion. See Chapter 6 in this volume.
48. CD III/2, 525.
49. CD IV/3, 364.

The hope of salvation for Barth is never grounded in humanity – whether that be human righteousness or human faith. Instead, it is in the victory of Jesus.[50] As I have noted earlier in this volume:[51] yes, it is true, for Barth, that Jesus stands at the door and knocks, but in the power of his resurrection he is able to make his way into locked rooms (cf. Jn 20).

Non-absolute actualistic anthropology

This section seeks to outline what are perceived as the underlying logics of Bonhoeffer and Barth's reasoning in order to relate the above discussions to the life of Christian faith. This move is termed here 'non-absolute actualistic anthropology'.[52] In this, there is a need to confess to a level of creativity in the reading offered here of Bonhoeffer and Barth – more the thoughts that their work, and that of others, stir: this section arises from taking a lead from their thinking and thinking with them, rather than repeating them. It concerns not what has been said but what can, may and (perhaps) should be said.

The wider hope that Barth and Bonhoeffer both seem to suggest appears to be grounded, as argued, in their recognition that even the saint is a sinner, and united to humanity's sinfulness; and that even the believer in her sin and doubt is faithless. Therefore, to offer any hope to the Christian at all, there is required a broader hope for all humanity not grounded generally in God's love, but most especially in the love expressed ultimately even towards the continued unloveliness of the Christian. As Paul puts it, 'What then? Are we any better off? No, not at all.'[53] But in addressing these themes we must surely ask a variety of questions. What of judgement? What of the clear biblical demand for decision, for ethical behaviour, for discipleship, indeed? If we are all depraved and faithless people, and if Christian depravity is potentially the most damning of all, what purpose does an attempted life of faith serve? Does an account such as I have sketched suggest no quest for growth and piety? Does this determine that I should just sin that grace might abound? Space does not allow a full discussion of these themes here, but the category of non-absolute actualistic anthropology helps to facilitate a response to such matters.

It is possible to detect in Barth and Bonhoeffer the sense that, while the eternity of the human being may be absolute (since this eternal determination is based in Christ, and its future determination is to be in him), there is a simultaneous need to recognize the non-absolute nature of human beings in time. Put briefly,

---

50. See ibid., 173–80, and Chapter 5 in this volume.

51. See Chapter 5.

52. For reflection on Bonhoeffer's *Act and Being* (DBWE 2) and the relationship between his thought between these concepts, see André Dumas, *Dietrich Bonhoeffer: Theologian of Reality*, trans. Robert McAfee Brown (London: SCM, 1971), 97–117.

53. Rom. 3.9.

this requires distinguishing but holding together the view from below and the view from above (or to borrow Bonhoeffer's terminology – the penultimate and the ultimate). As non-absolute beings, it is difficult to make absolute judgements about human lives. Were this otherwise, the finite would be made infinite.[54] As Rahner recognizes, each single human is an 'inwardly plural being' about whom various things can be said regarding the different aspects of her existence.[55] As a result, there is a sense in which human beings are determined by the acts in which they engage: our acts may well be determinative of our being.[56] Thus, in terms of thinking about a wider hope, we may say that all *acts* of sin and faithlessness (which is itself sin) impugn God's righteousness; and there is thus either a hope for all or a hope for none, as all are culpable of these acts. An understanding of non-absolute anthropology which is concerned with the manner in which acts determine being allows for a shared sense of the Christian's and the non-Christian's position before God, as those whose lives are full of ambiguity, contradiction and failed attempts. These are lives in which Paul's words ring true: 'For I do not do the good I want, but the evil I do not want is what I do.'[57] One might be forgiven, however, for suggesting that this means a return to the non-Christian idea of deeds from one's life being judged by some heavenly scales of justice – with blessings for those whose good deeds outweigh the bad, and damnation for those whose evil outweighs the good.[58] Certainly, that is a fear and a danger. However, returning to pessimism and shared sinfulness may help again here. Bonhoeffer reminds us:

> Because everyone, as human being, stands within the humanity of Adam, no one can withdraw from the sinful act to a sinless being; no, the whole of one's being a person is in sin. Thus, in Adam act is as constitutive for being as being is for act; *both* act and being enter into judgement as guilty. … Because sin is envisaged through the concept of 'Adam', in the mode of being 'person', the contingency of conduct is preserved, as the continuity of the person of humanity, which attests itself in action – the person that I also am.[59]

It is not so simple as to suggest that acts are free from beings: the co-responsibility for sin (original sin) determines that our being is identified with our acts, and

---

54. See here Paul Tillich, *Systematic Theology*, vol. 3, *Life in the Spirit; History and the Kingdom of God* (Welwyn: James Nisbet, 1964), 434.

55. Karl Rahner, SJ, 'Purgatory', in *Theological Investigations*, vol. 19, *Faith and Ministry* (London: Darton, Longman & Todd, 1984), 184.

56. The argument below seeks to demonstrate the relationship between the act of sin and being in Adam (i.e. being a sinner). In order to be a sinner, one must necessarily sin, but this very act is constitutive of the being of the human, making a human a sinner.

57. Rom. 7.19.

58. On the non-Christian nature of this view, see Jürgen Moltmann, *In the End – the Beginning: The Life of Hope*, trans. Margaret Kohl (London: SCM, 2004), 140–1.

59. DBWE 2, 146; emphasis added.

our acts with our being. The act determines the being, just as the being wills the act (even if against the being's better will). We cannot simply say that some acts are found wanting and some praiseworthy: this is eating from the tree of the knowledge of good and evil, judging for ourselves (rather than accepting God's judgement), and not realizing that an act of individual disobedience corrupts the whole of human nature. Once again to quote Bonhoeffer: 'If sin were no more than a free act of the particular moment, a retreat to sinless being would in principle be possible, revelation in Christ having become redundant.'[60] Each individual's co-fallenness with Adam determines this: 'As I am in Adam, so is every individual; but in all individuals the one person of humanity, Adam, is active. This expresses both the contingency of the deed and the continuity of the being of sin.'[61]

But within this, once more, how may we hold these two ideas together of the co-sinfulness of all humanity, and the call to the 'higher life'? The non-absolute nature of our being again helps here. In recognizing the relationship outlined above between act and being, we may say that – while a pessimistic view of human beings' (even or most especially Christian human beings') situation before God helps to underline the need to realize God's salvific purpose for all creation (or else none) – the variety of the acts in which these beings engage and the vast array of determinations that they bring about point towards a stronger sense of particularity than simple binary separationism allows.[62] Realizing that the good one performs in faith and obedience corresponds to the ultimate being destined for humanity from and to all eternity provides ample reason for the life of discipleship, as a life which responds and corresponds to God's act of grace and love towards humanity in Christ. In seeking to correspond to that life is found

---

60. DBWE 2, 145.

61. Ibid., 146. It is here that one can note the contrast with Rahner, with whom there are similarities on these themes. Firstly, Rahner is pessimistic primarily about humans *knowing* the difference between each other (Christian and non-Christian), as opposed to there *being* a difference between people: his concerns are epistemological rather than ontological. Secondly, this is because of the current argument's predominantly *pessimistic* view of the Christian's capacity not to sin (and, therefore, the being of the Christian in Adam), as opposed to a predominantly optimistic view on the part of Rahner of the non-Christian's capacity to engage in acts corresponding to Christ (though certainly this would be a theme to explore at another time). Furthermore, thirdly, Rahner's emphasis on the good of others who are 'anonymously Christian' still facilitates a distinction between (on one side) Christians and 'anonymous Christians' and on the other non-Christians or non-'anonymous Christians'; an emphasis on the relationship between being in Adam and individual acts of sin makes such distinctions of being difficult, and also does not allow for the prioritized situation of the Christian except in terms of knowing God's graciousness to the whole world.

62. I am thinking here of such passages in the New Testament as those about storing up treasures in heaven. For further detailed reflection on non-binary eschatological differentiation, see my *Barth, Origen, and Universal Salvation*, esp. 210–11.

the basis of being formed into the image of Christ in whom all human destinies find themselves. For those who realize their future lies in Christ, nothing other than this desire for correspondence (despite all propensities to sin and unbelief) could be imagined.[63] In this, therefore, is the act of becoming human proleptically (and inevitably imperfectly, given all that has been said above) in anticipation of the true human identity awaiting all humans in transformation at the eschaton. However, in simultaneously understanding human co-responsibility for sin in the world and the union of the believer and the unbeliever, we realize that these penultimate differences of degree cannot undermine the ultimate future of God; and no difference of degree can save any human from their responsibility for sin. How will this be so? That is entering into precisely the other-worldly realm of eschatology I – with Bonhoeffer – wish to eschew. Suffice it to say in Bonhoeffer's own words: 'It is beyond what we are able to conceive now as to how it will come to pass that all become one and yet each keeps their own identity.'[64]

Conclusion

In conclusion, by identifying the sin and unbelief of the believer, there opens a door to the possibility of universalism (even if only expressed as a sigh) which has otherwise been cut off by calls upon the seriousness of sin and the righteousness of God. Such an emphasis, moreover, protects universalism from still working within the bounds of separationist eschatology: the so-called 'others' are not added extras, but are as integral to the plan and purposes of God as any Christian might hope to be. Furthermore, in seeking to identify the Christian and the non-Christian, it has been possible to determine a non-absolute actualistic anthropology which arises from God's judgement of the act and being of an individual. In exploring this approach to humanity, it has been possible to find a place for human and Christian particularity within a schema which points towards universalism. Faith and obedience still find their place, especially as 'only faith itself can say whether God "is" also outside the act of faith'.[65] Epistemologically, there is a need to speak from the perspective of faith about these realities, albeit the distinction is between the Christians who know these realities for the world and the non-Christian who does not yet know them – *not* between the saved and the damned.[66] And there

---

63. Cf. Eberhard Jüngel, 'Humanity in Correspondence to God: Remarks on the Image of God as a Basic Concept in Theological Anthropology', in *Theological Essays I*, ed. and trans. John Webster (Edinburgh: T&T Clark, 1989), 124–53; and Eberhard Jüngel, 'On Becoming Truly Human: The Significance of the Reformation Distinction between Person and Works for the Self-Understanding of Modern Humanity', in *Theological Essays II*, ed. John Webster, trans. Arnold Neufeldt-Fast and John Webster (Edinburgh: T&T Clark, 1995), 216–40.

64. DBWE 1, 288.

65. DBWE 2, 93.

66. For further discussion of this theme from the perspective of pneumatology, see my *Barth, Origen, and Universal Salvation*, chap. 7.

remains an accountability for all actions as well as for the whole sin of humanity; neither original sin, judgement nor particularity is removed. But aware of her own sin and unbelief, and her own culpability for the sins and unbelief of humanity, the Christian is freed to realize that the depths of grace are the points at which forgiveness reaches her, as the last and least in everything. Kierkegaard pointed in this direction when he stated, 'If others go to hell, then I will go too. But I do not believe that; on the contrary I believe that all will be saved, myself with them – something that arouses my deepest amazement.'[67]

---

67. Cited and translated by Ludlow, 'Universalism in the History of Christianity', 208.

CONCLUSION

The essays in this book have been gathered together not only for the purpose of explicating Barth and Bonhoeffer on themes relating to the church and its speech in a post-liberal context but also to offer a contribution to the ways in which theologically we should speak to and about the context in which the church exists today in the hope that there might be ever more interventions by the theological community into the theological discussions of these themes, building from the wisdom of theologians from the past who wrestled with proximate issues. Indeed, we might consider that this kind of 'traditioned' reflection on the church in a post-Christendom context is the only wise approach available. Simply accepting maximally secular, pluralistically relativistic or liberal approaches to these themes leads to an intolerant atheism, a relativism without any sense of the authority of exclusivist claims or a failure to see liberalism itself as a traditioned mode of thinking with traditioned claims.[1] Theological engagements with the church and its proclamation must also not simply engage as if theology were in a vacuum with only internally orientated discussions which ignore the given spatio-temporal, quotidian existence of the church and the world at a given point; such approaches lead to sectarianism or at worst fundamentalism. There is wisdom to be found in Wolfhart Pannenberg's assertion:

> Christian theology in the secular world must not give up central elements in God's transcendence of the world and in his salvation or allow them to fade into the background for the sake of assimilation to the secular understanding of reality. On the other hand, Christianity may not be content with just securing the existence of the dogmatic content of the tradition. That would be merely to oppose a counter-world of faith to the secular world, not to bear witness to God as creator and reconciler of this world of ours.[2]

---

1. Cf. Alasdair MacIntyre: 'Liberal theory is best understood, not at all as an attempt to find a rationality independent of tradition, but as itself an articulation of an historically developed and developing set of social institutions and forms of activity, that is, as the voice of a tradition.' *Whose Justice? Which Rationality?* (London: Duckworth, 1988), 345.
2. Wolfhart Pannenberg, *Christianity in a Secularized World* (London: SCM, 1988), 56-7.

The church's life and speech are always ordered to the world to which the church witnesses to and proclaims the God of the gospel – the God of good news, of salvation, of *shalom*.

There will always be a degree of occasionalism about engagement regarding the church in relation to these themes. While there is a degree of systematicity in these essays, especially in the awareness of the horizon and taxonomy of proximate theological loci, the engagements in drawing on the theology of Barth and Bonhoeffer do not involve the kind of over-determined systematicity to which they were both opposed – for all of the theological architecture of both their works. The Spirit's own freedom is important to remember as the Spirit actualizes Christ in the here and now. Indeed, this is the way in which it is best to consider the manner in which a system can be best understood as Christian – in relation to the way in which God reveals Godself in Christ by the Spirit. Bonhoeffer's words are helpful here:

> Christ is not a principle according to which the whole world must be formed. Christ does not proclaim a system of that which would be good today, here, and at all times. Christ does not teach an abstract ethic that must be carried out, cost what it may. Christ was not essentially a teacher, a lawgiver, but a human being, a real human being like us. ... God did not become an idea, a principle, a universally valid belief or a law; God became human.[3]

The Christological personalism, actualized by the Holy Spirit, reminds theology that in drawing from the riches of the past, the engagement cannot be one of a principled and immutable system.

The world itself, as governed by and subject to the providential grace of God its creator and sustainer, is the theatre in all its particularity and givenness of the economy of God. The world's passing, changing and contingent nature is the locus in which the church witnesses to Jesus Christ. In this way, the church (which exists within the world) is always orientated in its ministry to the boundaries at which the church and the world meet. The church, therefore, has to speak and witness to the world in which it exists – not only in which it exists, indeed, but for which it exists. Barth helpfully reminds us:

> By believing in Jesus Christ and preaching Jesus Christ it [the church] believes in and preaches Him who is the Lord of the world as He is Lord of the Church. And since they belong to the inner circle, the members of the Church are also automatically members of the wider circle. They cannot halt at the boundary where the inner and outer circles meet, though the work of faith, love and hope which they are under orders to perform will assume different forms on either side of the boundary.[4]

---

3. DBWE 6, 98–9; cf. 231.
4. Karl Barth, *Community, State and Church* (Garden City, NY: Doubleday, 1960), 158–9. David Fergusson's work is helpful on this theme: 'By emphasizing the universal

Engagement with the world in its very givenness (indeed, in its political realities) is necessary for the church to be truly the church. Indeed, our engagement with the world and the neighbours we find in it is an affirmation of the world. This represents the church's necessary concern for others outwith the church beyond the concern the church might have for itself and its own existence. Bonhoeffer makes this point powerfully:

> The statements in the New Testament regarding Christian action, as well as the Sermon on the Mount, do not grow out of bitter resignation over the irreconcilable rift between the Christian and the worldly, but from joy over the already accomplished reconciliation of the world with God, from the peace of the already accomplished work of salvation in Jesus Christ.[5]

This recognition of the objective work that Christ has achieved in and for the world already (which is actualized in the present in the church by the redeeming Spirit) is the basis for the hope the church has for the world in its post-Christendom existence.

But this engagement with the world cannot be an engagement that presumes this eschatological consummation is already achieved. The reconciling grace of God in the world, in fact, occurs only proleptically and in anticipation. In this way, the church after Christendom has, in one sense, much more hope for the world than a church which believes in an overly realized institutional form of the presence of the kingdom within the world in the unity of church and altar. As Barth evocatively reminds us:

> The object of the promise and the hope in which the Christian community has its eternal goal consists, according to the unmistakeable assertion of the New Testament, not in an eternal Church but in the _polis_ built by God and coming down from heaven to earth, and the nations shall walk in the light of it and the kings of the earth will bring their glory and honour into it.[6]

This hope is a hope which lies ahead of both the church and the world. It is a hope, which the work of both Bonhoeffer and Barth reminds us, in which both the church and the world share in anticipation, even as the grace of God is made actively present by the Spirit's work in the here and now. The church in a post-liberal context can never forget this certain hope within which it lives in all of the complexity of the world in its fallenness and contingent forms.

---

significance of God's action in Christ from which the polity of the church derives, ecclesial isolationism may be avoided' (David Fergusson, *Community, Liberalism & Christian Ethics* [Cambridge: Cambridge University Press, 1998], 167).

5. DBWE 6, 238.
6. Barth, *Community, State and Church*, 154.

BIBLIOGRAPHY

Asad, Talal. *Formations of the Secular: Christianity, Islam, Modernity*. Stanford, CA: Stanford University Press, 2003.
Balthasar, Hans Urs von. *The Theology of Karl Barth: Exposition and Interpretation*. Translated by Edward T. Oakes. San Francisco, CA: Communio Books, Ignatius Press, 1992.
Barr, James. *Fundamentalism*. London: SCM Press, 1977.
Barrett, David B., George Thomas Kurian and Todd M. Johnson. *World Christian Encyclopedia: A Comparative Survey of Churches and Religions in the Modern World*. 2nd edn. Oxford: Oxford University Press, 2001.
Barth, Karl. 'An Prof. Dr. Hendrik Berkhof, Leiden, 1968'. In *Briefe 1961–1968*, edited by Jürgen Fangmeier and Hinrich Stoevesandt, 504–5. Karl Barth Gesamtausgabe V.6. Zurich: Theologischer Verlag, 1979.
Barth, Karl. 'Barth: May 7, 1968'. In *A Late Friendship: The Letters of Karl Barth and Carl Zuckmayer*, translated by Geoffrey W. Bromiley, 41–4. Grand Rapids, MI: Eerdmans, 1982.
Barth, Karl. *Evangelical Theology: An Introduction*. Grand Rapids, MI: Eerdmans, 1979.
Barth, Karl. *Fragments Grave and Gay*. Edited by Martin Rumscheidt. London: Collins, 1971.
Barth, Karl. 'From a Letter to Superintendent Herrenbrück'. In *World Come of Age: A Symposium on Dietrich Bonhoeffer*, edited by R. Gregor Smith, 89–92. London: Collins, 1967.
Barth, Karl. 'Gespräch Mit Rheinischen Jugendpfarrern (4.11.1963)'. In *Gespräche 1963*, edited by Eberhard Busch, 235–333. Karl Barth Gesamtausgabe IV.41. Zürich: Theologischer Verlag, 2005.
Barth, Karl. *God, Grace and Gospel*. Edinburgh: Oliver and Boyd, 1959.
Barth, Karl. 'Humanity of God'. In *God, Grace and Gospel*, by Karl Barth, translated by James Strathearn McNab, 31–52. Edinburgh: Oliver and Boyd, 1959.
Barth, Karl. 'Letter to Wilhelm Vischer, August 24, 1933'. In *Briefe des Jahres 1933*, edited by Eberhard Busch, Bartolt Haase and Barbara Schenck. Zürich: Theologischer Verlag Zürich, 2004.
Barth, Karl. *Letters 1961–1968*. Edited by Jürgen Fangmeier and Hinrich Stoevesandt. Translated by G. W. Bromiley. Edinburgh: T&T Clark, 1981.
Barth, Karl. *On Religion: The Revelation of God as the Sublimation of Religion*. Translated and introduced by Garrett Green. London: T&T Clark, 2007.
Barth, Karl. *Protestant Theology in the Nineteenth Century: Its Background and History*. Grand Rapids, MI: Eerdmans, 2002.
Barth, Karl. *The Epistle to the Romans*. Oxford: Oxford University Press, 1968.
Barth, Karl. *The Resurrection of the Dead*. Eugene, OR: Wipf and Stock, 2003.
Barth, Karl. *The Theology of John Calvin*. Translated by Geoffrey W. Bromiley. Grand Rapids, MI: Eerdmans, 1995.

Barth, Karl. *Theologische Existenz heute!* 8. Aufl. Theologische Existenz heute 1. München: Kaiser, 1933.

Barth, Karl. 'To Rector Eberhard Bethge, Rengsdorf near Neuwied'. In *Letters 1961–1968*, edited by Jürgen Fangmeier and Hinrich Stoevesandt, translated by G. W. Bromiley, 250–2. Edinburgh: T&T Clark, 1981.

'Being Christian in Western Europe'. Washington, DC: Pew Research Center, 29 May 2018. https://www.pewforum.org/2018/05/29/being-christian-in-western-europe/.

Berger, Peter L. 'The Desecularization of the World: A Global Overview'. In *The Desecularization of the World: Resurgent Religion and World Politics*, edited by Peter L. Berger, 1–18. Washington, DC: Ethics and Public Policy Center; Grand Rapids, MI: Eerdmans, 1999.

Berkhof, Louis. *Systematic Theology*. Grand Rapids, MI: Eerdmans, 1938.

Berkouwer, G. C. *The Triumph of Grace in the Theology of Karl Barth*. Translated by Harry R. Boer. London: Paternoster Press, 1956.

Bethge, Eberhard. *Dietrich Bonhoeffer: A Biography*. Edited by Victoria J. Barnett. Rev. edn. Minneapolis, MN: Fortress Press, 2000.

Bethge, Eberhard. *Dietrich Bonhoeffer: Theologian, Christian, Contemporary*. Edited by Edwin Robertson. Translated by Eric Mosbacher, Peter Ross, Betty Ross, Frank Clarke and William Glen-Doepel. London: Collins, 1970.

Bettis, Joseph D. 'Is Karl Barth a Universalist?' *Scottish Journal of Theology* 20, no. 4 (1967): 423–36. https://doi.org/10.1017/S003693060005314X.

Bonhoeffer, Dietrich. *Letters and Papers from Prison*. Edited by Eberhard Bethge. London: SCM Press, 1999.

Brierley, Peter. *UK Church Statistics*. 3rd edn. Tonbridge: ADBC, 2018. https://static1.squarespace.com/static/54228e0ce4b059910e19e44e/t/5a1591cb9140b7c306789dec/1511363021441/CS3+Page+0.2+Intro.pdf.

Busch, Eberhard. 'Indissoluble Unity: Barth's Position on the Jews during the Hitler Era'. In *For the Sake of the World: Karl Barth and the Future of Ecclesial Theology*, edited by George Hunsinger, 53–79. Grand Rapids, MI: Eerdmans, 2004.

Busch, Eberhard. *Karl Barth: His Life from Letters and Autobiographical Texts*. London: SCM Press, 1976.

Busch Nielsen, Kirsten. 'Community Turned Inside Out: Dietrich Bonhoeffer's Concept of the Church and of Humanity Reconsidered'. In *Being Human, Becoming Human: Dietrich Bonhoeffer and Social Thought*, edited by Jens Zimmermann and Brian E. Gregor, 91–101. Eugene, OR: Wipf and Stock, 2010.

Bush, George W. 'Remarks by the President to the Warsaw Conference on Combatting Terrorism'. Presented at the Conference on Combatting Terrorism, Warsaw, 6 November 2001. https://avalon.law.yale.edu/sept11/president_086.asp.

Calvin, Jean. *Institutes of the Christian Religion*. Edited by John T. McNeill. Translated by Ford Lewis Battles. 2 vols. Philadelphia, PA: Westminster Press, 1960.

Cavanaugh, William T. *Theopolitical Imagination*. London: T&T Clark, 2002.

Chase, Michael. 'Time and Eternity from Plotinus and Boethius to Einstein'. *ΣΧΟΛΗ* 8, no. 1 (2014): 67–110.

Chestnut, Glenn A. 'The Secular Parables of the Kingdom'. Presented at the Society for the Study of Theology, Leeds, 2006.

Chia, Clement. 'Is Barth a Supercessionist? Reconsidering the Case in the Historical Context of the Nazi Jewish Question'. Presented at the Society for the Study of Theology, Leeds, 2006.

Choueiri, Youssef M. *Islamic Fundamentalism*. Rev. edn. London: Pinter, 1997.
Choueiri, Youssef M. 'The Political Discourse of Contemporary Islamicist Movements'. In *Islamic Fundamentalism*, edited by Abdel Salam Sidahmed and Anoushiravan Ehteshami, 19–33. Boulder, CO: Westview Press, 1996.
Clifford J. Green. *Bonhoeffer: A Theology of Sociality*. Rev. edn. Grand Rapids, MI: Eerdmans, 1999.
Clough, David. 'Karl Barth on the Idolatry of Religion'. In *Idolatry: False Worship in the Bible, Early Judaism, and Christianity*, edited by Stephen C. Barton, 213–14. London: T&T Clark, 2007.
Colwell, John. 'The Contemporaneity of Divine Decision: Reflections on Barth's Denial of Universalism'. In *Universalism and the Doctrine of Hell*, edited by Nigel M. de S. Cameron, 139–60. Carlisle: Paternoster, 1992.
Crisp, Oliver D. 'I Do Teach It, but I Also Do Not Teach It: The Universalism of Karl Barth (1886–1968)'. In *'All Shall Be Well': Explorations in Universal Salvation and Christian Theology, from Origen to Moltmann*, edited by Gregory Macdonald, 305–24. Eugene, OR: Cascade Books, 2011.
Crisp, Oliver D. 'On Barth's Denial of Universalism'. *Themelios* 29, no. 1 (2003). https://www.thegospelcoalition.org/themelios/article/on-barths-denial-of-universalism/.
Davie, Grace. *Europe: The Exceptional Case: Parameters of Faith in the Modern World*. London: Darton, Longman & Todd, 2002.
Davie, Grace. *Religion in Britain since 1945: Believing without Belonging*. Oxford: Blackwell, 1994.
D'Costa, Gavin. 'Theology of Religions'. In *The Modern Theologians: An Introduction to Christian Theology in the Twentieth Century*, edited by David F. Ford, 2nd edn, 626–44. Cambridge, MA: Blackwell, 1997.
DeJonge, Michael P. *Bonhoeffer's Theological Formation: Berlin, Barth, and Protestant Theology*. Oxford: Oxford University Press, 2012.
DiNoia, J. A. 'Religion and the Religions'. In *The Cambridge Companion to Karl Barth*, edited by John Webster, 243–57. Cambridge: Cambridge University Press, 2000.
DiNoia, J. A. *The Diversity of Religions: A Christian Perspective*. Washington, DC: Catholic University of America Press, 1992.
Dramm, Sabine. *Dietrich Bonhoeffer: An Introduction to His Thought*. Translated by Thomas Rice. Peabody, MA: Hendrickson, 2007.
Dumas, André. *Dietrich Bonhoeffer: Theologian of Reality*. Translated by Robert McAfee Brown. London: SCM, 1971.
'Europe's Growing Muslim Population'. Washington, DC: Pew Research Center, 29 November 2017. https://www.pewforum.org/2017/11/29/europes-growing-muslim-population/.
Fergusson, David. 'Will the Love of God Finally Triumph?' In *Nothing Greater, Nothing Better: Theological Essays on the Love of God*, edited by Kevin J. Vanhoozer, 186–202. Grand Rapids, MI: Eerdmans, 2001.
Feuerbach, Ludwig. *The Essence of Christianity*. Translated by George Eliot. New York: Harper & Row, 1957.
Ford, David F. 'Abrahamic Dialogue: Towards Respect and Understanding in Our Life Together'. Presented at the inauguration of the Society for Dialogue and Action, Cambridge, 2006.
Ford, David F. *Barth and God's Story: Biblical Narrative and the Theological Method of Karl Barth in the 'Church Dogmatics'*. 2nd edn. Frankfurt am Main: Lang, 1985.

Ford, David F. 'Barth's Interpretation of the Bible'. In *Karl Barth, Studies of His Theological Method*, edited by Stephen Sykes, 55–87. Oxford: Clarendon Press, 1979.

Ford, David F. 'Conclusion: Assessing Barth'. In *Karl Barth, Studies of His Theological Method*, edited by Stephen Sykes, 194–202. Oxford: Clarendon Press, 1979.

Ford, David F. 'God and Our Public Life: A Scriptural Wisdom'. *International Journal of Public Theology* 1, no. 1 (2007): 63–81. https://doi.org/10.1163/156973207X194493.

Ford, David F. 'Gospel in Context: Among Many Faiths'. Presented at the Fulcrum Conference, Islington, 2006.

Glasse, John. 'Barth on Feuerbach'. *Harvard Theological Review* 57, no. 2 (1964): 69–96.

Godsey, John D. 'Barth as a Teacher'. In *For the Sake of the World: Karl Barth and the Future of Ecclesial Theology*, edited by George Hunsinger. Grand Rapids, MI: Eerdmans, 2004.

Graham, Jeannine M. *Representation and Substitution in the Atonement Theologies of Dorothee Sölle, John Macquarrie and Karl Barth*. New York: Peter Lang, 2005.

Green, Clifford J. 'Trinity and Christology in Bonhoeffer and Barth'. *Union Seminary Quarterly Review* 60, nos. 1–2 (2006): 1–22.

Green, Garrett. 'Barth on Religion'. Presented at the Society for the Study of Theology, Leeds, 2006.

Green, Garrett. 'Challenging the Religious Studies Canon: Karl Barth's Theory of Religion'. *Journal of Religion* 75, no. 4 (1995): 473–86. https://doi.org/10.1086/489678.

Greggs, Tom. *Barth, Origen, and Universal Salvation: Restoring Particularity*. Oxford: Oxford University Press, 2009.

Greggs, Tom. 'Being a Wise Apprentice to the Communion of Modern Saints: On the Need for Conversation with a Plurality of Interlocutors'. In *The Vocation of Theology Today: A Festschrift for David Ford*, edited by Tom Greggs, Rachel Muers and Simeon Zahl, 21–34. Eugene, OR: Cascade Books, 2013.

Greggs, Tom. *Theology against Religion: Constructive Dialogues with Bonhoeffer and Barth*. London: T&T Clark, 2011.

Gunton, Colin E. 'Karl Barth's Doctrine of Election as Part of His Doctrine of God'. *Journal of Theological Studies* 25, no. 2 (1974): 381–92. https://doi.org/10.1093/jts/XXV.2.381.

Gunton, Colin E. 'No Other Foundation: One Englishman's Reading of *Church Dogmatics* Chapter V'. In *Reckoning with Barth: Essays in Commemoration of the Centenary of Karl Barth's Birth*, edited by Nigel Biggar, 61–79. London: Mowbray, 1988.

Gunton, Colin E. 'The Triune God and the Freedom of the Creature'. In *Karl Barth: Centenary Essays*, edited by S. W. Sykes, 46–68. Cambridge: Cambridge University Press, 1989.

Hardy, Daniel W. 'Karl Barth'. In *The Modern Theologians: An Introduction to Christian Theology Since 1918*, edited by David F. Ford and Rachel Muers, 3rd edn, 21–42. Great Theologians. Oxford: Blackwell, 2005.

Hart, Trevor. 'Universalism: Two Distinct Types'. In *Universalism and the Doctrine of Hell*, edited by Nigel M. de S. Cameron, 1–34. Carlisle: Paternoster, 1992.

Hart, Trevor A. *Regarding Karl Barth: Toward a Reading of His Theology*. Carlisle: Paternoster Press, 1999.

Hartwell, Herbert. *The Theology of Karl Barth*. Studies in Theology. Bungay: Richard Clayton, 1964.

Hauerwas, Stanley. *With the Grain of the Universe: The Church's Witness and Natural Theology*. London: SCM Press, 2002.

Hick, John. *God and the Universe of Faiths: Essays in the Philosophy of Religion*. London: Macmillan, 1973.
Hunsinger, George. 'A Tale of Two Simultaneities: Justification and Sanctification in Calvin and Barth'. In *Conversing with Barth*, edited by John C. McDowell and Mike Higton, 68–89. Aldershot: Ashgate, 2004.
Hunsinger, George. *Disruptive Grace: Studies in the Theology of Karl Barth*. Grand Rapids, MI: Eerdmans, 2000.
Hunsinger, George. *How to Read Karl Barth: The Shape of His Theology*. New York: Oxford University Press, 1991.
Huntington, Samuel P. 'The Clash of Civilizations?' *Foreign Affairs* 72, no. 3 (1993): 22–49. https://doi.org/10.2307/20045621.
'In U.S., Decline of Christianity Continues at Rapid Pace'. Washington, DC: Pew Research Center, 17 October 2019. https://www.pewforum.org/2019/10/17/in-u-s-decline-of-christianity-continues-at-rapid-pace/.
'In Western European Countries with Church Taxes, Support for the Tradition Remains Strong'. Washington, DC: Pew Research Center, 30 April 2019. https://www.pewforum.org/2019/04/30/in-western-european-countries-with-church-taxes-support-for-the-tradition-remains-strong/.
Jenkins, Timothy. *Religion in English Everyday Life: An Ethnographic Approach*. Oxford: Berghahn, 1999.
Jenson, Matt. *Gravity of Sin: Augustine, Luther and Barth on* Homo Incurvatus in Se. London: T&T Clark, 2006.
Jenson, Robert. *God after God: The God of the Past and the God of the Future as Seen in the Work of Karl Barth*. Indianapolis, IN: Bobbs-Merrill, 1969.
Jüngel, Eberhard. *God's Being Is in Becoming: The Trinitarian Being of God in the Theology of Karl Barth: A Paraphrase*. 2nd English edn. Edinburgh: T&T Clark, 2001.
Jüngel, Eberhard. *Theological Essays I*. Edited and translated by John Webster. Edinburgh: T&T Clark, 1989.
Jüngel, Eberhard. *Theological Essays II*. Edited by John Webster. Translated by Arnold Neufeldt-Fast and John Webster. Edinburgh: T&T Clark, 1995.
Kelsey, David H. *Eccentric Existence: A Theological Anthropology*. Louisville, KY: Westminster John Knox Press, 2009.
Kirkpatrick, Matthew D., ed. *Engaging Bonhoeffer: The Impact and Influence of Bonhoeffer's Life and Thought*. Minneapolis, MN: Fortress Press, 2016.
Kittel, Gerhard, ed. *Theologisches Wörterbuch zum Neuen Testament*, vol. 3. Stuttgart: Kohlhammer, 1957.
Krötke, Wolf. *Karl Barth and Dietrich Bonhoeffer: Theologians for a Post-Christian World*. Translated by John P. Burgess. Grand Rapids, MI: Baker Academic, 2019.
Leahy, Brendan. '"Christ Existing as Community": Dietrich Bonhoeffer's Notion of Church'. *Irish Theological Quarterly* 73, nos. 1–2 (2008): 32–59. https://doi.org/10.1177/0021140008091690.
Leftow, Brian. 'Boethius on Eternity'. *History of Philosophy Quarterly* 7, no. 2 (1990): 123–42.
Leftow, Brian. *Time and Eternity*. Ithaca, NY: Cornell University Press, 1991.
Lindsay, Mark. 'Dialectics of Communion: Dialectical Method and Barth's Defence of Israel'. In *Karl Barth: A Future for Postmodern Theology?*, edited by Geoff Thompson and Christiaan Mostert, 122–46. Hindmarsh, South Australia: Australian Theological Forum, 2000.

Louth, Andrew. 'Barth and the Problem of Natural Theology'. *Downside Review* 87, no. 288 (1969): 268–77. https://doi.org/10.1177/001258066908728803.
Lovin, Robin W. 'Reinhold Niebuhr and Dietrich Bonhoeffer on Responsibility'. In *Engaging Bonhoeffer: The Impact and Influence of Bonhoeffer's Life and Thought*, edited by Matthew D. Kirkpatrick, 65–86. Minneapolis, MN: Fortress Press, 2016.
Ludlow, Morwenna. *Universal Salvation: Eschatology in the Thought of Gregory of Nyssa and Karl Rahner*. Oxford: Oxford University Press, 2000.
Ludlow, Morwenna. 'Universalism in the History of Christianity'. In *Universal Salvation? The Current Debate*, edited by Robin Parry and Christopher H. Partridge, 191–218. Carlisle: Paternoster, 2003.
MacDonald, Gregory. *The Evangelical Universalist: The Biblical Hope That God's Love Will Save Us All*. London: SPCK, 2008.
MacIntyre, Alasdair C. *Whose Justice? Which Rationality?* London: Duckworth, 1988.
Markham, Ian S, ed. *A World Religions Reader*. Oxford: Blackwell, 1997.
Marshall, Bruce D. Review of *Review of A Theology on Its Way? Essays on Karl Barth*, by Richard H. Roberts. *Journal of Theological Studies* 44, no. 1 (1993): 453–8. https://doi.org/10.1093/jts/44.1.453.
Martin, David. *Reflections on Sociology and Theology*. Oxford: Clarendon Press, 1997.
Martin, David. *The Religious and the Secular: Studies in Secularization*. London: Routledge & Kegan Paul, 1969.
McCormack, Bruce L. 'Grace and Being: The Role of God's Gracious Election in Karl Barth's Theological Ontology'. In *The Cambridge Companion to Karl Barth*, edited by John Webster, 92–110. Cambridge: Cambridge University Press, 2000.
McCormack, Bruce L. *Karl Barth's Critically Realistic Dialectical Theology: Its Genesis and Development, 1909–1936*. Oxford: Clarendon Press, 1995.
McCormack, Bruce L. *Orthodox and Modern: Studies in the Theology of Karl Barth*. Grand Rapids, MI: Baker Academic, 2008. http://books.google.com/books?id=wpVCAQAAIAAJ.
McDowell, John C. *Hope in Barth's Eschatology: Interrogations and Transformations beyond Tragedy*. Aldershot: Ashgate, 2000.
McDowell, John C. 'Learning Where to Place One's Hope: The Eschatological Significance of Election in Barth'. *Scottish Journal of Theology* 53, no. 3 (2000): 316–38. https://doi.org/10.1017/S0036930600051012.
Moberly, R. W. L. *The Old Testament of the Old Testament: Patriarchal Narratives and Mosaic Yahwism*. Minneapolis, MN: Fortress Press, 1992.
Moltmann, Jürgen. *In the End – the Beginning: The Life of Hope*. Translated by Margaret Kohl. London: SCM Press, 2004. http://www.vlebooks.com/vleweb/product/openreader?id=none&isbn=9780334048664.
Morris, Wayne, and Hannah Bacon, eds. *Transforming Exclusion: Engaging with Faith Perspectives*. London: Continuum, 2011.
Moseley, Carys. 'Karl Barth's Theology of Religion: Interpreting Religious Change Yesterday and Today'. Presented at the Society for the Study of Theology, Leeds, 2006.
Nayed, Aref. 'Al-Rahman: God the Compassionate'. Presented at the Society for the Study of Theology, Leeds, 2006.
Neder, Adam. *Participation in Christ: An Entry into Karl Barth's Church Dogmatics*. Louisville, KY: Westminster John Knox Press, 2009.

Nickson, Ann L. *Bonhoeffer on Freedom: Courageously Grasping Reality*. Aldershot: Ashgate, 2002.
Niebuhr, Reinhold. Review of *Ethics*, by Dietrich Bonhoeffer. *Union Seminary Quarterly Review* 11, no. 4 (1956): 57–8.
Nimmo, Paul T. *Being in Action: The Theological Shape of Barth's Ethical Vision*. Library of New Testament Studies. London: T&T Clark, 2007.
Nimmo, Paul T. 'Election and Evangelical Thinking: Challenging Our Way of Conceiving the Doctrine of God'. In *New Perspectives for Evangelical Theology: Engaging with God, Scripture, and the World*, edited by Tom Greggs, 29–43. London: Routledge, 2010.
Ochs, Peter. *Peirce, Pragmatism, and the Logic of Scripture*. Cambridge: Cambridge University Press, 1998.
O'Collins, SJ, Gerald. *Salvation for All: God's Other Peoples*. Oxford: Oxford University Press, 2008.
Ott, Heinrich. *Reality and Faith: The Theological Legacy of Dietrich Bonhoeffer*. London: Lutterworth Press, 1971.
Pangritz, Andreas. *Karl Barth in the Theology of Dietrich Bonhoeffer: A Clarification Whose Time Has Come*. Grand Rapids, MI: Eerdmans, 1999.
Pangritz, Andreas. 'Wilhelm Vischer's Contribution to the "Bethel Confession"'. Presented at the American Academy of Religion, Montreal, Quebec, 2010.
Pannenberg, Wolfhart. *Metaphysics and the Idea of God*. Grand Rapids, MI: Eerdmans, 1990.
Pannenberg, Wolfhart. *Systematic Theology*, vol. 1. Grand Rapids, MI: Eerdmans, 2010.
Parry, Robin, and Christopher H. Partridge, eds. *Universal Salvation? The Current Debate*. Carlisle: Paternoster, 2003.
Percy, Martyn. *Words, Wonders and Power: Understanding Contemporary Christian Fundamentalism and Revivalism*. London: SPCK, 1996.
Plant, Stephen. *Bonhoeffer*. London: Continuum, 2004.
Plant, Stephen, and Ralf K. Wüstenberg, eds. *Religion, Religionlessness and Contemporary Western Culture: Explorations in Dietrich Bonhoeffer's Theology*. International Bonhoeffer Interpretations 1. Frankfurt am Main: Peter Lang, 2008.
Puffer, Matthew. 'Dietrich Bonhoeffer in the Theology of Karl Barth'. In *Karl Barth in Conversation*, edited by W. Travis McMaken and David W. Congdon, 46–61. Eugene, OR: Pickwick, 2014.
Quash, Ben, and Timothy Jenkins. 'The Cambridge Inter-Faith Programme: Academic Profile', 22 August 2006. https://www.interfaith.cam.ac.uk/resources/journalarticlesandbookchapters/cipacademicprofile.
Rahner, SJ, Karl. 'Anonymous Christians'. In *Concerning Vatican II*. Theological Investigations 6. London: Darton, Longman & Todd, 1974.
Rahner, SJ, Karl. 'Purgatory'. In *Faith and Ministry*. Theological Investigations 19. London: Darton, Longman & Todd, 1974.
Roberts, Richard H. *A Theology on Its Way? Essays on Karl Barth*. Edinburgh: T&T Clark, 1991.
Roberts, Richard H. 'Karl Barth's Doctrine of Time: Its Nature and Implications'. In *Karl Barth, Studies of His Theological Method*, edited by Stephen Sykes, 88–146. Oxford: Clarendon Press, 1979.
Robinson, John A. T. *In the End, God*. London: Collins Fontana, 1968.
Rogers, Eugene F. 'Supplementing Barth on Jews and Gender: Identifying God by Anagogy and the Spirit'. *Modern Theology* 14, no. 1 (1998): 43–81. https://doi.org/10.1111/1468-0025.00056.

Sauter, Gerhard. 'Why Is Karl Barth's Church Dogmatics Not a "Theology of Hope"? Some Observations on Barth's Understanding of Eschatology'. *Scottish Journal of Theology* 52, no. 4 (1999): 407–29. https://doi.org/10.1017/S0036930600050468.
Schleiermacher, Friedrich. *The Christian Faith*. Edited by H. R. Mackintosh and J. S. Stewart. Translated by D. M. Baillie, W. R. Matthews, Edith Sandbach-Marshall, A. B. Macaulay, Alexander Grieve, J. Y. Campbell, R. W. Stewart and H. R. Mackintosh. English translation of the 2nd German edn. Edinburgh: T&T Clark, 1968.
Schwöbel, Christoph. ' "Religion" and "Religionlessness" in *Letters and Papers from Prison*: A Perspective for Religious Pluralism?' In *Mysteries in the Theology of Dietrich Bonhoeffer: A Copenhagen Bonhoeffer Symposium*, edited by Kirsten Busch Nielsen, Ulrik Nissen and Christiane Tietz, 159–84. Göttingen: Vandenhoeck & Ruprecht, 2007.
Selby, Peter. 'Christianity in a World Come of Age'. In *The Cambridge Companion to Dietrich Bonhoeffer*, edited by John W. de Gruchy, 226–45. Cambridge: Cambridge University Press, 1999.
Siddiqui, Ataullah. *Christian-Muslim Dialogue in the Twentieth Century*. London: Macmillan, 1997.
Smith, R. Gregor, ed. *World Come of Age: A Symposium on Dietrich Bonhoeffer*. London: Collins, 1967.
Sonderegger, Katherine. 'Response to Eberhard Busch'. In *For the Sake of the World: Karl Barth and the Future of Ecclesial Theology*, edited by George Hunsinger, 80–7. Grand Rapids, MI: Eerdmans, 2004.
Sonderegger, Katherine. *That Jesus Christ Was Born a Jew: Karl Barth's 'Doctrine of Israel'*. University Park, PA: Pennsylvania State University Press, 1992.
Soulen, R. Kendall. ' "Go Tell Pharaoh", or, Why Empires Prefer a Nameless God'. In *The Economy of Salvation: Essays in Honour of M. Douglas Meeks*, edited by Jürgen Moltmann, Timothy R. Eberhart and Matthew W. Charlton, 58–70. Eugene, OR: Cascade Books, 2015.
Tanner, Kathryn. 'Creation and Providence'. In *The Cambridge Companion to Karl Barth*, edited by John Webster, 111–26. Cambridge: Cambridge University Press, 2000.
Thompson, Geoff. 'Religious Diversity, Christian Doctrine and Karl Barth'. *International Journal of Systematic Theology* 8, no. 1 (2006): 3–24. https://doi.org/10.1111/j.1468-2400.2006.00180.x.
Thompson, Geoff, and Christiaan Mostert, eds. *Karl Barth: A Future for Postmodern Theology?* Hindmarsh, South Australia: Australian Theological Forum, 2000.
Thompson, John. 'The Humanity of God in the Theology of Karl Barth'. *Scottish Journal of Theology* 29, no. 3 (1976): 249–69. https://doi.org/10.1017/S0036930600029148.
Tietz, Christiane. ' "Nur der Glaubende ist gehorsam, und nur der Gehorsame glaubt." Beobachtungen zu einem existentiellen Zirkel in Dietrich Bonhoeffers "Nachfolge" '. In *Dietrich Bonhoeffer Jahrbuch 2, 2005/2006*, edited by Christian Gremmels, Hans Pfeifer and Christiane Tietz, 170–81. Gütersloher: Gütersloher Verlagshaus, 2005.
Tillich, Paul. *Life in the Spirit: History and the Kingdom of God*. Systematic Theology 3. Welwyn: James Nisbet, 1964.
Torrance, Alan J. *Persons in Communion: An Essay on Trinitarian Description and Human Participation with Special Reference to Volume One of Karl Barth's Church Dogmatics*. Edinburgh: T&T Clark, 1996.
Torrance, Thomas F. *Royal Priesthood: A Theology of Ordained Ministry*. 2nd edn. Edinburgh: T&T Clark, 1993.
Torrance, Thomas F. *Space, Time and Resurrection*. Edinburgh: T&T Clark, 1998.

Torrance, Thomas F. 'Universalism or Election?' *Scottish Journal of Theology* 2, no. 3 (1949): 310–18. https://doi.org/10.1017/S0036930600004713.
Webster, John. *Barth's Moral Theology: Human Action in Barth's Thought*. Edinburgh: T&T Clark, 1998.
Webster, John. 'The Grand Narrative of Jesus Christ: Barth's Christology'. In *Karl Barth: A Future for Postmodern Theology?*, edited by Geoff Thompson and Christiaan Mostert, 29–48. Hindmarsh, South Australia: Australian Theological Forum, 2000.
'When Americans Say They Believe in God, What Do They Mean?' Washington, DC: Pew Research Center, 25 April 2018. https://www.pewforum.org/2018/04/25/when-americans-say-they-believe-in-god-what-do-they-mean/.
Williams, A. N. *The Architecture of Theology: Structure, System, and Ratio*. Oxford: Oxford University Press, 2011.
Wüstenberg, Ralf K. *A Theology of Life: Dietrich Bonhoeffer's Religionless Christianity*. Grand Rapids, MI: Eerdmans, 1998.

INDEX

actualism 15, 54, 56 n.32, 87 n.28, 206–9
analogia relationis 46, 173–5
Anselm 51, 72
apokatastasis 83, 85, 99 n.66, 97, 195, 198, 199
Aquinas, Thomas 17 n.20, 55 n.26, 68, 70, 86 n.17, 163 n.1
Asad, Talal 22 n.36, 100 n.5, 138
Athanasius 51, 63, 175 n.50
atheism 98, 111, 113, 156, 204, 211
atonement 42, 57–62, 191
Augustine 67, 69, 72, 86 n.17, 166–7
autonomy 22, 93, 134–5, 143

Balthasar, Hans Urs von 54
baptism 61, 201–2
Barmen Declaration 39
Berger, Peter 140 n.38, 147 n.2, 148, 151 n.23
Berkhof, Louis 69
Berkouwer, G. C. 40 n.28, 56 n.31, 63 n.69, 78 n.57, 85, 86 n.23, 89–92, 96, 203 n.36
Bethge, Eberhard 14, 20, 24, 31, 37, 39, 197–8
Boethius 65–70, 72, 81–2
Brunner, Emil 45, 46, 48
Bultmann, Rudolf 29–31, 37, 48

Calvin, John 12–14, 27 n.61, 48 n.64, 53–4, 55 n.26, 82, 88, 180 n.71
Christological personalism 5 n.6, 19–20, 212
church
   as Christ 179, 184
   community of confession 176–7
   and Israel 88
   locus of true religion 103–4, 107–8
   and world 126–7, 129, 178–9, 188–92, 200, 212
Church Struggle 16, 39

command 21, 42–6
communion of saints 4, 46–8, 198
covenant 52, 55–60, 75, 81–2, 86, 95, 123, 129–30, 190
creation 52, 76–7, 120, 128–9, 173–4
Crisp, Oliver D. 5 n.6, 63 n.69, 203 n.36

damnation 96, 201, 207
DeJonge, Michael P. 16 n.18, 19 n.27, 35 n.1, 166 n.2, 172 n.34
Dilthey, Wilhelm, 12, 27, 30, 32
discipleship 41–3, 208–9
divine (*see also* God)
   constancy 71
   eternity 55–6, 67–9, 71–7, 81, 94–5
   liveliness 73–4
   mystery 56 n.33, 144, 157
   simplicity 68, 70, 73, 75
   sovereignty 94, 127, 141–2, 157–9
   suffering 158
Dumas, André 21 n.35, 22 n.38, 26 n.58, 27 n.59, 164 n.3, 206 n.52

ecclesiocentrism 164–5
election
   decretum absolutum 55–6, 87, 94
   double predestination 19, 56–7, 87–8, 96, 119
   electing God 54–7, 86–9
   of humanity 55, 57, 64, 84, 88, 93
   of Jesus Christ 55–7, 66, 79 n.63, 81, 86–90, 94–5
enhypostasis 19, 66, 76, 93
eschatology 92, 95–6, 129, 152, 197–8, 200–1, 209
ethics 43–6, 61
evil 91–2, 94, 97, 151 (*see also* nothingness)
exclusivism 103, 105, 107, 119, 122–5, 129
extra Calvinisticum 17, 27
extremism (*see* fundamentalism)

faith 59, 61–2, 64, 96, 126, 128, 169, 201, 202–6
Feuerbach, Ludwig 21, 22 n.35, 26, 99, 102, 158
Ford, David 3 n.1, 5 n.7, 151
freedom
　of God 15, 46, 55–6, 64, 71, 74, 87, 94, 174
　of humanity 46, 93, 95–6, 127, 166, 187, 196
　of the Spirit 212
Freud, Sigmund 21, 22 n.35, 26, 27 n.59
fundamentalism, 98, 105, 114, 116 n.62, 133, 138–43, 149–59, 162, 211

God
　for us 28 n.67, 51–2, 87, 174
　speech about 144, 153–4, 156–7, 159–60
　Trinity 26 n.57, 71, 74–5, 82, 128
　Word of 17 n.20, 18, 19 n.26, 51–2, 143, 159
Godsey, John 14, 21 n.34, 83 n.1
Green, Clifford 22 n.35, 24, 26 n.54, 27 n.62, 164 n.3, 173 n.43, 176 n.57, 186–7

Hart, Trevor 55 n.21, 59 n.54, 78 n.56, 98 n.90, 195 n.1, 196
Holy Spirit 15, 33 n.100, 47–8, 61–2, 104, 126–7, 180–1, 186, 212–13
hope 61–2, 84, 97, 129, 195–6, 201–2, 205–7, 213
Hunsinger, George 26 n.57, 53, 56 n.32, 62 n.66, 63, 84 n.7, 87 n.28, 103 n.17, 106 n.33, 108 n.41, 119 n.6

idolatry 108–9, 111, 128, 144, 153–4, 157, 159, 160 n.60
imago dei 46, 173–5
incarnation 15, 17, 19–20, 51–2, 58, 66, 71, 75–6, 79–82, 175
Islam 101, 105–6 115, 124–5, 128, 137, 139, 152 n.27
Israel 88–9, 122–3

Jauss, Hans Robert 11
Judaism 16 n.17, 39–40, 89 n.39, 101, 115, 124–5, 128, 143, 152 n.26

Jüngel, Eberhard 86 n.22, 93 n.68, 171 n.28, 209 n.63
justification 42–3, 59, 103

Kant, Immanuel 12, 15, 78 n.57
Kierkegaard, Søren 12, 210

liberalism
　political 105, 139, 156, 211
　theological 6, 29–31, 34, 38, 196–7
love
　divine 54–6, 86–7, 124–5, 196–7, 200, 202, 206
　human 14, 106–7, 111, 188
Luther, Martin 12, 17, 27, 166 n.6, 167 n.10, 169, 183, 189, 190, 201 n.28, 204, 205 n.46

MacIntyre, Alasdair 114 n.59, 161 n.64, 211 n.1
mandates 21, 45
Marsh, Charles 28 n.67, 29
Marx, Karl 21, 26, 99
Mathewes, Charles 6
McCormack, Bruce 5 n.8, 19, 26 n.57, 56 n.32, 65, 69 n.20, 70 n.21, 77 n.50, 78 n.57, 87 n.28, 173 n.41
metaphysics 7, 65, 68, 70 n.21, 93 n.66, 168–9, 173
mission 104, 112, 114, 127 (*see also* witness)
Moberly, Walter 149, 156 n.42
monotheism 123, 128
munus triplex 52, 58
mysticism 111, 113, 156

Nayed, Aref 115
Niebuhr, Reinhold 44
Nietzsche, Friedrich 21, 27, 99
Nimmo, Paul T. 56 n.32, 63 n.69, 120 n.9
nothingness 91, 121

obedience 42–4, 62, 126, 208
Osborn, Robert 28

Pangritz, Andreas 15, 16 n.17, 20, 23 n.39, 26 n.55, 27 n.61, 35, 40 n.26, 99 n.2
Pannenberg, Wolfhart 24 n.43, 66 n.6, 69, 211

participation
    in Christ 53–7, 62, 88–9, 92–3, 190–1
    in divine providence 125–9
    in sin 168, 192, 207
Percy, Martyn 139, 151 n.24, 158 n.47
personhood 172
    of Christ 91, 94
    of God 55, 87, 172–4
    of the human 172–3, 175–6, 187–8
Plant, Stephen 22 n.35, 133 n.1, 135 n.11, 142 n.47, 148 n.1
Plato 66–7
Plotinus 66, 69, 77
politics 6, 40–1, 142, 148, 150–4
pluralism, 5 n.7, 6, 98, 108, 129, 138, 159, 196
prayer 126–8, 183
providence 67–8, 119–29

Rahner, Karl 202 n.33, 207, 208 n.61
reconciliation 41–2, 51–2, 57–61, 92, 104
relationality
    of church 184, 189–90
    of God 82, 171, 173–4
    of humans 46, 170–2, 174, 176
religion
    critique of 21–34, 99–100, 102, 105, 107, 109, 110 n.45, 111–16
    religionless Christianity 21–3, 28–9, 33, 37–8, 140–4, 147–9, 154–61, 191
    religious conflict 119, 127, 147, 158, 162 (*see also* fundamentalism)
responsibility 42, 167, 171, 184, 189, 191, 207, 209
revelation 15, 17, 32, 51, 73, 123, 125, 155–6
    and religion 33, 102–4, 107–10, 114
    positivism of 24–8, 32–3, 37
Roberts, Richard 33 n.100, 78 n.57, 94 n.74
Robinson, J. A. T. 37, 196

salvation
    as *anthroposis* 175, 187, 208–9
    as community formation 186
    human response to 61–2
    objectivist 53–4, 57, 61–3, 90, 92–3, 213
    of non-Christians 98, 197, 201, 205
sanctification 42, 58, 60, 199
Schleiermacher, Friedrich 17 n.20, 31–4, 69, 196
Schwöbel, Christoph 148 n.7, 149
sectarianism 5–6, 211 (*see also* fundamentalism)
secularism 3, 6, 22, 98, 100 n.5, 116, 134–45, 148, 150–2, 158, 160–2, 211
separationism 98, 119, 195, 196 n.9, 201–2, 208–9
simultaneity 66, 68–71, 73, 74–5, 78, 82
sin
    confession of 42, 176–8
    as corporate 166–70
    forgiveness of 176–9, 191–2
    horizontal 170–75, 180
    original 159 n.55, 166–7, 199–200
    total depravity 197–202
    as unbelief 202–206
sociality, *see* relationality.
Sonderegger, Katherine 89 n.39, 116 n.63
systematic theology 2, 4, 5, 8, 36, 117–18, 163–5, 179–80

time 78–81, 94–5
tolerance 106–7

Webster, John 1, 2, 4, 93, 97
Williams, A. N. 8 n.14, 36, 164 n.2, 165 n.4
witness 60–1, 64, 88, 190, 212
Wüstenberg, Ralf K. 22 n.35, 23 n.41, 27 n.60, 28 n.66, 32, 99 n.2, 133 n.1, 141 n.40, 160

www.ingramcontent.com/pod-product-compliance
Lightning Source LLC
Chambersburg PA
CBHW062215300426
44115CB00012BA/2072